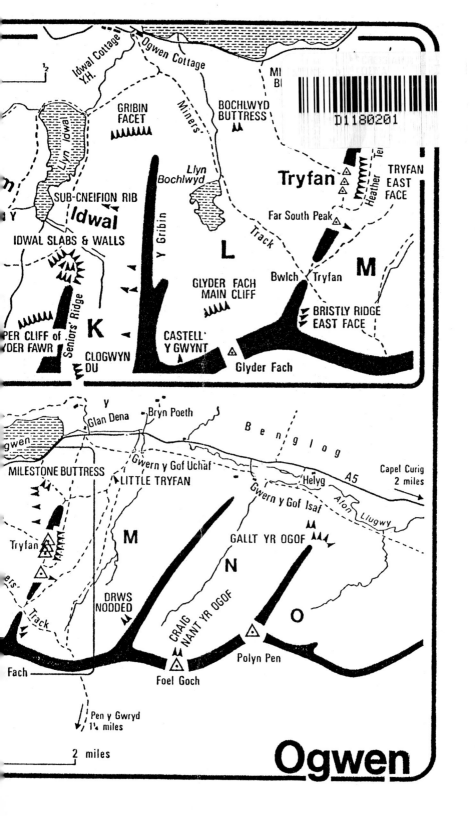

Ogwen

HANDS OF A CLIMBER

A Life of Colin Kirkus

Lot's Groove, Glyder Fach. The route follows the right-angled corner just left of the seated figure.
Photo Graham MacPhee

HANDS
OF A CLIMBER

A Life of Colin Kirkus

Steve Dean

 THE ERNEST PRESS

Published by The Ernest Press 1993
© Steve Dean

ISBN 0 948153 21 0

British Library Cataloguing-in-Publication Data.
A Catalogue record for this book is available
from the British Library.

Typeset by EMS Phototypesetting, Berwick upon Tweed.
Printed by St. Edmundsbury Press.

Contents

HANDS OF A CLIMBER (to C.F.K.)

Faces fade with too much emphasis.
The blank illumination of yearning,
nebulous with shadows, loses touch
with sane reality – a dream remains.

Could I but catch one windswept moment
to energise my desolation
into the ecstasy of remembered love!
And yet, one vision leaps exultant.

Hands of a climber, vital, tense.
Fingers, conscious of reach, exploring smoothness,
as a blind man touches inanimate loves
for the last time, moving forward gladly.

Passion expressed by the body poised
on the edge of vastness, motionless, unyielding,
until the rapture passes, hold roughen upwards,
delightfully, towards the impassive summit.

Only now, hands idle, laid aside,
all reckoning over, endeavour pauses.
Eyes receive the muscles' lost nobility
gratefully, softened by a new hill dream.

Guy Kirkus (1945)

Foreword

To most of the people presently climbing, many of whom I hope will read this book, Colin Kirkus can only be a legendary figure of fifty or so years ago. Yes, they may remember he was a chap who put up a most remarkable series of first ascents in Snowdonia and a very important one in the Lake District during his short climbing career, before he was killed on active service with the R.A.F. in 1942. But to me, he gave years of warm friendship, and the opportunity to climb with the greatest pioneer of his era.

He was undoubtedly one of the greatest British climbers this century. Nearly all his first ascents, such as Dinas Mot's *Central Route*, (now called *Nose Direct*) *Great Slab* on Clogwyn Du'r Arddu and *Mickledore Grooves* on Scafell's East Buttress, were done straight from the floor with no immoral initiation on a top rope from above. To me, as one of the few people still alive who climbed with him, he was more than a great climber – he was a good friend and jolly companion on the hill, in the hut and elsewhere.

This book, prepared by Stephen Dean, a keen climber himself, resulted from lengthy research into Colin's life and involved seeking out those still alive who knew him and might have climbed with him, which was no easy task. The book tells you the full story of Colin's climbing from his earliest days, through the trauma of the tragic accident on Ben Nevis in 1934 when he lost his good friend Maurice Linnell and was himself physically and psychologically damaged, to his career in the R.A.F. during the Hitler War.

It is a story well worth telling, because Kirkus was not only a great climber and a truly significant figure in the development of British rock-climbing, but also a very interesting and worthy person – he deserves such a memorial.

Alan (AB) Hargreaves
Ulverston, Cumbria.
May 1993.

Acknowledgements

The assistance I have been given in writing this book has been enormous, and I am extremely grateful to all those who provided information, photographs, anecdotal material and just pure encouragement at different times! I would particularly like to thank Guy Kirkus, AB Hargreaves and Bill Stallybrass for much laughter and genuine inspiration, particularly in the early stages of this work. In addition, many thanks are due to Jim Perrin and to Geoff Milburn, who despite their own heavy workloads, found time to offer much help and encouragement when it was needed, and were often able to point me in the right direction over specific problems. I would also like to express my gratitude to Peter Hodgkiss and Jack Baines of The Ernest Press, for their patience and encouragement, and to my old friend Sid Geake for painstakingly printing high-quality black and white photographs that form the bulk of the illustrations in this book.

It is impossible to assess every contribution, but the list of those who have helped is as follows: Alpine Club Library, Berta Andrews, Hugh Banner, Arthur Birtwistle, Alastair Borthwick, BBC archives, Joe Brown, the late Rennie Bere, Harry Calvert, Climbers' Club, Heaton Cooper, Sid Cross, Fell & Rock Climbing Club, Peter Fleming, Hermione Fletcher, Ifor Freeman, Jim Gavin, Sid & Pauline Geake, Tony Greenbank, Earl of Halsbury, Des Hannigan, Peter Harding, Alan (AB) Hargreaves, Richard Hargreaves, Hal Jacob, Guy & Jenny Kirkus, Liverpool College, Liverpool Central Public Library (Local History Section), John Llewellyn, Sir Jack Longland, Jo Longland, John Lumb, Geoff Milburn, Richard Nicholson, the late Marco Pallis, Jim Perrin, Public Records Office, RAF Museum Hendon, Jim Reace, Ruth Janette Ruck, Rucksack Club, Matthew Shaw, Tony Smyth, Bill and Margo Stallybrass, Showell Styles, Les Swindin, Ian Thomson, Elliot Viney, Ivan Waller, Charles Warren, David Watson, the late John Watson, Mary Watson, Wayfarers' Club, Paul Williams, the late Paul Orkney Work.

I offer my apologies to anyone I have inadvertently omitted.

Particular thanks are also due to Pam Sharpe, Janet Marshall and Shirley Magee, for turning my biro-written scrawl into workable typed text, and to my wife Janet for enduring long periods of my preoccupation with the climbing world of many years ago!

SJD
Derby 1993

1 Let's Go Climbing

Had you been walking on the Carneddau on Midsummer's Day in 1931, the chances are that you would have had the hills to yourself. The great post-war expansion in outdoor activities was still many years away. For most of the time, this lovely range of mountains to the north of the Ogwen Valley and the A5 road, would have been deserted except for the hill-farmers and shepherds, striving the year round to make a living out of this hard land. But if, that afternoon, you had been making your way up the shoulder of Carnedd Llewelyn above the dark waters of Ffynnon Llugwy, it is possible that the cloud may have lifted to reveal the impressive, steep cliffs that form the upper wall of Craig yr Ysfa. Together with the Amphitheatre Wall below it, these are some of the most spectacular and finely positioned mountain crags in Wales, rarely crowded with climbers even to this day.

From the vantage point of the ridge to the summit of Llewelyn, you might just have seen a young man climbing alone on the upper wall, steadily making his way upwards to the main feature of the face, an obvious partly-detached pinnacle. A slim youth of medium height, only a couple of days past his twenty-first birthday, he is wearing a tattered navy-blue sweater, a ragged pair of old flannels, cheap black plimsolls, and is carrying a small rucksack. Tied around his waist is a climbing rope, which he trails behind him in the absence of a companion. His thick brown hair tumbles forward on to his brow now and then, but barely disturbs his concentration as he carefully tries the next move, stepping up slowly but with a certain sureness and composure that serves to reassure the witness to this solo adventure. Occasionally the young man balances on his footholds and flaps one or other of his hands behind him in an almost nervous gesture, but his constant upward movement, although slow, is assured and executed smoothly despite the lack of the mental support a companion could offer in such a place. A particularly exposed step brings him to the top of the pinnacle, where an equally open set of moves takes him on to the short rough wall above it. Beneath lies a drop of more than 200 feet to the scree in the gully-bed below, but as the angle of the wall above him eases and a series of good holds arrives, he steps up to the grassy ledges above, released now from his solitary journey. He glances at the fine mountain view for a few moments, seeks out a spot to sit down out of the wind and then eats some food carried up in the rucksack. After a while, he lights a cigarette held in a small holder and then builds a small cairn of stones before coiling the rope and shouldering the

sack, to set off back down the ridge towards Ogwen. It is late in the afternoon, his valley base is almost an hour's walk away and from there he faces a journey of ninety miles on his bicycle, back to his home in Liverpool

The young man is Colin Kirkus. At the time of which I write, he was already acknowledged as the outstanding climber in the mountains of North Wales, having made a series of daring first ascents over the previous two summers. Only the day before this climb was made on Craig yr Ysfa, he had completed another hard new climb, (*Lot's Wife*), on the cliffs of Glyder Fach in the Ogwen Valley. This was a companion route to one of his earlier climbs, *Lot's Groove*, already regarded as one of the most difficult in the British mountains. It is possible that this particular solo ascent on the cliffs below Carnedd Llewelyn, was prompted by a visit to the crag two weeks previously by Colin and two companions. On that day they had completed a new climb called the *Amphitheatre Rib*. Finishing it their eyes would have been drawn to the upper wall and its striking pinnacle. A true pioneer, Colin had returned at the first opportunity to investigate.

Much of this is conjecture, but within it I hope there lies something of the truth. Colin did indeed make the first ascent, alone, of what became known as the *Pinnacle Wall* on that Sunday afternoon in June 1931. The climb subsequently became very popular and is now regarded as a classic of the area. This particular image of him climbing alone in the mountains of Snowdonia sixty years ago, is one that has endured in climbers' minds over the years. In the two years which followed, Colin had established himself not only as one of the major figures in the history of British rock-climbing, but as a unique character in that particularly esoteric field. His name is still recalled with great affection and regard, both by those who knew him and climbed with him and by climbers aware of the history of the sport. And yet, although a central figure in the evolution of pre-war climbing, Colin has remained a rather shadowy figure; an embodiment of a now distant era. It is my intention here to examine something of his unique contribution to British mountain-eering and to look at the period and the social context in which he, together with a number of other talented characters, shared the exciting period of exploration in the years leading up to the Second World War – a period which, in the opinion of some, saw the birth of modern rock-climbing in Britain.

Colin Fletcher Kirkus was born in Liverpool on June 19th, 1910, to Cecil and Muriel Kirkus. He was their first child, being followed by Nigel and Guy. Colin's father, Cecil Kirkus, was a self-employed automobile engineer

Pinnacle Wall, Craig yr Ysfa.   *Photo C. F. Kirkus (AC coll.)*

Muriel Kirkus with her sons Colin, Nigel and Guy.   *Photo courtesy of Guy Kirkus*

and, together with his wife, they provided the three boys with a strict but very happy upbringing in the framework of a typical Edwardian middle-class family. The name Kirkus is unusual, and is thought to be Dutch or Nordic in origin. The family lived in a variety of locations in the Liverpool area, prior to settling at Acre Lane in Heswall in 1934. A good-natured, trusting and meticulously honest man, Cecil Kirkus had developed a great love for the countryside and particularly for the mountains of North Wales, and was himself a considerable walker. By virtue of being largely self-employed, he was able to take his young family to North Wales for four or five weeks most summer holidays and the effect this had on the boys, and on Colin in particular, was considerable. The family's usual practice was to rent a small cottage or farmhouse near Carrog in the Vale of Llangollen. This family trait of Welsh holidays was shared by Cecil Kirkus's cousin Frank Noyce, who was the father of the celebrated mountaineer Wilf Noyce. In his book 'Mountains and Men',[1] Wilf Noyce refers to similar early holidays in the Welsh Hills, and happily recalls his early adventures with his cousins, the Kirkus brothers.

Early photographs of Colin and his family are typical of the time; his mother wears the blouse, long skirt and hat of the period, while the boys run ahead on a country walk. There is something in Colin's pose and in his

1 'Mountains and Men'. Wilfrid Noyce (Geoffrey Bles – 1947).

expression that sets him a little apart from his brothers – the hint of a more serious and intense nature, and the suggestion of a slightly more solitary and self-reliant character. Already there is a strong facial resemblance to his mother.

At home in Liverpool Colin first attended Caldy Grange Grammar School in West Kirby, before being sent to Liverpool College as a day boy in the autumn of 1923 at the age of thirteen. Colin remained at home during his period of formal education, while both Nigel and Guy attended boarding schools. Guy went to Ellesmere College, while Nigel was sent to Christ's Hospital in Sussex, where he particularly loathed the school's old-fashioned traditional uniform. Perhaps as a result of this arrangement, and the periods of separation it involved, the two younger brothers, Nigel and Guy, formed a very close relationship, while Colin was more solitary in character. Guy Kirkus recalled that both he and Nigel had the greatest regard and admiration for their elder brother, but felt that their similar form of school experience bound them a little closer to each other than to Colin.

At the time that Colin enrolled, Liverpool College was already established as a very significant institution in the city. The school had been founded in the early years of Queen Victoria's reign – during a period of affluence in which Liverpool shed its role as a fishing port to take the national lead as a major trading city. With the rapid increase in the wealth of the city came a demand for a first-class educational establishment. The wealthy of the city subscribed and in 1843 the Liverpool Collegiate, as it was then known, was opened. It has remained a proud claim of the school that it maintains a close and mutually valuable link with the city, in providing a public school education based on the principles of the Church of England. In the early 1920s the senior boys' school was located in Sefton Park Road, but gradually the whole school became established on the fine site at Mossley Hill, very close to Sefton Park. The philosophy of the school was based on sound religion and useful learning and it was the proud boast of the school that, even in the depressed years of the 1930s, less than 3% of boys leaving were without suitable work and that there was actually a demand for 'Old Lerpoolians' in the job market at that time.

Colin was above average academically, although not outstanding enough to be considered university material. He was in Butler's House and seems to have quite enjoyed school life. An early influence appears to have been a Mathematics teacher, B.F.K.O'Malley, who was himself an experienced mountaineer and a member of the Liverpool-based Wayfarers' Club. O'Malley encouraged Colin's interest in mountains, already firmly established by family holidays in North Wales, long walks on the Wirral, and extensive reading on the subject. Guy Kirkus remembers Colin being tremendously interested in climbing even at the age of eleven or twelve.

An inspiration at home for both Colin and his brothers may well have been a magnificent late-Victorian oil painting by Peter Ghent of Lyn Idwal and the cliffs of Clogwyn y Geifr that hung in the family sitting room. Clouds tumble over the Devil's Kitchen and along the ridge to Y Garn, while sunlight shafts down on to the hillside that encloses the lake, picking out the snow remaining in Cwm Clyd. The view is unquestionably Welsh, the mountains dark, grand and mysterious, yet somehow it seems to invite you to make your way along the path by the side of the lake, to reach out to the friendly rock and to climb it. As a child and as a young man, Colin would have seen it daily in the house.

Colin's father, Cecil Kirkus, had been educated at Sedbergh School where he had been an outstanding cross-country runner. This athletic ability was passed on to the three boys in turn. While Nigel was quite muscular in appearance, Colin and Guy were both slight in build, taking after their mother. Muriel Kirkus shared her husband's love of the hills and countryside and was herself a keen hill-walker. Nigel was later to run at a very good standard for the RAF, while Guy remembers seeing Colin win the school Five-Mile Cup with some ease at the School Sports day in March 1927 – a day blighted by dreadful weather. The event was reported in the school magazine thus:

> 'The pulling in the tug-of-war was very good this year: some stubborn contests and some surprising recoveries were seen, and often the results were most unexpected. As usual, the coaches were very prominent. Bovenizer behaved with a completeness of deportment which suggests that the gain of Cambridge will be the loss of Hollywood. Craig risked apoplexy heroically, if unavailingly, and Petty screeched the Junior Team of Brook's to victory with a devotion which he gives but rarely to his geometry. In the long-distance races, the start of the five-mile race was made sensational by the hurried disappearance into the distance of Wylie and Gaskin. "They had their day, and ceased to be" in the race, and it was eventually won by Kirkus, Cox gaining second place, and G.H. Moffat third place.'

Later that same afternoon, Colin was also placed second in the Senior Mile, to the aforementioned Wylie. That same year he also received his school colours for rugby football. Guy was also a very keen runner in his youth, regularly turning out for Clayton Harriers (now Clayton-le-Moors) in league, County and National Championships. He returned to the sport at the age of sixty-eight, and is still a very fit-looking man who recently ran a half marathon in 1 hour 41 minutes. These same family qualities of stamina and determination were to serve Colin well as a mountaineer, and Jack Longland amongst others has been quick to testify to Colin's considerable toughness and resilience.

In broad terms, therefore, Colin grew up in an ordinary middle-class family of the period, attending a local and quite notable public school. The three brothers appear to have enjoyed a happy childhood and adolescence and Colin continued to live with his parents until he married in 1940. Of the three brothers, Guy had a childhood somewhat troubled by sickness and he remembers taking long walks with Colin both in Sefton Park and out in the Wirral whilst recovering from illness. Guy also recalled Colin taking him to Helsby crag for the first time and the thrill and delight of enjoying a pint of beer on the way home despite both being well under age! Their middle brother, Nigel, was a strikingly handsome boy, and very much the 'dare devil' of the three brothers. More practical than academic, Nigel shared his father's love for cars and machines, and joined the RAF as an apprentice straight from school, in due course becoming a pilot. On more than one occasion, Nigel commandeered their father's car in order to whisk the brothers away for a day in the country or on the crags. Years later the myth began to circulate that Colin was a 'working-class' climber. Guy humorously pointed out that although Colin would certainly not have objected to such an idea, it was in fact far from being the case. The Kirkus family members were the type of hard-working middle-class people who formed the core of commercial life in Britain in the early part of the century.

In 1941 the publishers Thomas Nelson issued a book called 'Let's Go Climbing!' written by Colin in 1939, when he was 29, as an instruction book for young people. Frequent reference will be made to this delightful book: it contains some interesting recollections of Colin's early holidays in the Welsh mountains. He first recalls being taken up:

> '....a rocky 2000-foot lump called Manod, near Ffestiniog. ... That was a great day in my life, and ever afterwards I gazed at all mountains with longing.'

At the age of nine Colin was taken up Snowdon by the Glaslyn track, and it made a vivid impression on the young boy:

> 'It was wonderful to be at last actually on a slope composed entirely of rocks, surrounded by terrific precipices that exceeded my wildest expectations. I had provided myself with a stout and knobbly stick, which I had cut myself with loving care; it had rather the appearance of a petrified snake or a giant corkscrew. But in my eyes it was an indispensable companion, and I decided that some young men we saw coming down at breakneck speed without sticks of any kind must be very ignorant of mountain-craft. The whole day was one orgy of continuous rapture which I have never since been able quite to recall.'

By the age of eleven Colin had been taken along the knife-edge rib of Crib Goch and at the age of twelve his enterprising parents allowed him to wander over the hills alone.

> 'This shows the value of training one's parents from the very earliest age. I found that, properly managed, they gave very little trouble.'

This humorous aside in Colin's book hid an important truth; his parents' love of the hills and trust in him enabled the boy to develop, from an early stage, a self-reliance and sense of judgement that was to serve him well in the future, when breaking new ground in the mountains. Nonetheless there were a number of notable adventures whilst still a schoolboy, often with his long-suffering brothers in tow! An early attempt at rock-climbing in the Berwyns with the inevitable length of clothes-line was followed by similar escapades on the sterner cliffs of Arenig Fawr and Cader Idris. At the time of some of these exciting exploits, Guy Kirkus was only eleven years old. At Christmas 1924, aged fourteen, Colin was given a copy of 'British Mountain Climbs' written by George Abraham and this became not only his bible, but persuaded him to dispense with the clothes-line and purchase a proper climbing rope for future adventures. A lone photograph survives of Colin climbing, in what appears to be his school uniform (i.e. blazer, cap and short trousers), somewhere in Wales. The location would seem to be the cliffs of Arenig Fawr. The concentration and sureness of touch of the young man is already in evidence – Colin looks to be about fourteen years old, the photograph probably having been taken on a family holiday.

During the summer holidays from 1920 until 1926, Cecil Kirkus arranged for his young family to stay at a farmhouse called Carreg Afon, close to the A5 road and a short distance to the west of Carrog. In the autumn of 1991, I returned to the farm with Guy Kirkus who recognised it immediately. "....there it is, the steep slope down to the main road where we all rode our bikes!" Guy was delighted to discover that the farm was still in the same family; the present owner, Mr Thomas, informing us that in the early 1920s when the Kirkus family visited on their holidays, the farm was owned by his father's uncle, and had subsequently passed to him, and would in turn pass to his son who was already working the farm with him.

Guy pointed out the barn where the three brothers had played together seventy years ago and the farmyard overlooking the valley of the Dee and the picturesque hills beyond. Their father was very fond of fly-fishing, and would fish for trout in the Dee as the boys played on the riverbank; just a few yards away the trains would chuff past on the GWR line from Ruabon to

First steps: Colin climbing on Arenig Fawr.   *Photo courtesy of Guy Kirkus*

Barmouth and the Cambrian coast. One of Guy's outstanding memories of
the place was the boys' first visit to the cinema (or rather a picture-house.)
This took place one evening in Corwen, and the silent film they all went to
see was a western. The walk back along the riverbank to Carrog was then
enlivened by the three brothers' ambushing each other and their parents –
reliving the adventures on the screen, as they made their way back to the
farm in the evening with sunshine illuminating the lovely valley of the Dee
and the slopes of Llantysilio Mountain away to the east. As they climbed up
to the farm from the road, the last evening train might have steamed past on
its way to Corwen then on to Dolgellau and the coast.

Colin was only ten or eleven years old on his first visit to the farm at
Carreg Afon, and the family returned there for several years, before
switching to a holiday base at Trefriw. By that time Colin was spending most
of his leisure time at Helyg. It was from Carreg Afon that Colin began to set
off on his bike, armed only with a burning enthusiasm for the hills and a
packed lunch, to explore the hills and valleys of the Arans and the Berwyns.

Each night Colin would return leg-weary and hungry to the cosy comfort
of the farmhouse, a welcome meal and a bath. From this modest beginning,
encouraged by his parent's trust, was to develop gradually a great talent as a
rock-climber and mountaineer. In truth, the Kirkus boys were very fortunate
in that era (the 1920s) to be able to spend four or five weeks in the Welsh
hills every summer. Their parents were by no means wealthy people, but
both adored Wales and felt that the time spent there would be beneficial to
the boys' development. Often, such lengthy holidays were made possible by
letting the family home in Sefton Park, such was the family fondness for
North Wales. Most of the time, Cecil Kirkus was self-employed and chose
to spend as much time as possible with his young family during the summer
months. Before the rapid growth of tourism, this part of Wales around
Carrog must have been idyllic, with little or no traffic on the A5 and few
people in the hills.

Similar summer holidays followed in North Wales, including much time
spent walking and scrambling in the Berwyns and the Arans, until the time
came for Colin to leave school in the summer of 1927. By then he was
determined to devote his leisure time to climbing and, although not yet
seventeen, he managed to persuade his parents to take that year's holiday not
at Carrog, but at Betws-y-Coed. For a keen young climber, armed only with
a rope, a sense of adventure and a bicycle, this would be a huge improvement
as the village of Betws-y-Coed is situated much nearer the great mountains
and crags of central Snowdonia. Guy Kirkus remembers Colin trying hard to

persuade their father to change the holiday plans, and Cecil Kirkus finally agreed to forsake Carrog for that year as Colin was about to leave school and take up full-time employment. This family holiday at Betws-y-Coed was to be a most important milestone in Colin's life, as it marked the beginning of his serious rock-climbing. It was also to be a hazardous period for him, as Colin made quite clear in 'Let's Go Climbing!' He lacked a partner for most of the time, but undeterred he proceeded regularly to cycle down the A5 to Ogwen, and took to the crags alone.

'I spent practically the whole of this holiday in continuously breaking a rule that is being constantly hammered into beginners – climbing alone while still a novice. But what else could I do? I did not know any climbers, and it was only occasionally that I could get my father or brothers to accompany me. There was only one alternative – not to climb – and that was unthinkable. The ambition of my life at that time was to do some recognized rock-climbs; not just casual little scrambles, but real routes that had names and were described in the guide-book.

Though wrong as a policy, this early solo-climbing taught me an immense amount. I knew that if I made a mistake I had no-one to help me; I had to rely entirely on my own skill and my own judgement.'

As mentioned earlier, Colin was an assiduous reader of 'British Mountain Climbs', a book written very much in the era of gully climbing before climbers ventured out on to the sunlit slabs and faces. It was whilst gully climbing on this holiday that Colin had his first serious brush with danger, alone on the cliffs of Craig yr Ysfa. His own account leaves one in no doubt that the young man did not lack ambition or drive, but that these were dangerous allies until some sharp lessons had been absorbed and some prudence learnt.

'On the occasion in question I had cycled the ten miles from Betws and then slogged for an hour-and-a-half across the grassy slopes of the Carnedds, over the saddle below Pen Helig, and down to the grand precipice of Craig yr Ysfa. My objective was the Arch Gully, which was classified as difficult, so I was all keyed-up for a great struggle. The lower pitches – pitches are the stretches of actual climbing between the easier sections – went quite easily, and I arrived at the foot of the 50-foot chief obstacle. This was a vertical, three-sided cleft, about a yard across and had scarcely any holds, or so it seemed to me. The only way to get up is to put the back against the right wall and the feet against the left. Then you have to raise one foot a few inches, then press with the palms of your hands on the wall behind until your back goes up a bit. This type of problem is known as a chimney; it is strenuous but usually safe, since you are firmly wedged. You can quite easily practise this technique in an ordinary doorway at home.

It was drizzling and the chimney was streaming with water and made more slippery by a coating of thick green moss. However, I arrived quite safely underneath the small chockstones which closed up the top of the chimney and overhung a little. I reached up cautiously with one hand and felt about until I found a fine sharp hold. One hard arm-pull and a struggle, and with a gasp of triumph I landed at the top of my first difficult rock-climb. It was a very small triumph really, for there are three harder standards, but it seemed a notable victory to me.

I descended a moderate gully into the Amphitheatre, a magnificent hollow in the centre of the cliff. Nothing easy would do for me in my exultant state of mind, so I made a bee-line for B. Gully. This has one very awkward pitch, a steep slimy crack overhung by a smooth chockstone. It was raining heavily now, and muddy water was dripping down dismally on every side.

I climbed the crack with a good deal of difficulty and felt for holds on the boulder above, hanging backwards from one hand. It all seemed as smooth as glass and my fingers were so cold that I had lost all feeling in them. My supporting hand was getting tired and I felt I must do something quickly. I did. I scraped the mud out of a slight crevice on top of the overhanging boulder and decided to make it do. I let go with my left hand, my right hand slipped numbly from the boulder, and before I had time to think I found myself lying in the bed of the gully.

My first feeling was one of pained surprise that it should have been possible for me to have fallen off. Then I wondered how many bones I had broken, and found that I was completely uninjured. Finally I was overcome by such a feeling of baffled rage at being thus ingloriously beaten that I rushed at the pitch again, like a mad bull at a gate.

The same thing happened again, only this time I fell and slid about 30 feet and stopped dangerously near the edge of the pitch below. I decided it was quite time to stop.

It was a very chastened and rather shaky climber that made his way back to Betws that evening. Needless to say I did not breathe a word of the affair to any one. It was a disgraceful secret, to remain locked in my guilty bosom.

It is very easy to discover the causes for this little mishap – over-confidence, inexperience, and complete lack of judgement. It was bad enough to fall off once, but to go and do it again in a spirit of reckless petulance was sheer madness and showed that I was not really fit to be a climber. In climbing, everything should be considered calmly, and each move carefully thought out beforehand. Still, the whole thing did me a great deal of good. It showed me my limitations, made me think a lot, and made me much more careful in future. It was lucky for me that the fates picked on a nice safe place to teach me a lesson.'

Later in the same holiday, Colin made a solo attempt on the climb called *Lazarus* on Idwal's Holly Tree Wall. He only succeeded in extricating himself by lassoing a bollard with the rope he always carried, and then swarming up it past the crux. He carried out a number of other solo climbs at that time, wandering all over the Tryfan buttresses and the Milestone, and it is a measure of his natural ability that he survived unscathed.

Needless to say, the full details of these adventures were not revealed to the remainder of the family. In later years Colin was to conceal often quite painful injuries from his parents following falls at Helsby or in Wales; notably broken fingers and cracked ribs. His own accounts of these early adventures are fascinating and, reading between the lines, Colin was lucky to survive this early period of solo climbing, often on remote and deserted crags. The early years of lonely wandering and scrambling in the hills had paid off and helped Colin to develop a strong sense of survival. Certainly, by his late teens he had gathered a knowledge of Snowdonia the equal of any other activist in the area at the time. This intimacy was to pay dividends in the years ahead.

Whilst examining Colin's progress as a climber up to this point, it is important to examine the accepted levels and perceptions of difficulty in British rock-climbing in the mid to late-1920s. It was still widely accepted that the highest level of attainment was Herford and Sansom's ascent of Scafell's Central Buttress, together with, some years later, Roper's fierce routes on Dow Crag. It is safe to say that in North Wales, this standard of difficulty had not been approached by the summer of 1927, except in the case of Pigott's bold new route on Clogwyn Du'r Arddu climbed at the Whitsun of that year. In general, young climbers were expected to proceed with very great caution, due to the dire penalties likely to be exacted in the case of a fall and the consequent disgrace should he survive. A traditional and protracted period of following ponderous leaders up Moderates and Difficults was the usual introduction to the sport, followed by an equally pedestrian approach to leading. Added to this air of caution, was the established social climate that permeated the sport. At the end of the 1920s, mountaineering was still most definitely a sport of the professional and upper middle-classes. It required time in the form of long holidays, as activity on the rocks of Tryfan or Gable was viewed only as practice for the more serious business of Alpine climbing. In 'Menlove'[2], Jim Perrin touches on this point accurately:–

> The Alpine peaks were pretty much analogues for their ascensionists' situations in society during this period; mountaineering was capitalism and privilege geographized. There was a process of democratization beginning, particularly in the Peak District of Derbyshire where its representatives were working-class men like Frank Elliott and Eric Byne, but not until after the next war was there sufficient social change for it to be consolidated.

2 'Menlove' – Jim Perrin (Gollancz – 1985).

It was apparent from the outset that Colin did not really conform to the accepted pattern in the sport as a whole, both in terms of social position and approach to the physical act of climbing. Colin's background and occupation were not typical of most young men climbing in North Wales and the Lake District at this time, the public school/university background still being very much the norm. Similarly, his early exposure to climbing alone and to outcrop climbing near to his home in Liverpool had enabled Colin to develop quickly a level of technical proficiency and boldness on rock unusual for the period. Notwithstanding a certain amount of luck in avoiding serious injury up to this point by virtue of his natural ability, Colin had largely side-stepped the 'strait jacket' of the traditional approach to climbing outlined earlier. In this respect, he was the forerunner of a new generation of climbers such as Maurice Linnell and Menlove Edwards, who were similarly quick to grasp the essentially physical nature of rock-climbing whilst at the same time understanding the need for a highly developed sense of judgement to take the sport forward in relative safety.

Following that holiday in North Wales in the summer of 1927, Colin, at the age of seventeen, commenced work as a trainee clerk in the offices of the Royal Insurance Company (Liverpool and London and Globe Group). Their offices were located at the corner of North John Street and Dale Street in Central Liverpool, just a short walk from the Pier Head, and Colin would travel in from Sefton Park each day either on his bicycle or by train. By the latter part of the 1920s work was already becoming scarce in Liverpool and his family was pleased that Colin was able to obtain an office position straight from school. The Royal was to remain Colin's only employer until he joined the RAF some thirteen years later.

The year 1927 was significant for Welsh climbing primarily because it heralded the first major route on Clogwyn Du'r Arddu, the great cliff on the north side of Snowdon long viewed with awe as being impregnable. This major breakthrough came with the ascent of the East Buttress Route (now called *Pigott's Climb*) by the gritstone-trained team of Fred Pigott, Morley Wood, Lindley Henshaw and John Burton. Following on from the establishment of the Climbers' Club hut at Helyg in 1925, this ascent marked the beginning of a Welsh ascendancy in British climbing after a long period of Lakeland dominance. Elsewhere in Wales that summer a young climber from Cambridge University called Ivan Waller made two short hard routes, *Fallen Block Crack* on Clogwyn y Ddysgl and *Belle Vue Bastion* on Tryfan's Terrace Wall, that represented a real step forward in concept and execution and gave a foretaste of what was to come in the next few years.

By the spring of 1928, Colin had become more associated with members of the Wayfarers' Club and was making regular weekend trips to Snowdonia. The Wayfarers' Club, founded in 1906, was already a well-established organisation for climbers and walkers in the Liverpool area and was at this time looking to increase its membership by advertising for suitable candidates. The club was expertly organised at this time by its Honorary Secretary, Basil Alferoff, and had a core of keen active members. It was an ideal organisation for Colin, not yet eighteen, as it put him firmly in touch with like-minded people, and led him away from largely solo activity and its attendant dangers. Describing the club at this time, A.B. Hargreaves later wrote:–

> 'I have the clearest of recollections of the Wayfarers' Club as it was at that time – very small, very friendly, very enthusiastic and most welcoming to young and upcoming climbers. This was particularly shown by the generosity of the older members in providing transport between Liverpool and the hills. Hardly any young climbers at that time had transport of their own – we certainly hadn't. We were dependent for the main part on rail journeys followed by long walks, or in the case of Kirkus, cycling overnight from Liverpool.'

In addition to its own activities, the Wayfarers' Club had strong links with the Climbers' Club, and the Manchester-based Rucksack Club, both of which had club huts, Helyg and Tal-y-braich respectively. It is around this time that Colin's initials appear for the first time in the visitors' book at Helyg. Before very long he was a member of the Climbers' Club, itself undergoing a period of rejuvenation following the 1925 establishment of Helyg as a base in the Ogwen Valley. For their persistence and foresight in this matter, succeeding generations of climbers owe much to Herbert Carr and his friends in the Climbers' Club. From its opening, until the outbreak of World War II, Helyg became not only a meeting place for members of the club but the very hub of Welsh climbing. In his fine biography of John Menlove Edwards, Jim Perrin describes Helyg at this time with frankness and affection:

> 'Helyg lies in a grove of trees between the A5 and the Afon Llugwy in the Nant y Benglog. Just across the stream is the bulky vegetated mass of Gallt yr Ogof. More elegantly, Tryfan stands face-on a little down the valley, with all the grander hills around Llyn Ogwen massed behind it. In the 1930s, for all the intellectual and sporting glitter of its habitués – Longland, Wager, Greene, Auden, Kirkus, Hargreaves, Watkins, Shipton, Smythe all stayed here – it was rather a seedy place. George Borrow's description of it as a "miserable hovel" was still not wholly inappropriate. Sooty oil lamps offered poor illumination to its grubbier recesses. Cooking was carried out on primus stoves. It was a male preserve and it

showed it, by a cavalier unconcern for any of the dictates of tidiness or hygiene. The log-book was filled with inter-factional sniping over responsibility for mouldering rubbish in the grate or excreta in the incinerator. A bus, a rattling green boneshaker of a Crosville Foden diesel, passed to and fro each day between Bangor and Betws-y-Coed, whence the branch line ran to Llandudno Junction and the main coastal railway.'

Colin was typical of a whole new generation of mountaineers who were able to take advantage of Helyg's ideal location, and were the forerunners of a new type of climber, outcrop trained with rapid and frequent access to the crags of Snowdonia. The outcome of this combination of factors was to be a magnificent crop of new climbs in an exciting period of exploration.

Colin had already become a regular visitor to the sandstone outcrop above the village of Helsby, only some eighteen miles from his home in Liverpool. Colin's usual practice was to cycle to and from Helsby, and the tough training he received there was to influence profoundly his climbing career. We will return to Helsby in the next chapter, as it is true to say that the real significance of outcrop training on mountain crags was at this time just starting to emerge. Now approaching his eighteenth birthday, Colin had developed into a slim but wiry youth of medium height (about 5ft 9ins) with a shock of thick brown hair and with large soulful eyes. As is often the case with those naturally gifted, Colin's ability as a climber developed very quickly in his later teens. By this time, all three Kirkus brothers were smitten by the climbing bug, but Nigel and Guy rarely climbed with Colin, who was already becoming a quite outstanding cragsman.

It was during the summer of 1928 that Colin pioneered his first major routes in North Wales. One was on Clogwyn yr Oen in the Moelwyns, which was climbed with his brother Guy and is now regarded as a fine steep 'V. Diff'. The other was a solo ascent of a crack-line on the sombre crag of Craig Lloer, above the Ogwen Valley. It was to be an ascent that almost cost Colin his life and his own account, taken from 'Let's Go Climbing!' is disarmingly honest about his motivations and his subsequent experiences on the climb.

'I now had no difficulty in obtaining climbing companions, but this time it happened that I was on my own. I had an urge for exploration, and probably also wished to make a name for myself, so I decided to have a look at Craig Lloer, a crag above Ffynnon Lloer, a lonely little lake set deep in one of the wild hollows of Carnedd Dafydd. I picked on the West Buttress, the shortest but steepest of the three sections of the cliff. It was about 200 feet high and had never been climbed.

The main feature of the route I had planned was a sinister-looking crack, some 80 feet up. So the first thing to do was to find a way to the foot of this crack.

Things started quite easily but grew much more difficult when I reached the airy crest of the buttress, overlooking the vertical wall that dropped dizzily into the depths of the gully on the left. I climbed straight up the steep edge and gained the sloping ledge at the bottom of the crack by a very awkward movement.

The crack was about 40 feet high and overhung at the top. It looked very difficult. I tied the rope round my waist, with the other end hanging free, and started up. The crack was just about wide enough to fit a boot, and I progressed chiefly by jamming my hands and feet. In places there were small chockstones jammed in the crack and these were a great help, though I had first to test them very carefully to make sure that they were firm.

After an exhausting struggle I arrived at the overhang. I felt tired, because when you are climbing a pitch that is really vertical the arms get no rest at all. And now I had the overhang to tackle, where my whole weight would come on my hands. There was a convenient little stone here, jammed firmly in the crack, and I threaded the whole length of my rope down behind it, hanging on meanwhile with my left hand only. Then I tied myself on to the chockstone and was able to rest my arms, hanging more or less bodily on the rope.

Before I started off again I untied the rope from the chockstone but still left it hanging down behind, hoping that it might jam and hold me if I did happen to fall off the next section. Then I started up the overhang. It was very strenuous, and I struggled frantically. Then, just at a crucial moment, my rucksack jammed in the crack. With a despairing effort I worked it off my shoulder and abandoned it, precious camera and all. Another blind struggle and I was up, surprised and relieved to find the rucksack still hanging over the other shoulder.

Conditions looked much easier above and I continued gaily. There was an innocent-looking bulge ahead, and I got half-way up without thinking very much about it. Then I realized that it was much more difficult than it had seemed. I could see a good handhold a little higher and made rather a grab for it. That was all very well, but there were no footholds, so that I was hanging from my hands alone. There were no holds above and I could not descend. My arms were getting tired. I looked down and saw a sheer drop of nearly 200 feet below me. My arms were aching now and I felt that I could not hold on much longer. I just hung there and waited for the end. Then I got into a panic and made a sudden convulsive spring round the corner on the left, where my hands mercifully landed on a hold.

I count that as one of my narrowest escapes. It was a foolish affair, because I don't think it was really such a very difficult place. I made the mistake of acting first and thinking afterwards.'

Stirring stuff indeed, sight-soloing a new route, with a rucksack on a deserted mountain crag! Today, *Kirkus's Route* on Craig Lloer is graded Very Severe, and in its cleaned-up state gives a pleasant climb, the best on this esoteric crag. At this time Colin had began to acquire something of a reputation for daring solo exploits, which, coupled with his detailed knowledge of Snowdonia, made him a climber of formidable potential. This

An Idwal Christmas party: Colin, Mrs Hilda Gadd, 'AB', Connie Alexander and Alf Bridge

potential was to be realised over the next couple of years with some of the finest first ascents yet seen on British rock.

Elsewhere in North Wales, the principal climbing event of the summer of 1928 was the continuing exploration of Clogwyn Du'r Arddu, and Jack Longland's bold lead into the unknown with the first ascent of the West Buttress Route (now known as *Longland's Climb*) at Whitsun. Longland was accompanied on the climb by Fred Pigott, Frank Smythe, Bill Eversden and Morley Wood and a new golden age of Welsh climbing was finally heralded by this most important ascent, achieved by a combination of Oxbridge men and northern climbers from the Manchester Rucksack Club.

2 'The Suicide Club' A.B. Hargreaves

By the autumn of 1928, Colin had gained considerable experience in the mountains of Snowdonia and was a regular visitor to the sandstone outcrop at Helsby. As luck would have it, he was about to meet a climber who was to help channel his talents over the next few years, somebody already quite well established in the climbing world. The man in question was Alan Hargreaves, known almost universally in climbing circles as 'AB'. Six years older than Colin and a member of both the Wayfarers' Club and the Climbers' Club, 'AB' was a crucial character of the period. Now in his late eighties, he remains one of the great names of British climbing, a past president of both the Climbers' Club and the Fell and Rock C.C. and a tireless worker over the years for the Friends of the Lake District Society and as a member of the Executive Committee of the Lake District National Park Planning Board. A mercurial figure, possessed of a sharp mind and an acid wit, 'AB' recalls his many adventures with Colin with great affection and relish.

Alan Hargreaves was born in Blackburn, and had trained as an engineer before moving to the Liverpool area to work as an articled clerk for a firm of Chartered Accountants. 'AB's initial passion had been cycling, but after a particularly unsuccessful trip to the Lake District in the summer of 1926 that was plagued by bike problems, he became seriously interested in rock-climbing and joined the Wayfarers' Club soon after. Once involved in the club 'AB' came under the guiding influence of people such as Robertson Lamb, W.R. Reade, Basil Alferoff and Marco Pallis. The following year he got to know various members of the Climbers' Club's northern section, including J.M. Davidson, and like many Wayfarers of the time also joined the C.C. In addition 'AB' also became a member of the Fell and Rock Climbing Club, so forming what was to be a most important link between the climbers of North Wales and those of the Lake District. He was to be something of a catalyst amongst the key figures of the period, associated not only with Colin, but with Jack Longland, Ted Hicks, Menlove Edwards, Alf Bridge, Maurice Linnell, Graham MacPhee, and Albert (A.T.) Hargreaves (no relation). 'AB' had worked hard at his craft and by 1928 had become a fine rock-climber in his own right, having led a number of Severe routes that year. In terms of keenness and ambition, he was a good match for Colin, and it was not surprising that the Climbers' Club regulars at Helyg encouraged the partnership between these two young 'thrusters' with whom they were

19

rather unsure what to do! Years later, in his book 'Mountains and Men', Wilf Noyce commented:

> Climbing friends "crop up" and the climbs done depend very much on their quality. For example, Colin Kirkus's early meeting with A.B. Hargreaves, though the meeting was perhaps inevitable at some time, was a cause assuredly of his later supremacy as a rock climber. For Hargreaves knew perfectly the way of coaching a brilliant leader.

Writing in the Climbers' Club Journal in 1943, 'AB' recalled his first meeting with Colin and how they came to climb together:

> The Climbers' Club people seemed to think that he (Colin) was a bit mad and our introduction was on that basis – possibly they thought I was too – anyway we were promptly dubbed "The Suicide Club" because our first climb together was the Holly Tree Wall in nails on a nice wet day. I certainly think we would have been "disapproved of" by Charles Marshall who, for some time, had been a kindly but dominating mentor to the young climbers who were beginning to use Helyg, and whose fine career had come so tragically to an end a few months before. However, not only did we survive this rash expedition but founded thereon a partnership which was to flourish.

Certainly the combination was to be beneficial for both, 'AB's drive and determination coupled with Colin's outstanding ability. Colin's brother Guy remembers the rather abrasive young Hargreaves visiting the Kirkus home in Liverpool, and not being altogether approved of by Colin's parents. Nonetheless, Guy agreed that 'AB' was the ideal partner for Colin because of the two men's different but complementary characters.

It was 'AB' who finally proposed Colin for membership of the Wayfarers' Club, seconded by G.A. Dawson. Colin's entry to the club was duly recorded in the minutes of a committee meeting held on September 13th, 1928. Amongst those on the Wayfarers' Committee at that time were 'AB' himself, Marco Pallis and Basil Alferoff. 'AB' had already been a member of the club for some eighteen months and he was able to provide Colin with a number of good contacts within the membership.

Colin had for some time been a regular visitor to the sandstone outcrop at Helsby, with its attendant 36-mile round-trip by cycle, and was becoming something of the local expert. Nearer home he worked to strengthen his fingers with training at Irby Quarry or at a quarry at Heswall, both popular haunts of the Wayfarers at that time. 'AB' had also become a devotee of Helsby and throughout the winter of 1928-29 he and Colin climbed there a great deal, as weekends in Wales or the Lake District were still only an occasional luxury for young men on limited incomes. At one time, prior to the development of the fierce little crag at Pex Hill, Helsby was the local practice ground for Merseyside climbers. Although rather neglected in recent years, Helsby was at that time a most important outcrop and by the standards of the day was already well developed. It is safe to say that the standard of climbing there was as high as anywhere in the country, and Colin (and later Ted Hicks and Menlove Edwards) were to push the standards still further in the early Thirties, making Helsby very much the forcing ground of its day. This bluff of red sandstone, mostly 30-60 feet in height, was to have a substantial influence on Colin's development as a climber since it made great demands on finger strength, gymnastic ability and agility, whilst giving in return steep, fierce climbing with little or no protection. In 'Menlove', Jim Perrin summarised the uncompromising nature of Helsby climbing:

> Although only a short outcrop, there was an air of gravity about it. Because the rock was fragile, most climbs were initially done on a top-rope. The seriousness of leading them was good preparation for the longer but less technical run-outs on the hardest Welsh climbs. To add to the respectful manner in which the place was treated, fresh in memory would have been the death of C.W. Marshall on the cliff in the spring of 1928. He was a well-liked and competent climber, and the first custodian of Helyg, who had died after a fall whilst attempting to lead the Flake Crack – a long and strenuous layback high above the ground.

The original exploration of Helsby was carried out by John Laycock, and his book 'Some Gritstone Climbs' published in 1913, contained accounts of some twenty-five routes at the crag. In about 1925 C.W. Marshall became active at the crag and prior to his tragic death, produced a number of classic routes including *Wood's Climb* and *Marshall's Route*. Marshall and other members of the Wayfarers' Club had already begun guide-book work on the crag, and, during the winter of 1928-29, Colin and 'AB' took on the bulk of this work to produce the 'Guide to Helsby' published in the Wayfarers' Club Journal for 1930. The work on this guide produced some very bold climbing on the crag, with a crop of new routes that are test-pieces to this day and compare favourably with those from the period of gritstone exploration in Derbyshire and Yorkshire. The locals were very proud of Helsby and, writing in the Wayfarers' Club Journal, C. Douglas Milner once described Almscliff Crag in Yorkshire as 'a miniature Helsby with a better view'! Over the years Helsby and in more recent times Pex Hill, have helped produce some very notable rock-climbers from the Merseyside area: Ted Hicks, Menlove Edwards, Bob Frost, Arnold Carsten, Hugh Banner, Jim O'Neil, Alan Rouse, Phil Davidson. There is little doubt that the sandy, delicate climbing at Helsby helps develop great skill in a cragsman; in addition it demands the coolness to make hard moves well away from the reassurance of protection.

Two routes at Helsby.   *Photo C. F. Kirkus (AC coll.)*

The 1930 guide to Helsby, co-written by 'AB' and Colin, was a very thorough piece of work and the result of frequent visits. At this time 'AB' had to work on Saturday mornings and would rush from his office to catch the 12 noon train from Lime Street station to Helsby to meet Colin for an afternoon on the crag. The story is told of how they used to change in a public house, the Robin Hood, but often on returning they would cover the floor in Helsby sand and were eventually asked to make alternative arrangements! 'AB' recalled this episode with great mirth:

> There was a succession of landlords at the pub, and they were quite happy to have us because we drank a little beer, and we'd usually buy some tea or something when we came down – but, we did make a mess! Helsby is a dirty place you see, wet and dirty and it smells as well! Eventually we were kicked out, and went to a little café down the road and they didn't like us much either, so we ended up having to change in the railway station.

Colin and 'AB's writing in that guide of sixty years ago is surprisingly modern in some respects and not without humour, reflecting the good times the place must have given them. The routes which they described have given a lot of pleasure to many, particularly in the years prior to the war.

Jericho Wall...."Above the bulge the body may be braced across the gulf, and without further serious impediment a junction can be effected with the top of the storm-scarred precipice."

Undertaker's Buttress...."and one is able to reach the ledge to the right of and above Bad Corner. Here is a fair stance with several small belays, which can be made effective if line is in use and there is a Heath Robinson imagination in the party."

Grooved Slab...."Of the two starts to this charming climb, that on the right, a mantelshelf, is so well scratched as to be easily identified from so far away as Helsby Station – a sure sign of strenuosity."

Referring to the humorous tone of much of the writing in the guide, 'AB' had this to say:

'With regard to the comments about the storm-scarred precipice and so on. This was really a joke on our part! At that time every young climber used to read "British Mountain Climbs" by the Abraham Brothers, and they went in for colourful language, exaggerating and talking about vertical cliffs, huge precipices and so on. Our comments were by way of a skit on the writing of Ashley and George! Colin and I argued a bit about their inclusion. I wanted to include them because I thought they would amuse a lot of people and I think they did!'

The resulting guide to Helsby contained descriptions of almost sixty climbs and formed a solid basis for future exploration on the crag. In his conclusion, 'AB' summed up his and Colin's efforts:–

The new climbing found during the past year may be summarised as follows:– 23 climbs amounting to about 1000 feet, consisting of 11 Very Severes, 3 Severes, and the remainder Very Difficult. All but four of these climbs were first led by C.F. Kirkus, those four by F.E. Hicks.

Amongst the new routes were *Jericho Wall* (now graded HVS 5b), *Eliminate II* (now VS 5a), *Golden Pillar* (now VS 5a) and *Eliminate I* (now HVS 5a). Thus the 5a technical grade, and above, was very well established on this outcrop as early as 1929 – significant climbing for that period. A classified list was included containing 13 Very Severes, and the top routes were *Eliminate I, Eliminate II, Omega, Cinderella, Flake Crack* and *Jericho Wall*. The guide also contained a number of photographs all taken by Colin. Following on from the publication of this guide, Helsby was to be a great influence on the climbing of the young Menlove Edwards, and further hard routes, including the boldly desperate *Morgue Slab*, were catalogued in the further guides of 1935 and 1946. (Some years after the publication of Colin and 'AB's guide, Guy Kirkus cycled out to Helsby and attempted to solo the Flake Crack, the climb from which Charles Marshall had fallen to his death. Guy remembers reaching the difficult layback moves near the top of the route and then parting company with the rock, hitting the ground and crashing into the rhododendron bushes below the crag. He lay there, looked up to see that the sky was still blue and marvelled at how wonderful it was still to be alive! However, the journey back to Liverpool in a sidecar was very painful, as the impetuous young climber had sustained a fractured pelvis. On hearing of his youngest brother's close call, Colin was understandably not pleased. 'AB' ruefully recalled: 'Guy was damn lucky that time!'

Their sustained activity throughout that winter had made 'AB' and Colin very fit and on an early trip to Wales on March 10th, Colin served notice of his increasing talent. Climbing solo on the East Face of Tryfan, he set off up the 1911 classic *Grooved Arête*, adding two variation pitches of his own *en route*. The first was a Severe pitch of 60 feet from *The Haven*, the second a far more imposing pitch of 80 feet taking the arête more or less in its entirety in a very exposed situation. In the current guide-book this pitch still warrants a grading of VS 4c and was a very bold venture for a solo climber at that stage of the season. That Easter of 1929, Colin and 'AB' travelled down to Wales for a Climbers' Club meeting at Helyg, recorded humorously in the Climbers' Club Journal by T.R.W. Deakin as being notable for the quality and quantity of food consumed by the eleven members present. In the early days of his membership, Colin acquired an amusing reputation as a considerable eater, and was known at one time as Fido due to his ability to clean up anyone's left-over food at the end of a weekend. E. Stuart Chantrell, the Helyg Custodian from 1928 until 1957, and a good friend of Colin, once recorded that:

> Those of us who made regular visits to Helyg will never forget the sight of his sitting at the table on a Sunday evening, polishing off everything left uneaten. He might commence with a tin of bully, go on to a large plate of porridge, liberally spread with syrup and butter, and then proceed to clear the table systematically. It was a most impressive spectacle.

Chantrell took great pride in his work at Helyg and was present there most weekends, gently bullying the members into keeping the place neat and tidy. Aside from his service to the club as hut custodian, Chantrell had the rare gift of being able to produce a friendly atmosphere at Helyg and by making sure that everyone felt involved, was particularly good at helping young and inexperienced people to become accepted amongst the established members. To a shy young climber like Colin, this must have been most beneficial at a time when he was still feeling his way in the climbing world.

Returning to the subject of Colin's renowned appetite, 'AB' had this to say:

Helyg.   *Photo C. F. Kirkus (AC coll.)*

As a young man, Colin had enormous energy, and I put this down to the amount he could eat! He was always hungry, and would eat anything that was going. Climbing mountains and eating were Colin's main interests at this time. I recall one day in particular, when he and I were up in Wales during the week and there was no one else about. We made our way to Helyg after a day on the crags, and I remember that we hardly had any food with us. Anyway, somebody had left a kipper on a window ledge at the hut. It was well dried out, and had gone an ominous shade of blue! (laughter) Old Colin wasn't bothered by any of that; he cooked the kipper and ate it without any hesitation! (joyous laughter) Damn funny that was.

Amongst the climbs done by Colin and 'AB' that Easter was an ascent of the *Direct Route* on Glyder Fach, by *Gibson's Chimney* (now graded VS 4c) which had not been repeated for several years and was considered to be quite notable at the time. Indeed C.F. Holland had declared it the hardest route in Wales until the mid-Twenties. This was an ascent that made the Helyg regulars sit up and take notice, and it displayed just how much Colin and 'AB' had developed as rock-climbers over the past winter. 'AB' remembers that particular climb with pleasure:

In the original guidebook to the Ogwen Valley they wrote it up as being Exceptionally Severe and all that, in a terrifying place. A real write-up! Consequently no-one had done it for years. Anyway, we thought we'd better go and have a look at this damn place, and it was a beautiful climb. In those days it was covered in grass and loose rock, a lot of which we shifted. H.B. Gibson of course was involved in the first ascent of the Flake Crack on Scafell's Central Buttress and this climb on Glyder Fach was a jolly fine piece of work. You could of course dodge it by doing the hand-traverse, but that was harder than the Chimney! It of course became a very well-known useful climb, but when Colin and I did it, it was quite an event.

Some weeks after the Easter meet, Colin and 'AB' spent a fortnight climbing a number of well-established hard routes in the Lake District. It is important to examine the relative positions of climbing in Wales and in the Lake District at that time, for the ascents achieved by Colin and 'AB' on this trip had much to do with what was to follow shortly on the crags of Snowdonia. It is fair to say that in the spring of 1929, despite the beginnings of a revival in Welsh climbing over the previous two years, rock-climbing in the Lake District was still considerably further advanced. This situation had largely followed on from the 1914 ascent of *Central Buttress* on Scafell by Herford and Sansom, and the production of the 1924 Scafell Guide by C.F. Holland. Dow Crag was another cliff that had been developed to a high standard, with the magnificent *Great Central Route* and *Black Wall* climbed by the gifted Joe Roper, and the *Eliminates A, B and C* climbed by H.S. Gross. In addition, two hard climbs had been done in Langdale the year previously, *Hiatus* and *Gimmer Crack*, and Harry Kelly and his friends continued to transfer the standards of difficulty achieved on Peak District gritstone to the crags of Cumbria. In general, the activities of Climbers' Club members in the Lake District had been only cursory in recent years, with the exception perhaps of C.F. Holland, Fergus Graham, and C.G. Crawford.

The routes that Colin and 'AB' did on that trip to the Lake District served still further to demonstrate their continuing progress as climbers. They made the third ascent of Esk Buttress (by *Bower's Route* and including a variation of their own) together with early repeats of *Eliminate B* and *Eliminate C* on Dow Crag, *North West* on Pillar, and the *Pinnacle Face Climbs* and *Botterill's Slab* on Scafell. It was a most important trip for Colin, not yet nineteen, and 'AB' was to write in his obituary of Colin:

> I think Colin really found himself as a climber during this holiday, and although impressed with what was then the much higher standard of climbing in the Lake District as compared with Wales, he obviously began to feel that in due course he would be able to tackle anything. It will be appreciated that at that time very few people indeed were leading Very Severes – round about half a dozen.

Glyder Fach, Final Crack.   *Photo C. F. Kirkus (AC coll.)*

Recalling that joyful holiday in the mountains of Cumbria sixty years ago, 'AB' recounted an amusing story that served to demonstrate the prevailing attitudes, and something of the mental barriers young climbers had to try to break down in order to take the sport a stage further:

> Now, in those days no-one ventured on to the Pinnacle Face of Scafell, not since Herford and Sansom wrote it up. It had a big hoodoo on it following the terrible accident in 1904 when four climbers were killed on the thing. It was most definitely taboo for most Fell and Rock people. I remember that Colin and I had been all over the Pinnacle Face, we'd done *Jones's Route, Hopkinson's Gully*, the *Direct Route* by Herford's Slab which everyone fell off, and another out to the right – we did the lot! We were two cocky young climbers! Anyway, we met this chap in the village pub in Wasdale who was a vice-president of the Fell and Rock, and we said what we'd done and he was absolutely horrified, horrified! He said it was a job for experts with twenty years' experience behing them. "You silly young buggers," he said, "you'll cause another fatal accident." Anyway, we went off and did *Botterill's Slab*. We were using line of course, and we'd discovered that you could do funny things with line; it hooked over things well for belays. On Dow Crag, *Eliminate B* and *Eliminate C* were top climbs at that time, and were hardly ever done. We didn't get to do A at that time though.

The late spring and summer of 1929 were notable for warm, dry sunny weather that encouraged climbing still further, even on the high mountain crags. The stage was set for Colin's first major breakthrough in Wales, and the story of the deeds of June 25th/26th is now part of British climbing history. Writing in the Climber's Club Journal, Rennie Bere remembered that particular trip to Helyg with his friend Ted Hicks, and gives an amusing insight into Colin's character:

> In June 1929 Ted and I were at Helyg with Charles Warren and Archie Spence. After a day's climbing, Ted decided that he wanted to spend the night alone on the Heather Terrace and to walk there barefoot. Would we meet him next morning on the top of Tryfan bringing his boots with us and a pair of "rubbers" in case we should feel like climbing anything interesting. Ted then left us. There was no-one else in the hut, and while we were breakfasting next morning a stranger arrived from Liverpool on a bicycle. As he did not seem to have any food with him, we reluctantly asked him to share our meal. With deadpan face the stranger said "I usually just eat bread fried in vaseline". And that was my introduction to Colin Kirkus.

Unaware of Colin's considerable ability, the group led by Charles Warren set off up one of the Tryfan ridges, with Colin securely roped up. However, it was soon realised that they had a most capable climber amongst them and on the summit of Tryfan they met up with Ted Hicks. Along with Warren,

Bere and Spence, Hicks was at University, studying at Cambridge. He was no mean climber himself and had already put up new routes in Wales. He had first come to notice the previous year when an early repeat of *Gimmer Crack* in Langdale and a new route on Idwal's Holly Tree Wall (*Piton Route*) established his credentials. Ted Hicks and Colin were to become firm friends, and climbed together a great deal over the next few years, usually with 'AB'. In 1933 Colin was to travel to the Himalaya with both Hicks and Warren.

The introductions over, Colin took charge of the 'Cambridge party' and, from Adam and Eve on the top of Tryfan, they descended to the Terrace Wall where he led them up *Belle Vue Bastion*. This route had been established some two years previously by the talented Ivan Waller and the bold nature of its crux moves had made it one of the current touchstones of Welsh climbing. Colin's cool lead of this climb greatly impressed Hicks and Warren, who were well acquainted with the better Welsh routes of the time. Nevertheless, better was to follow as the party made its way to the Main Cliff of Glyder Fach. In 'Mountaineering in Britain'[1] Clark and Pyatt describe what happened on arrival at the crag:

> Here, much to their astonishment, Kirkus pointed to a narrow groove on the East Buttress, slightly to the left of *Chasm*, one of the trade routes of the cliff, and said that he would like to try it. Some members of the party obliged by going up one of the easier routes and reaching the top of the groove, a position from which they would be able to provide the support of a rope from above if necessary. The climb, which today, nearly thirty years afterwards, is still ranked as a good class Very Severe, consists of a 90-foot groove which grows consistently harder the higher one gets and which ends in an overhang. "The last twenty feet are extremely severe", it was stated in the Climbers' Club Journal following the first ascent. "After the struggle with the initial overhang, the human limit is almost reached in the desperate bridging above, where the climber is exposed over a 200-foot drop." To the party's astonishment Kirkus climbed the groove without looking back, first on a rope from above and then without it, and *Lot's Groove* it became for ever more. Hicks followed, but none of the other members of the party could tackle the problem successfully.

For perhaps the first time the current standard achieved on outcrops had reached the mountain crags of Snowdonia. The climb rapidly acquired a big reputation and was not repeated until 1931, when Menlove Edwards battled up it in wet conditions. It was considered at the time to be one of the hardest routes in the country, and was described in Colin's 1937 guide to Glyder Fach thus:

[1] Phoenix House Ltd 1957

110 feet. A climb of great severity, including one of the most difficult pitches in Wales. A preliminary inspection on the rope is probably advisable. Skill and confidence are necessary and strong fingers are an asset. The groove is vertical and is both strenuous and delicate. Standard: Very Severe (exceptionally so). Rubbers.

The fearsome reputation of *Lot's Groove* was further enhanced by comments that appeared in the Helyg log-book after Ted Hicks and 'AB' top-roped the climb later that summer.

> *Belle Vue Bastion* and *Javelin Buttress* are comparative walks! The name that seems best is *Lot's Groove*, because there is no looking back!

Over the years *Lot's Groove* has lost its initial aura and, although very steep, has succumbed to modern protection techniques. It is now a delightfully clean 90-foot pitch of Very Severe (4c) standard, climbed mostly by jamming and bridging. Rumour has it that Colin laybacked much of the pitch which may have added to its reputation! Certainly the climb was steeper and more holdless than had been climbed at that time, and pointed the way to the future – perhaps the first of the great corner cracks climbed in Wales. In the opinion of some, it is one of the finest pitches of its standard in Wales. The delicate moves out onto the arête before moving back into the corner are still thrilling, and are a real link with climbing history. It is fair to say that *Lot's Groove* would have been regarded by North Wales regulars at that time with much the same awe as later generations conferred upon Joe Brown's *Cenotaph Corner* of 1952, and Pete Livesey's *Right Wall* of 1974. Although a little devalued now, it pointed the way forward at the close of the 1920s to a whole new approach to the exploration of British rock.

The following day saw the same team in action on Tryfan, and again a hard new route resulted from their efforts. It would appear that in his solitary wanderings Colin had had one or two problems in mind, and this time his attention led in the direction of the Terrace Wall. Colin picked out a line to the left of *Belle Vue Bastion*, which gave an unremittingly hard pitch up a corner through some overhangs. He belayed after 80 feet and took in the rope, but this time none of the party was able to follow, not even the gifted Hicks. In the current Ogwen guide-book, *Central Route*, as it was called, is graded Very Severe (5a) and at that time was probably the boldest and most difficult pitch in Wales. Thus was Colin's reputation as a rock gymnast finally established and word of these deeds spread quickly through the then predominantly Oxbridge based Climbers' Club. In 'Mountaineering in Britain' Clark and Pyatt summed up this episode and the direction in which it then led Colin:

Colin at the mid-point on the first ascent of Lot's Groove.   *Photo Renie Bere*

Both these climbs were examples of exceptional mastery of technique; but the rock-technician who made them might have lacked the judgement necessary for greater, longer and more complicated climbs. That Kirkus had this quality as well, even at the age of 19, was demonstrated three days later when he went round to Clogwyn Du'r Arddu with A.B. Hargreaves and made the second ascent of Longland's Climb on the West Buttress, a four-and-a-half-hour climb during which considerable gardening had to be carried out, and which must have had much of the feel and quality of a first ascent.

The two existing routes on Clogwyn Du'r Arddu, established in 1927 and 1928, were then regarded as the ultimate challenges to climbers in North Wales. Fred Pigott had repeated his route on the East Buttress, but Longland's West Buttress route was as yet unrepeated. This second ascent of the route by Colin, 'AB', and fellow Wayfarer E.W. Stewardson took place on June 29th. It was their first visit to this finest of Welsh cliffs, where over the next few summers (1930-32) Colin was to earn his place in climbing history, his name to be forever associated with the development of the Black Cliff, along with that of Joe Brown a generation later.

It must have been a satisfied young Kirkus who faced the long, tiring cycle ride back to Liverpool at the end of that week at Helyg. Not only had he achieved two quite outstanding first ascents of a difficulty not previously achieved in North Wales, but he and his friend 'AB' had gone to the great cliff of Clogwyn Du'r Arddu and made an important second ascent of one of only two hard routes established there, both of which were still regarded with awe. Perhaps more important for a young man of barely nineteen was the fact that he had been somewhat lionised by the glittering group of University men at Helyg. Removed in background and class from the University students and professional men who made up most of the membership of the Climbers' Club, Colin was unusual in that despite his modest employment as a clerk, his involvement in the club was wholly justified on the basis of his outstanding climbing ability. Somewhat diffident in his youth, it is possible that Colin found the confident, assured and academic atmosphere prevalent at Helyg more than a little daunting. The successes of the past few months would probably have warmed his spirit, as he pushed the bike hard over the Denbigh Moors and on towards Queensferry. No doubt also he would have been mindful of the need to make it to Birkenhead before the last ferry left for Liverpool at 11 p.m., and then it would be the final pull out of the city centre up to Sefton Park, and at last some sleep.

'AB' describes the general feeling towards Colin at this time, and something of his own relations with his friend:

Colin was really from a different class to many of those in the Climbers' Club. He was usually very quiet with not a great deal of conversation, unlike many of the students at Helyg with their almost constant babbling! You won't hear a bad word about Colin, he was the most amiable, friendly co-operative chap you could meet. I doubt if he made an enemy in his whole life, and really just about everybody liked him. Our common interest was really climbing. We weren't able to socialise much in Liverpool, as we were on opposite sides of the river. I also had night classes as I was busy swotting for exams, so I usually only saw him at weekends and sometimes on Mondays for a chat. He was a man I had a great liking for, as did a lot of people. He was a very charming, amusing bloke!

'AB' recalled that throughout 1929, 1930 and prior to his departure from Liverpool to live in Barrow in May 1931, he would often meet Colin at his office at lunchtime on Mondays to discuss what had happened over the weekend, or to plot future deeds:

I was working as an Articled Clerk in a firm of Chartered Accountants in Liverpool. I was somewhat freer in my movements than Colin was, and would often go over to his office at Dale Street. I would usually go on a Monday after he'd got back from Wales. I knew what his working hours were, and I'd go along to see what he'd been up to. He'd have probably walked or cycled back from Helyg the night before, and I'd find him sitting at his desk, supposedly writing renewal notices or whatever. He'd be sitting there apparently working, but in fact he'd be asleep! (much laughter). I'd then sneak up alongside him, and give him a dig in the ribs! He was a delightfully quiet, unassuming, friendly sort of chap. He seemed to have no ambition at work, he just loved the mountains.

It was during the spring of 1929 that 'AB' introduced Colin to two friends of his, who up to that time had done most of their climbing in the Lake District. The men in question were Alf Bridge and Maurice Linnell, both at the time resident in Manchester and slightly older than Colin. They had established highly impressive credentials on the gritstone edges of the Peak district, and Linnell in particular was an outstandingly bold rock-climber: both were to become important characters in Colin's life in the years ahead. On this particular weekend they all got to know each other, enjoying some classic routes at Idwal.

Three weeks after he and Colin had climbed Longland's West Buttress Route on Clogwyn Du'r Arddu, 'AB' returned to the Black Cliff. Again he had Stewardson with him, and this time they teamed up with Ted Hicks. Armed with a route description cribbed from the hut book at Tal-y-braich, they made the true second ascent of *Pigott's Route* on the East Buttress. Their climb that day rapidly turned into an epic, and 'AB's account of it in the Climbers' Club Journal is well worth quoting to give a taste of the atmosphere of climbing at the end of the 1920s:

I came again to Helyg on July 19th and there I met Ted for the first time. We began talking about Clogwyn Du'r Arddu and its wonderful opportunities. I had brought with me a crib (from the Rucksack Club log-book at Tal y Braich) of Pigott's Climb on the East Buttress which Kirkus and I had already thought of having a go at after his second ascent of Longlands. Ted became enthused with this idea and we said. "Let's go tomorrow". This we did – walking over the Glyders and Snowdon, again with Stewardson. We found the climb difficult, and time-consuming, particularly in its lower reaches, and I thought fit to thread a new sling round Morley Wood's artificial chock-stone of two years before. It was not only the first climb Ted and I had together but was very nearly the last climb for all three of us .... When Ted and I got to the grass ledge at the top of the crack it was raining and blowing. The original finish was up the steep wall of about fifteen feet at the right-hand end of the ledge, and the Pigott and Morley Wood instructions were for the second to go round the corner to the right and from there flip the leader's rope over the top of this wall, where there was a notch. Thus the party would be secured and the leader could use the rope as a handhold when getting up the holdless part of the wall at the top. The crack in the corner at the left-hand end of the ledge had not then been cleaned out and we were not to know that there was a perfectly good chock-stone belay at the foot of it; so the party was dependent, for security, on the rope manoeuvre prescribed by Pigott and Wood. After many attempts we did succeed in getting the rope over the top of the wall and it seemed to have caught securely. Ted set off up, but the moment he started pulling on the rope as a handhold the thing came off and it was only by a split second's adjustment and grab for the top that he escaped falling off. If he had done so we would all three have been at the foot of the crag within seconds. This was one of the narrowest shaves I ever remember in more than forty years of climbing with many hazardous incidents. On subsequent ascents I found the crack in the corner much easier and, of course, there is the security of that chock-stone. As this was the first lead after Fred Pigott's two, I think it virtually ranks as a second ascent.

This was quite a day because, by the time we had finished, it was getting dark and we were very wet and tired so we went down to P.Y.G. to consider how to get back to Helyg. There, in the bar, we had the good luck to meet with one J.E. Grosvenor, later to become a Vice-President of this club – particularly notable for coming to Helyg in a chauffeur-driven car bringing hampers full of delicacies for the party. On this occasion, when he realised what we had done, he kindly offered us a lift to Helyg, thus saving us a tiresome further walk.

A word here in praise of our third man, Stewardson, who, as was the case when he had been with Colin and me on the second ascent of Longland's, had been subjected to a constant bombardment of turf mixed with stones as we gardened our way up. Present-day climbers can hardly appreciate what Cloggy was like in those early days, literally covered with turf.

As outlined earlier, Ted Hicks became a great friend of both Colin and 'AB'. Strongly built and athletic, he and Maurice Linnell were probably

Colin's only equals, until the dramatic emergence of Menlove Edwards in 1931. He was a natural athlete who could do almost anything; climb, ski, row, swim, all extremely well, and was particularly at home in boats. Following a number of climbing exploits, notably some important first ascents at Idwal and some early repeats of the first Clogwyn Du'r Arddu routes, Hicks climbed in the Himalaya with Charles Warren and Colin in 1933. Following an accident on Scafell a few years later, he moved away from climbing and turned his attentions to the sea, becoming an expert sailor and making a dozen crossings of the Atlantic. Hicks became a school-teacher after leaving Cambridge, and for many years was a distinguished Housemaster at the Dragon School at Oxford. He died in 1978, aged 70, preparing for his thirteenth Atlantic sailing. Discussing Ted Hicks, Marco Pallis told me:

> Ted Hicks, Colin and AB made the most perfect climbing team I ever knew of. They had all the qualities, both athletic and human.

Following this epic ascent of Pigott's Route, Colin and 'AB' teamed up with Ted Hicks for the remainder of that summer, and they did a great deal of climbing together both in Wales and at Helsby. In September, a visit was made to the Lake District. The great climbing test-piece of the day was still the Central Buttress (CB) on Scafell Crag established as early as 1914 by the brilliant team of Herford and Sansom. Ted Hicks had made an attempt on the climb with Rennie Bere and Charles Warren but bad conditions had defeated them. However, Colin, 'AB' and Hicks set out for the route on the morning of September 7th. Writing in the Climbers' Club Journal, 'AB' described their adventures that day:

> On September 6, 1929 Ted, Colin and I got a lift to Langdale from another very kind man, R.O. Griffiths, a Wayfarer and a Senior Lecturer at Liverpool University, and on the following day we did C.B. Not without incident (!) as Colin slithered off the lower part of the crack, which was wet. We fielded him on the Oval! It was then Ted who led to the chockstone, after which Colin, having recovered, did the upper part of the flake. Accurate counts of ascents of C.B. had been by then lost, but I then made this to be about the seventh or eighth and it was certainly the first ascent by an entirely C.C. party (who were also Wayfarers). On his form that day Ted was probably capable of leading the top part of the flake without aid at the chock-stone but we restrained him from trying to do so because we wanted to do the climb in the then orthodox fashion. It remained for Menlove Edwards a year or two later to be the first to perform the feat of leading the upper part without aid or even a thread at the chock-stone!

Talking about this incident recently, 'AB' highlighted how well Hicks was climbing that summer:

We changed the lead, Colin was going to go on to the chock-stone, and he probably would have wanted to go on, but he slithered off and we did a rugger tackle on him (laughter!) on the Oval, which isn't a very big place. We got him tidied up, and then we put Ted up to go at the chock-stone. Now, Ted was in very good form that day, and I'm pretty sure he could have done the thing free. He was a splendid chap, a man of extraordinary ability as a schoolteacher, climber, skier, and yachtsman. Good old Ted!

As 'AB' recalled, this was the seventh or eighth ascent of CB, and they then followed it with the fifth ascent of Gimmer Crack, which still retained an aura of difficulty at that time. On returning to Wales, Hicks was particularly interested in the many new route possibilities around the Idwal Slabs. Their probings produced a number of new routes including the very bold and delicate *Rowan Tree Slabs* (led by Hicks on September 26th) which was thought to be even harder than Colin's *Central Route* on Tryfan. The same afternoon that Hicks completed this climb, with C.V.A. Cooper and W.E. Woosnam Jones, he also pioneered the *Girdle Traverse* of Holly Tree Wall, another exciting route for the period. That same month, Hicks led the fourth ascent of the West Buttress Route (Longland's) on Clogwyn Du'r Arddu. At the very end of September Colin returned to the fray and on the 28th climbed *Central Rib* on the Idwal Slabs with 'AB', a pleasant and delicate variation between the established lines of *Hope* and *Charity*. In addition both Colin and Hicks made attempts on what was to become *Suicide Wall Route 1* (Chris Preston's masterpiece of 1945) at Idwal. 'AB' recalls a strong attempt by Hicks, following a climb on Clogwyn Du'r Arddu and the walk back over Snowdon and the Glyders to Idwal:

> Suicide Wall was an obvious challenge even in our day, and everybody wanted to do it. I well remember going there with Ted Hicks, and we struggled up that first hard bit on to the grass ledge where I had a small spike belay. Then Ted started off up the final wall, and like a lot of climbs at Idwal it rapidly gets smoother the higher you go, very much smoother, like an elephant's backside as I used to say! Anyway, Ted got stuck some way up the final wall and told me I'd better get round to give him a top rope. Imagine the situation (laughter), I had to unhook, get back down that hard wall, and while Ted stood on a tiny foothold, I had to run round with the rope to the top of the Slabs, get a belay and drop him a loop. By this time Ted's hands had got very cold, and I had to assist him up that smooth elephant's bottom. He had got very near to doing it, but Ted was a very good and careful climber and there was nothing rash or desperate about him. I'm sure that Colin and Menlove tried as well at some point.

Colin, 'AB' and Ted Hicks continued climbing together into the latter part of that eventful year. In addition, that autumn Colin met someone who

Ted Hicks and Colin on Belle Vue Bastion.   *Photo Renie Bere*

was to be an important climbing companion and friend for the remainder of his life. The person in question was Graham MacPhee and Colin was introduced to him by 'AB'. MacPhee recorded that they first met on October 14th:

> ABH came round for the evening, and brought Kirkus who is about eighteen, and a quiet youth. They stayed until midnight, so they must have enjoyed themselves.

MacPhee was twelve years older than both 'AB' and Colin, having been born in 1898 and, already in his early thirties, was a notable mountaineer of the period. A Scot, of trenchant wit and sometimes caustic tone, he was, like 'AB', a major character of the time. A member of The Scottish Mountaineering Club (S.M.C.) and the Rucksack Club, he had got to know 'AB' through their common connection with the Fell and Rock C.C. MacPhee was a successful dental surgeon, with a practice in Liverpool and an academic post at Liverpool University. His credentials as a rock-climber were impressive, with a number of first ascents (notably *Gimmer Crack* and *Hiatus* on Gimmer Crag) and early repeats to his credit. MacPhee's achievements in the climbing world were to be many, although he is probably best remembered for his associations with Colin, and his numerous first ascents on Ben Nevis during the production of the excellent 1936 S.M.C. guide-book. From 1952-54 he was President of the S.M.C. and in 1955 became the twentieth person to complete the Munros. He died in 1963, in an accident whilst climbing alone in the Canary Islands.

A fortnight later on October 27th, Colin and 'AB' were climbing together on Tryfan and added a new pitch to Ivan Waller's Long Chimney of 1927. Someone who recalls that particular weekend, and his own introduction to Colin, is Bill Stallybrass.

> I first met Colin in Wales in October 1929. I first took to rock-climbing that summer, having had numerous holidays in the hills with my parents who were keen hill-walkers. One of our neighbours in Heswall, Peter Brown, was a cousin of Ted Hicks the well-known Cambridge man. Ted taught Peter to climb, and took him to the Idwal Slabs a few times. The Browns had a cottage in the Nant Ffrancon at the time. Peter joined us that summer for a fortnight at Wasdale, and four of us climbed together on a sixty-foot rope – rather with the speed and motion of a caterpillar! Immediately after that I went up to Liverpool University, and I joined the Wayfarers' Club, sometimes having lunch with AB who was also a member. AB arranged for me to go on a weekend in Wales, a joint meet of the Wayfarers' Club and the Rucksack Club at Tal y Braich. Colin and some of the Climbers' Club people were staying nearby at Helyg. AB introduced me to the Idwal Slabs on the Saturday, and by the Sunday I had decided to join the

Graham MacPhee, underneath the Douglas Boulder in 1927.   *Photo courtesy of Matthew Shaw*

Climbers' Club. There wasn't any great qualification required at that time, but I hadn't actually led a climb so a chap called George Radcliffe let me lead him up the Milestone. On the way up we were passed by Colin and AB going at a rate of knots unroped. I was rather shocked, because up to then I had been rather wrapped up in the old Abraham Brothers tradition. I think they realised I was a little taken aback, because as they sped past one called to the other "Do you think it will go Ashley?" and the other said "Yes, I think so George!" They were on their way up to do *Long Chimney*. I have to be honest, I was a little bit disappointed when I first met Colin, because I was expecting someone who was outstanding to look at! I had already heard of him, as a lot of people were talking about him in the climbing world. To meet him and to see this ordinary, undistinguished person didn't live up to my expectations!

Bill Stallybrass was at this time a student at Liverpool University. A cheerful extrovert character, he was to be a leading light in the Liverpool University Rock Climbing Club and a sometime climbing partner of Menlove Edwards. Bill later worked with Colin on the production of the 1937 Glyder Fach guidebook, and they became close friends for the remainder of Colin's life. Bill became a notable linguist and, in later life, occupied a senior lecturing post at the Royal Military Academy at Sandhurst, where amongst his students was a young man called Christian Bonington.

A week later, at the Climbers' Club Dinner at the Adelphi in Liverpool, Bill takes up the story again and describes his first day on the crags with Colin:

I can remember that there were a lot of younger people at the Dinner, from Cambridge and so on, and there was some fairly heavy drinking going on! By the end of the evening Colin had had a little more than was good for him (laughter) and was not terribly capable. It so happened that I was in a University Hostel in the Sefton Park area, and Colin only lived about a quarter of a mile away. We went back on a tram, and I saw him to his door to make sure he got in safely (laughter). He'd mentioned the idea of climbing together sometime before we parted. Next morning at breakfast, one of my fellow students told me that there was an odd-looking chap outside looking for me, and it was Colin. I was very surprised to see him up and about so early after the night before, but he asked me if I'd like to go climbing at Helsby with him. It was a bitterly cold morning, but we set off on our bicycles and after a stop for a pint, did twenty routes at Helsby in an afternoon. Nothing very startling, but as a final thing he led me up *Wood's Climb*, a lovely little route, and I fell off the overhang three or four times before finally giving up and saying "...not another thing today Colin!" We then cycled back to Liverpool. We really hit it off right away, and it's funny but we never talked about anything serious in those days, like politics. We were just friends enjoying a day on the crags together. A fortnight later I went back to Helsby with Colin and AB, and again failed on *Wood's Climb*. I was pushed in at the deep end really!

The following weekend, Colin, 'AB' and Hicks were back in Wales staying at Helyg. On this particular trip they established, on November 9th, a new climb on the East Wall at Idwal. The route was called *Rake End Chimney* and it was quite a handful on the day, as 'AB' later recorded:

> For a time this was thought to be the hardest route on the East Wall. The corner was wet. Hicks failed on the overhang and the party was about to give up and try a severe-looking traverse on to the Ash Tree Wall. Kirkus, however, was not to be beaten and took off his boots and the overhang "went" after a struggle .... This must have been one of the boldest leads ever undertaken as the rocks were greasy and the possibility of exit doubtful.

The modern grade for the climb – parts of which have fallen down over the years, making it easier – is Very Difficult, and it is described as having '...a solid mountaineering feel.'

A fortnight later, following the Wayfarers' Club Dinner on Saturday November 23rd, Colin climbed with Graham MacPhee for the first time. MacPhee was the Fell and Rock C.C. representative at the dinner, and noted that 'Solly made a particularly good speech.' After the dinner, MacPhee drove Colin and 'AB' down to Wales in his Sunbeam, reaching Helyg at 1.30 a.m. It was a typically miserable morning when they arose, cold and with more than a hint of drizzle in the air – an average Welsh Sunday! Nonetheless, the three of them, in the company of Ted Hicks, set off for the Idwal Slabs. 'AB' led MacPhee up *Hope*, while Colin climbed with Hicks. Colin then led MacPhee up the *Original Route* on the Holly Tree Wall, a fine climb that has entertained thousands of climbers over the years since the first ascent by I.A. Richards, C.F. Holland, and Dorothy Pilley in May 1918. On that particular occasion, the Richards party started up what was to become *Piton Route*. However, the present notoriously difficult start was added by Ted Hicks in March 1929. It was an auspicious opening to the partnership of Colin and MacPhee, not least because it was one of Colin's favourite routes. MacPhee found it hard work, and recorded: 'I was just about at my limit!' On reaching the top of the wall, the two of them were drenched by a deluge of rain and sleet and scuttled back to Helyg with Hicks and 'AB' for a welcome brew of tea. One reason for MacPhee struggling on the Holly Tree Wall that day was that he was just finding his way back on to rock having recovered from a climbing accident sustained the previous February. He had smashed his ankle badly in a fall at Black Rocks near Cromford in Derbyshire, whilst climbing with Ivan Waller. This ankle injury was to trouble MacPhee periodically for the remainder of his life. Graham MacPhee took his climbing very seriously, and worked hard at keeping fit.

His daily routine always included physical jerks followed by a cold bath, and he was a regular visitor to the gymnasium and swimming pool at the Adelphi Hotel, often meeting 'AB' there. This habit of training at the Adelphi was later adopted by Menlove Edwards prior to some of his finest performances on rock, and it is likely that he was encouraged in this by MacPhee.

The meeting of Colin and 'AB' with MacPhee brought a most important factor into their climbing activities – namely a reliable motor car. The whole issue of transport, particularly to North Wales and the Lake District, was of course a major problem to young climbers at that time. Indeed car ownership amongst even the largely middle-class climbers of the time was far from common and, as 'AB' recalls, they often had to rely on the kindness of senior club members:

> You must remember that we young climbers simply did not have motor cars. We were absolutely dependent upon older club members, most of whom were very kind and ferried us about. The Wayfarers were particularly good at this side of things. MacPhee of course did have a car, but he was already an established professional and somewhat older than us. Colin, Ted, myself and no doubt many others were just glad to be carted along! We simply couldn't have got to Langdale or to Ogwen otherwise. Some years later Menlove had a car, but he was an absolute menace, didn't have a clue! He would just fling the car round corners, and after a couple of rides with him I vowed never again! I don't think that Colin ever owned a car.

Some weeks after their ascent of Holly Tree Wall, Colin returned to Helyg with Graham MacPhee on Saturday December 14th. The night before they had passed a pleasant evening looking at photographs of the Alps with fellow Wayfarer Marco Pallis. Ted Hicks and 'AB' were at Helyg when Colin and MacPhee arrived, and the Sunday morning saw them all climbing together again at Idwal. MacPhee recorded in his diary:

> Ankle sore. Relayed climbers in car to Ogwen cottage, making two trips. Kirkus led GGM and FEH up *Heather Wall*, and nearly came off. It was far too difficult a climb given the greasy conditions! Later Kirkus led ABH up a new climb, *Grooved Wall*. Drove back to Liverpool in the Sunbeam, in 2 hours 23 minutes, including three stops...

This was obviously a good day out for the time of year, and Colin made what was possibly the second ascent of *Heather Wall* on Idwal's East Wall. The first ascent had been made some six months previously by Ted Hicks, E.A. Stewardson and 'AB'; it had proved to be a hard climb as 'AB' recalled:

> An apparently weak spot was attacked light-heartedly in boots; after about an hour's hectic work, in which the Helyg poker played its part nobly, and during

which the leader changed into rubbers, a heaven-sent belay was reached ... after
several abortive attempts on the holdless corner above, an inspired lead across a
rickety traverse and up an impossible-looking bulge gave us *Heather Wall.*

In Menlove Edwards's guide to Cwm Idwal, published in 1936, *Heather
Wall* was described thus:

> This is one of the finest routes on the East Wall. Starting easily, it gets steadily
> harder to the finish, steep and exposed. The rock is clean and good with very little
> grass, yet it is not very often that rubbers can be kept dry through the whole of it.
> Very clean face climbing with a light touch, even on the stances. Rubbers are
> usual. Standard: Hard Severe. Easily becomes Very Severe in imperfect
> conditions.

The climb is still graded Very Severe in the current Ogwen guide-book,
and must have given Colin an exciting lead that cold morning. In the
afternoon Colin teamed up with 'AB', and made a new climb at the top end
of the East Wall, approaching from Ash Tree Wall. The pitch they climbed
is of good quality and is exposed. It was climbed in socks, 'using all possible
stances', and they called it *Grooved Wall.* It is now graded Severe, with the
addition of a first pitch done in 1942.

Bill Stallybrass remembers visiting Helyg with Colin, 'AB' and fellow
Wayfarer, R.O. Griffiths, at the very end of that year. Conditions proved to
be particularly cold and wintry:

> I recall that there was a great deal of snow about, and it was bitterly cold. Griffiths
> and I got hauled up the Central Buttress on Tryfan, and I remember swearing
> that I'd never go out again in the winter! Of course, by the time we got back to
> Helyg, I thought what a wonderful day we'd all had despite the cold.

There is no doubt that it had been quite a year for Colin. Life in the
Insurance Office might have been rather dull, austere and restrictive during
the week, but the weekends had certainly been wonderful. Almost constant
climbing at Helsby or in North Wales, coupled with two successful holidays
in the Lake District, had vastly increased Colin's experience as a rock-
climber. The raw and often erratic talent of a year previously had blossomed
into a near mastery of Welsh rock. The tenuous marriage of judgement and
flair that Colin was now developing, so crucial in that period before climbs
could be safely protected, was to be the corner-stone of his climbing in the
years ahead. Much credit here is obviously due to 'AB', as his guidance and
thorough knowledge of the current British climbing scene would have
proved invaluable to the nineteen-year old Kirkus, still finding his way in the
world in many respects. During that summer and autumn, Ted Hicks had
also proved to be a staunch ally in some exciting deeds, while, within the

Wayfarers' Club, Colin's friendship with Marco Pallis was to do much to broaden the young man's outlook to the wider mountain world. Perhaps of the greatest significance, at this stage of Colin's life, was his introduction to the vastly experienced Graham MacPhee – a climber with whom he was to share some notable adventures in the next few years. MacPhee's mobility and continuing ambition as a climber were to be key factors in Colin's climbing activities from this point forth, as was Colin's growing friendship with Alf Bridge and Maurice Linnell.

It is possible to imagine Colin outside the hut at Helyg at the end of that year, following the wild day on Tryfan with 'AB', Bill Stallybrass and R.O. Griffiths. He might well have paused for a minute or so and glanced up at the lovely form of Tryfan, smothered in snow and ice and glittering in the moonlight against a dark starry sky. Perhaps he had time to reflect for a moment that he had indeed come a long way from his solitary wanderings in the hills of a few years before, until his contemplations were broken by a bitter wind blowing up the Ogwen Valley and a cry from the warmth of the hut telling him that the tea was ready. He crunches across the frosty ground and closes the door behind him; the great hills look on impassively, and the dark Welsh night closes in at the turn of the decade, and the passing of the 1920s.

3 The Birth of a Golden Era

The opening months of 1930 saw Colin's climbing activities continue in a similar pattern to that of the previous year, with weekends at Helyg interspersed with finger-toughening trips to Helsby, usually on the trusty bicycle. An increasingly frequent feature of his mid-week social life was evening visits to Graham MacPhee's home, usually in the company of 'AB', Marco Pallis or Ted Hicks. At this time Colin's family lived at Croxteth Grove, not far from MacPhee's lodgings near to Sefton Park. These mid-week meetings, usually to look at photographs, drink tea, listen to music or to plot future deeds in the hills, would no doubt have been very stimulating and valuable to someone of Colin's age and background. In particular Marco Pallis and Graham MacPhee were cultured and urbane men, somewhat older than their youthful companions, and probably they would have attempted to broaden 'AB's and Colin's outlook on the mountains, away from pure rock climbing and towards an interest in the Alps and the Himalaya. Certainly at this time, MacPhee had great knowledge of both summer and winter climbing in Scotland through his links with the S.M.C., and was also an experienced Alpinist, having had some notable adventures with Frank Smythe, amongst others. Marco Pallis also shared this broader view of the mountains but his major interests were in the direction of music and Buddhism. He had formed a close friendship with Colin through mutual activity with the Wayfarers' Club and they were to share a number of adventures in the early 1930s.

Marco was born in 1895 in Liverpool, of Greek parents, and acquired from them a deep interest in India and its culture – itself a result of family business links with the sub-continent. He was educated at Harrow and, after a period in the Grenadier Guards during which he was wounded on the Western Front in the Great War, he attended Liverpool University. It was here that he started to develop his main interests in music, mountaineering and metaphysics, to which was added a talent for languages. By 1925 he had become a pupil of Arnold Dolmetsch and here he not only met Richard Nicholson who was to become his friend and companion for life, but also began the study of Tibetan Buddhism in which field, after his acceptance into its practice in the mid-Thirties, he became the acknowledged expert in Britain. When Colin first met him, Marco was a leading light in the Wayfarers' Club, and although only possessing a modest mountaineering

Colin and Marco Pallis in the early 1930s.   *Photo courtesy of Marco Pallis*

ability, was himself well liked and respected by many key figures of the period. He was to be a considerable influence on Colin at this stage of his life and I suspect that much of Colin's philosophy towards the mountains stemmed from his shared experiences with Marco. Two years before his death in 1989 at the age of ninety-four, I had the very great pleasure of meeting Marco Pallis, together with Richard Nicholson, at their flat in central London. Marco talked very happily of his adventures with the Wayfarers' Club, and in particular of his high regard for Colin, both as a mountaineer and as a man. It is very likely that, not yet twenty years old, Colin's life then consisted almost entirely of his job and his climbing activities: it is unlikely that his modest wages as an Insurance Clerk would have run to very much more, after regular visits to North Wales or Helsby and the necessary upkeep of equipment. Certainly Bill Stallybrass, amongst others, did not recall Colin going very often to the theatre, the cinema or to concerts, and a little of the class and material differences between him and many of his University-based climbing friends becomes more evident here. In this respect, Colin's social contact with Graham MacPhee and Marco Pallis, together with others in the Wayfarers' Club, must have been particularly valuable to him as he developed as a young adult. No doubt the same could be said for 'AB', although much of his leisure time was now taken up with evening classes and hard study to qualify as an accountant. Nonetheless, their work-day grind in the office would be broken up by the lunch-time get-togethers which the Wayfarers regularly held in central Liverpool, and which served further to help young climbers find their feet in the club.

January 1930 was a particularly bleak wintry month and Bill Stallybrass remembered a bitterly cold visit to Helsby with Colin and 'AB'. Cycling home must have been colder than the climbing itself but there was no doubting their keenness even in the depths of winter. Colin also paid a couple of visits to Helyg with MacPhee that month, the first on the weekend of January 4th/5th. MacPhee drove the party, consisting of Colin, 'AB', and Hicks down to Wales on the Saturday afternoon. That evening they adjourned to a Capel Curig pub to celebrate MacPhee's 32nd birthday, which was the following day. The Sunday found the party a little the worse for wear and the weather was distinctly unfriendly. MacPhee described the day in his diary:

> Hargreaves was up early cleaning as usual. We went up to Idwal in a blizzard and got soaked to the skin. Even the easiest route would not go.

No doubt the party was glad of the heater in MacPhee's redoubtable

Sunbeam, on the journey back to Liverpool that Sunday evening! A week later, MacPhee again drove Colin and 'AB' down to Helyg, once more in a blizzard! They awoke on the Sunday to a really wild morning, with thick snow on the ground and the wind screaming up the Ogwen Valley. Undeterred the party breakfasted and set off for the hill, as described by MacPhee:

> We left the hut at 10.30 in sleet and wind, and made for the Heather Terrace of Tryfan. We then followed *Bristly Ridge* up on to the Glyders. Far too much for my ankle.

A couple of weeks later Colin and 'AB' accompanied MacPhee to the Climbers' Club Northern Dinner at the Liverpool University Club. MacPhee recorded that: 'It was quite a good do, but Kirkus and co. got drunk!'

Next day, well past lunch-time, 'AB' and Colin called round to see MacPhee and were delighted to find him still in bed recovering! The remainder of the afternoon was enjoyed looking at MacPhee's extensive collection of Alpine photographs.

Whatever problems Graham MacPhee's ankle had been causing him in Wales, he managed to put them aside some weeks later when he was involved in a superb first ascent in the Lake District, on Deer Bield Crag in Far Easdale, with A.T. Hargreaves. The climb in question was the excellent and highly strenuous *Deer Bield Crack*, which they climbed on Sunday February 16th following a number of weekends of exploration and gardening. In particular, the weekend previously they had got a long way up the route and had cleaned off a lot of loose material before being defeated by the crux-chimney. This time, they were not to be denied, and MacPhee recorded how pleased he was with their success:

> Hargreaves led in magnificent style. We took four hours, and I then did a bit of stage-managing by abseiling down the climb afterwards to take photographs. It was a perfect day to do a first ascent in my present condition, with the ankle playing up, and I enjoyed every minute.

The crux of this route is an infamous struggle up a chimney, which still warrants a technical grade of 5b. Beyond this lies a further sting in the tail, with a difficult final pitch up an overhanging corner. Even today, the climb is graded 'Hard V.S.' and the first ascent was clearly a magnificent achievement, given the meagre protection at their disposal. There is no doubt that MacPhee was a very fine rock-climber, and his companion that day quite exceptional. Some years later 'AB' commented that:

Deer Bield Crack in Easedale is one I rank harder than 'Central Buttress' – a really fine climb of great difficulty and a very strenuous one at that. It has almost a Clogwyn Du'r Arddu flavour about it and is, perhaps, as hard as *Piggot's Climb* or the *Pedestal Crack*.

'AB' was involved in an early repeat of the climb, with A.T. Hargreaves and Bill Clegg, and their ascent was an eventful one with much changing of the lead! MacPhee returned to *Deer Bield Crack* with A.T. Hargreaves and A.B. Reynolds only a fortnight later to make the second ascent. They followed this by climbing *Deer Bield Chimney*, and then strolled up to Easdale Tarn. Here the thick ice was broken, and in the tradition of the time they all enjoyed a swim!

MacPhee's companion on this climb, A.T. Hargreaves, was an outstanding rock-climber, and subsequently became a friend and climbing companion of both Colin and 'AB'. Albert Hargreaves, no relation to 'AB', had been born in Rochdale in 1903 and began climbing in his mid-twenties mainly on Peak District gritstone. Initially he climbed with Roy Horseman and Arthur Chisman and later they were joined by Herbert Hartley and Maurice Linnell, to form a powerful team on the rapidly-developing gritstone edges. Amongst the new climbs they pioneered were fine Stanage classics such as Hargreaves' *Black Slab*, the *Trinity Routes*, *Rusty Wall*, *Green Crack* and *Christmas Crack*, together with *Tower Arête* at Laddow. *Deer Bield Crack* was the first of many new routes which Hargreaves pioneered in the Lake District, where he was a regular partner of MacPhee. He was to become a major figure in the sport during the 1930s, climbing important new routes on Scafell with Linnell and on Ben Nevis with MacPhee, as well as being involved in a whole new series of Fell and Rock C.C. guide-books and the opening of Brackenclose, the club's first hut, in 1937. Sadly he was to die in a skiing accident in Austria in 1952, at the age of 49.

Of great significance for the Wayfarer's Club that February was the opening of the Robertson Lamb Hut in Langdale. This was to be a most considerable facility in the district and preceded the Fell and Rock C.C. huts by some seven years. This proved to be a most valuable asset to the club and its setting up was due in no small measure to the efforts of the club President, Lawson Cook with the aid of a generous gift from Robertson Lamb himself, followed by later gifts from his family after his death. 'AB' was particularly involved in these proceedings and commented:

> This was a tremendous development for the Wayfarers and I was enthusiastically involved, so that when the Hut was eventually set up I was appointed to be the first Hut Secretary/Custodian. Actually I was not very good at that job, because I was

far too involved then in active climbing to give the time needed to look after and run the Hut. But very soon, there appeared one Harry Spilsbury who soon showed a genius for Hut management, Hut maintenance and general organis-ation, which was needed and he took over from me after about a year and did this job splendidly for a great many years.

Colin became a regular user of the hut on his visits to the Lake District and, later this same year, it was the base of operations for one of his most famous first ascents.

Towards the end of March Colin made a couple of visits to Helyg with MacPhee. The first weekend, March 22nd/23rd, saw him walking up to the Bochlwyd Buttress below Glyder Fach, on a cold snowy morning with MacPhee and 'AB'. Here they made the third ascent of Ted Hick's charming route of the previous year, *Wall Climb*. On a bitterly cold morning, this exposed little route must have been quite difficult but, undeterred, Colin led the party up it; then they did *Chimney Climb*, the original route on this pleasant crag. By this time the weather was becoming distinctly unpleasant and Colin elected to go for a 'snow bash' and a walk. Meanwhile 'AB' persuaded MacPhee to climb on the Idwal Slabs, where they climbed a combination of *Faith* and *Charity* in increasingly poor conditions that caused them considerable delays.

The following weekend MacPhee again drove down to Helyg accom-panied by Colin and C.J.Astley Cooper. Maintaining a proud tradition amongst climbers, MacPhee was stopped by a policeman in Llandudno for what was described as dangerous driving! They continued to Helyg at a slightly reduced speed. On the Sunday (March 30th) MacPhee drove the three of them round to the Llanberis Pass, where they examined the possibility of a new climb on the virtually unexplored Nose of Dinas Mot – the great bastion of dolerite buttressing the north ridge of Crib Goch. Colin proceeded to make a lead of the first part of what is now known as the *Direct Route*, when a way was then found to the left to join what later became the line of the *Cracks Climb*. What Colin attempted on this occasion was to complete the central groove of *Direct Route*, but he was forced out to the left, probably by wet rock. Nonetheless they seem to have enjoyed the climb as MacPhee noted: 'A very fine first lead and a Severe climb, most enjoyable.

Writing in the Climbers' Club Journal, Colin recorded:

This climb, about 250 feet in height, is very similar in character and difficulty to the Pinnacle Face on Scafell – a Hard Severe. There is hardly a trace of vegetation or earth except on the last two stances, and the rock is perfect, whilst the whole climb is most delightfully exposed and delicate, without being in the slightest degree of a desperate nature.

Following their climb on the Nose, Colin and MacPhee spent the afternoon attempting another new route farther to the right, but were finally driven back to Helyg by the rain.

Easter that year came quite late in April and, while MacPhee set off for the Highlands, Colin travelled up to the Lake District with 'AB', hoping for some spring weather on the higher crags. On Good Friday, April 18th, they walked up to Dow Crag to make an attempt on *Great Central Route*, Joe Roper's great (and fearsome!) classic of 1919, a route that is unfortunately often wet. Colin had almost completed the second pitch, the renowned *South America Crack*, when he missed a crucial hold and fell seventy feet. 'AB', who fortunately had a genius for constructing safe belays, succeeded in holding the fall and in doing so almost certainly saved Colin's life. 'AB' commented:

> Colin fell completely free you see, nothing to stop him except the rope, and as soon as the load came on me and the belay the rope twanged as you can imagine, and he just hit the scree with his feet and luckily not his head. The stretch in the rope brought him up again, and he was finally dangling just above the scree. Hitting the screes had broken one of his big toes, which proceeded to go a delightful range of purple, green and yellow over the next few weeks (laughter). Colin was very lucky indeed that he didn't hit his head, and that I had a very good belay and was able to get some rope in. It could very easily have been the end of the lad!

As the impact of Colin's fall came onto 'AB', he was pulled savagely on to his belay and had his hands torn and burnt to the bone by the rope. As the shock came on the rope, he was also twisted into the rock and sustained a smashed nose. The couple managed to retreat from the crag when the abseil must have been agony for 'AB' with his damaged hands. Eventually they made their way to Coniston where a doctor helped them to patch up their injuries. Colin's broken toe and a few aches and pains did not keep him out of action for very long, but the damage to 'AB's hands was very serious. He was forced to undergo a most unpleasant treatment involving scrubbing carbolic acid into the wounds with a toothbrush, and it put him out of action for some considerable time. In retrospect, 'AB' took the view that the accident was caused by a combination of over-confidence, youthful inexperience and perhaps a slight lack of fitness. It was one of Colin's very few serious errors of judgement, but it had indeed been a close brush with disaster for them both.

Colin later wrote an account of this accident in 'Let's Go Climbing', which is quite disarmingly honest:

The Crack was terribly strenuous, and near the top the holds seem to give out completely. My only support was my left arm jammed in the crack; I hung outwards from it and clawed at the rock with the other hand. I made a bad mistake here; if I had looked around I should have seen a good hand-hold on the right.

I squirmed up again until my head came against the overhang; my balaclava helmet dropped noiselessly to the bottom. I slipped down again and hung there exhausted. I was dimly conscious of a watching crowd of climbers, away on the left. There were good holds below me; I could still have descended. But I was too tired to think. I had to go on struggling – for ever and ever it seemed.

I jerked myself up again in a last despairing effort. I was so close that I could hardly see. Everything went black.

The next thing I knew I was 30 feet lower down, hurtling head-first through the air. My arm had slipped out and I had fallen backwards. I passed about 4 feet outside Alan's stance.

All fear disappeared as soon as I started falling. The struggle had been ghastly, but now it was all out of my hands; nothing I could do would make any difference. Now I'm in for a nasty smash, I thought; I knew I might be killed. All I could do was to wait and see what happened. Strangely enough it did not seem to concern me at all. My interest was quite detached. Somebody was crashing down to earth, but somehow it seemed to have nothing to do with me.

I fell 70 feet. The first thing I hit was 50 feet below. I can still remember every detail. The rock rushed up and flung me out into the air again. The rope tightened and jerked my head uppermost, then ran out again and I continued on my downward way.

I landed on the scree at the bottom, with my hips wedged in Hopkinson's Crack. I was conscious of no pain until I stopped; then my hips hurt fiercely for a few moments, and I thought something must be broken. But I could move, and I soon found that I could walk. I seemed to be uninjured. I climbed straight up to A.B.H. so that I should not lose my nerve .... It was over a year before I dared to attempt G.C.R. again. This time I found the crucial hold, and the crack went quite easily. I even managed to lead the wall above the Bandstand without a shoulder, which had not often been done. So I had my revenge.

On the occasion of Colin's successful lead of Great Central Route, Sid Cross remembered being at Dow Crag:

I was only once on a climb with, or rather at the same time as, Colin Kirkus. In my very early climbing days, my partner Charlie Tatham and I stood aside to let the great Kirkus, Linnell and Bridge pass on Great Central Route on Dow Crag. I think that A.B. Hargreaves was also in the same party. It's funny, but the thing I remember most clearly was watching Colin open a large tin of corned beef and then consuming the lot in the Dow Crag cave. That quartet were always very helpful to us rather scruffy youngsters, and I later climbed a little with Maurice Linnell, as we both lived in Kendal at the time.

In North Wales, that Easter saw two highly significant first ascents, one at Idwal and the other on Dinas Mot in the Llanberis Pass. The first of these new routes was the ascent of *Javelin Blade* on the Holly Tree Wall by Jack Longland and Courtney Williams. This route, the crux of which was a thin committing groove with poor protection, was a new step forward in difficulty and perhaps heralded the introduction of the 5b technical grade to Welsh climbing. The true worth of this climb was not fully realised for many years, but it was without doubt one of the hardest routes in Britain prior to Chris Preston's ascent of *Suicide Wall* in 1945. But for his wider interest in higher range mountaineering it is likely that Jack Longland would have made a greater contribution to Welsh climbing. At the time he was very fit, and probably the equal of Ted Hicks or Colin in terms of technique and daring. Longland only climbed with Colin a few times, but remembered him with great affection and commented particularly on Colin's toughness and stamina. The other first ascent of note that Easter was that of *The Cracks* on the Nose of Dinas Mot, by B.L. and H.C.H. Bathurst. The lower part of this climb had been explored some years before, and that first ascent must have been exciting.

> The party traversed in from the foot of the Eastern Gully, and climbed the heather-filled crack direct to the twin cracks by means of two pitons, a bolt and a top rope.

Colin himself completed the first free ascent later that year. *The Cracks* initially had quite a reputation as did most of the early routes in the Pass, but fully cleaned up it became an amenable Hard Severe, and a very popular Welsh classic.

Colin's toe gradually mended and, just over a month later, he paid a visit to the Lake District on the weekend of May 24th/25th, staying at the Robertson Lamb Hut in Langdale. With him on this occasion, and in the absence of the injured 'AB', were Marco Pallis and Ivan Waller. The weather had been dry and the scene was set for the successful ascent of one of Colin's finest and most famous climbs, which virtually opened up a major climbing ground, namely the East Buttress of Scafell. In his history of climbing in the Lake District,[1] Alan Hankinson sets the scene particularly well:

> Although climbers had been active on Scafell Crag since the earliest days of the sport, nothing of any note had been done on the other side of the Mickledore

1   'A Century on the Crags' – (Dent 1988)

Gap, on the massive bulging cliffs of the East Buttress. They must have seen them frequently and wondered about the possibilities there. Perhaps they were repelled by the bleakness and steepness of the prospect and the usual wet and greasy state of the rock. Whatever the reason, in half a century of climbing only two routes had been made – Mickledore Chimney at the northern end and Slime Chimney at the southern, neither of them of much merit. Between these two lines of weakness lies nearly a quarter of a mile of high and forbidding rock, specially designed by nature, it would seem, to attract the interest of men who had trained on "Cloggy".

Colin, Ivan and Marco set off that Saturday morning on the five-mile approach from Langdale. It was warm slogging up Rossett Ghyll and they stopped for a bathe in Angle Tarn, before making for Scafell. Writing in the Fell and Rock C.C. Journal, Ivan Waller recalled that memorable day:

> Colin was a thin untidy-looking lad with wiry hair and slightly sunken features. He looked neither strong nor athletic, and quite unprepossessing. In fact he was incredibly tough, determined and completely dedicated to the mountains.
>
> On arrival at the foot of the East Buttress, then unclimbed, Colin led the first two pitches just as if he were on a well-trodden route. Each pitch had a strenuous fingery move which I thoroughly enjoyed.... For the main pitch the second man sits on a good ledge with an overhanging wall above, behind which goes the slab up which the pitch starts. After about a quarter of an hour Colin made an excursion to the left edge of the slab and his head appeared above me. He was happy and relaxed and assured me that all was going well. After a further half hour all the rope was out, Colin was at the top and it was my turn to follow.
>
> I imagined during those 45 minutes that Colin must have found various ledges where he could rest and was surprised to find the difficulty sustained throughout without anywhere to stand in real comfort. Colin had just pottered from hold to hold in a completely relaxed manner where many climbers would have been thoroughly gripped.

Ivan Waller touched on Colin's style of climbing as 'pottering', and enlarged on this:

> Colin was an effective but inelegant climber : he pottered. He'd a funny way of standing to rest on a foot hold and flapping his hands against his thighs. Then he'd potter to another hold and stand there for a bit. He did it in a series of moves, like playing chess, like the hard climbers of the 1980s.'

Without doubt the climb they made that day, which Colin called *Mickledore Grooves*, was the great break through on this famous cliff. The route takes a strikingly direct line up the right flank of the crag and, after a steep wall and a groove pitch, the climber arrives at the foot of a magnificent slab which gives a sustained 140-foot pitched to the top. Their ascent, wearing socks in the damp conditions, was a masterpiece of route-finding and bore the mark of outstanding talent on Colin's part. The climb is delicate and very exposed and at that time entirely unprotected. Previous attempts had been made by Harry Kelly, who had tried to climb the slabs out of *Mickledore Chimney* (this is now the variation start climbed by R. Barry and C. Collin in 1936 which also forms part of the *East Buttress Girdle*). Like the early routes on Clogwyn Du'r Arddu, *Mickledore Grooves* was a considerable psychological break through and led the way for the series of great routes on the cliff, pioneered by Maurice Linnell, A. T. Hargreaves and Jim Birkett. In the current guide-book *Mickledore Grooves* is graded Very Severe (4c) but in anything other than dry conditions, it feels considerably harder: it was destined to be the scene of a serious accident some years later in the summer of 1937, when Colin's cousin, Wilf Noyce, was seriously injured in a fall when attempting the route with Menlove Edwards.

Its ascent was a magnificent achievement on the part of Colin, who was still not yet twenty, and talking to his companions many years later it was obvious that they had been very impressed with his cool lead that day. Strangely enough, this was to be his only major first ascent in the Lake District and in this respect he is not dissimilar to a later genius on Welsh rock, Joe Brown. Both men climbed fairly extensively in the Lake District, but it was North Wales that was the real centre of their activities, and which exerted the much greater attraction for their unique talents.

After they had completed the climb and returned to the foot of the buttress, Marco Pallis elected to go for a walk up Scafell Pike. Colin and Waller were so thrilled by the climb that they then went round and did Harry Kelly's *Moss Ghyll Grooves*, 'which by contrast seemed very easy and we climbed at great speed with enormous enjoyment'.

It must have been a wonderfully satisfying walk back over to Langdale for Colin that May evening, with the hills deserted in the late sunshine. The party was probably tired as they clattered down Rossett Ghyll to the valley and perhaps to a welcome pint in the Dungeon Ghyll hotel, before strolling back to the hut. Possibly Colin took the time to reflect on the success of his first really major route in the mountains – and one that has stood the test of time and become a genuine classic. Their ascent that day was duly written up in detail in the Robertson Lamb Hut log-book, and the same account later appeared in the Climbers' Club Journal. The account in the log-book was later augmented with a photo of the crag (taken by Colin), and one of Ivan Waller on the long top pitch, taken by another Wayfarer, A. M. Uttley: they remain there to this day. Colin's description went thus:

> Very Severe; rubbers; leader needs 150 feet of rope or preferably line. First ascent 24/5/30; C. F. Kirkus, I. M. Waller, M. Pallis.

On the left of the lower part of Mickledore Chimney is a large slab, about halfway along which, near to the left-hand edge, will be noticed a small piece of turf. The route comes up to this from the left, goes up the slab, and finishes up the groove to the left of the overhang at the top of the slab.

(i) 30 feet. Start about a hundred feet to the left of Mickledore Chimney at a scoop sloping to the right (Cairn). A slight struggle up the initial overhang and a delicate step to the right across a slab brings one to a stance and inadequate belay at the foot of the groove.

(ii) 60 feet. Climb groove above with difficulty, at the top make an awkward step into another groove on the right. Two difficult problems in the bed of this groove lead to a small stance with good belay.

(iii) 30 feet. The groove is climbed without serious difficulty to a large grass platform (Belay round large boulder on right).

(iv) 140 feet. Step round corner on right and traverse horizontally to turf ledge on face of slab above Mickledore Chimney, out of sight of second man. From left end of turf ledge make a series of very difficult steps on to arête overlooking stance. Then follow a diagonal crack to right, and surmount overhang by small holds. Climb with slightly less difficulty to foot of groove on left of big overhang. The groove is climbed with great difficulty for thirty or forty feet, the hardest part being at the top, after which a tricky swing is made to a grass ledge on the right [it was the departure of this grass ledge which caused Noyce's near-fatal fall seven years later], ninety feet above the second man. (Half-way up the groove the leader can gain moral support by flicking the rope over a loose-looking spike on the left – a difficult manoeuvre). As there is no belay on the grass ledge a slightly awkward step is made round a corner on the right and an easy horizontal traverse taken until a convenient place is found to ascend the greasy wall above to the grassy summit of the cliff. A descent can then be made to a good stance in a deep crevasse at the actual top of the groove (thread belay).

For some reason, when the 1936 guide-book to Scafell was prepared, Colin's ascent of Mickledore Grooves was credited as having been done in 'May 1931', and this has remained the same in all subsequent guides to the area. This is not the case, as the entries in the RLH Log book and the Climbers' Club Journal clearly show. Over forty years later, when in his mid-sixties, Ivan Waller returned to repeat the route with another leader. Ivan recalled:

It was a superb climb, and I was delighted to do it again. That chap Mattheson was taking his mother up it on the day we were there!

On returning to Liverpool, Colin 'phoned 'AB' to tell him about this exciting new climb. 'AB' duly took note, and made the second ascent of Mickledore Grooves with Bill Stallybrass in August 1931. 'AB' also led the third ascent, which he made with Alf Bridge sometime later. (On one of these occasions 'AB' went straight back down and soloed the route.)

The week after his ascent of *Mickledore Grooves*, Colin spent a couple of evenings in the company of MacPhee. Graham MacPhee was, like Colin, a keen photographer and had his own darkroom. An evening was spent developing and printing a number of photographs which Colin had taken that year. These were mostly crag photos, some of which later appeared in the Climbers' Club Journal. The following evening, Friday May 30th, MacPhee drove them over to Manchester where he gave a lecture to the Rucksack Club, entitled 'Recent Climbing in the Lake District'. It would seem that he and Colin were in a particularly good position to discuss that very topic! That same evening, an amusing incident occurred when MacPhee gravely sought the advice of Wilson Hey regarding his increasingly troublesome ankle. Hey, a founder member of the Manchester University Climbing Club, a noted medical man and a close friend of A. T. Hargreaves, is reported to have looked at MacPhee and then at Colin with some considerable deliberation, before concluding his consultation. MacPhee was duly advised that the best and only treatment for such an injury was to continue with regular rock-climbing!

The following weekend (June 7th/8th) was the Whitsun Bank Holiday and both Colin and MacPhee were in Wales, climbing on Clogwyn Du'r Arddu, but not together. MacPhee spent the weekend at Tal-y-braich with A. T. Hargreaves, the latter taking him up *Longland's Route* on the West Buttress. Meanwhile, Colin was staying at Helyg and, on the Sunday, proceeded to increase his knowledge of Clogwyn Du'r Arddu by making the fourth ascent of *Pigott's Climb* on the East Buttress, accompanied by A. B. Hargreaves.

On the previous ascents, which had been led by Fred Pigott (twice) and by Ted Hicks, the leader had seen fit to use aid in the form of a shoulder in order to scale the infamous and holdless ten-foot corner on pitch two, still regarded as one of the crux sections of the route. On this occasion, Colin boldly dispensed with the shoulder and free-climbed the whole pitch with some ease. It was, however, clearly not a simple matter, as 'AB' later wrote:

> The ten-foot corner was for the first time led without the second on the ledge below. The grassy landing at the top of this pitch is becoming increasingly loose and the final movements are decidedly risky.

Colin thus became one of the very few people at that time who had successfully led both existing routes on Clogwyn Du'r Arddu. Not yet twenty years old, he was clearly in magnificent form, and reducing the aid used on *Pigott's Climb* must have further boosted his confidence. The following

Tuesday evening more mundane matters intervened when MacPhee
recruited Colin to help him as he went flat-hunting in the Sefton Park and
Grassendale areas of Liverpool. The reason for this was MacPhee's recent
engagement and forthcoming marriage, none of which appears to have been
mentioned to Colin prior to that evening! The following day Colin wrote to
him offering congratulations, and hinting at some excitement on the crags
for the forthcoming weekend:

> 18 Croxteth Grove,
> Liverpool
> 11/6/30

Dear MacPhee,
Congratulations on your engagement! If you had told me last night I might have
been much more helpful in looking over the flat. I see now why you were so
anxious that I should not disturb the elaborate packings of the slides before I left
you.

I hope this will not mean an end of your climbing career. Next Sunday I will
nobly sacrifice myself not only by getting you on the rocks again (Ha! Ha!), but
also by taking special pains not to kill you (or myself incidentally).

Once again congratulations. I am very glad and wish you a long and happy
married life.

> Yours ever
> C. F. Kirkus

P.S. You will be able to pull out all your children's teeth yourself!

What a delightfully light-hearted letter from a young man just approaching his twentieth birthday, to an older and obviously dear friend. The trip on
the 'next Sunday' referred to was to be significant, for as we shall see,
climbing history was to be made that day. It was less than a fortnight to
MacPhee's wedding, and this was to be his last weekend at Helyg as a
bachelor! They set off from Liverpool at lunch-time on Saturday June 14th
and drove down the Pass to the cliffs of Dinas Mot. Here Colin led
MacPhee up *The Cracks*, the route established by the Bathursts that Easter.
This time Colin led the route in dry conditions, using none of the aid
employed on the first ascent. However, he did baulk at the top pitch,
regarded by some as the crux of the climb. MacPhee took over, led the
awkward and exposed mantelshelf and then the easy rocks to the top. Well
pleased, they descended to the road and drove round to Helyg.

Sunday June 15th dawned dry and warm and after an early breakfast,
MacPhee and Colin elected to go round to Clogwyn Du'r Arddu, both
having climbed there only a week before. Within the context of climbing in
North Wales, the pre-eminence of Clogwyn Du'r Arddu was already firmly

established by 1930. It was recognised as the finest cliff south of the Scottish border, and its sombre location above a dark lake on the north side of Snowdon, linked with the steepness of the East Buttress and the seeming inaccessibility of most of the West Buttress, had given the place a very considerable reputation and aura. Up to this time very few people had climbed there, and the two routes already established (by Pigott and Longland respectively) were seen as perhaps the ultimate in vision, daring and technique, and were held in considerable awe by most climbers. Certainly, the possibilities for any new routes looked few and far between and were likely to be of a high order of difficulty and danger. Nonetheless, Colin's continuing development as a rock-climber was such that he was about to find himself in the wonderful position where his own ability and daring coincided with what was required to continue the development of the cliff; the same thing was to happen to Joe Brown some twenty years later, at a higher grade again. Just as Archer Thomson will always be associated with the exploration of the cliffs of Lliwedd, so Colin's name will forever be linked with the early development of the finest mountain crag in Wales. That association really began on that sunny Sunday afternoon, more than sixty years ago.

Colin and MacPhee walked up from Llanberis alongside the Snowdon Railway and, not surprisingly, found that there were no other climbers on Clogwyn Du'r Arddu. The quiet brooding atmosphere of the place is not difficult to imagine, as even with the June sunshine they were soon in the shadows beneath the cliffs. Despite the fact that MacPhee had climbed it the week before, they elected to make an ascent of the West Buttress Route. However, this time MacPhee led the climb and they made a very rapid ascent in 2¼ hours. This was something of a triumph for MacPhee, since it was not only his first lead on this great cliff, but was the first climb which he had led in its entirety since breaking his ankle eighteen months previously. MacPhee noted in his diary that the climb had been a great restorer of confidence, and he must have been well satisfied as they returned to the base of the crag and commenced sun-bathing by the Llyn. Possibly MacPhee thought the day's work was over, but Colin had other ideas! He cast his eye over the other possibilities on the West Buttress, which he had studied carefully on his previous visits to the cliff. It occurred to Colin that he might be able to find an entry below the Great Slab, longest of the leaning slabs on the west, at a point where both Longland and Pigott had tried in 1928. What happened that afternoon has passed into climbing folklore and Colin's account, which appeared in 'Let's Go Climbing!', gives a gripping indication

Colin en route to Cloggy for the first ascent of the Great Slab.
Photo Graham MacPhee courtesy Matthew Shaw

of the physical and mental stresses involved, as well as the joy they shared at the top. Graham MacPhee must have wondered if he was ever going to make it to his wedding in a week's time!

On the upper half of the buttress was a huge slab. If only it could be reached! Below, the rocks were almost vertical. But the main problem was in the first few feet. All the way along the foot of the cliff the rocks overhung. It was a genuine overhang, too; it formed a kind of covered corridor, with a roof that projected in places for 20 feet or more. Nobody had yet succeeded in overcoming this overhang. There seemed to be a faint chance in the middle, where a pile of blocks formed a kind of natural ladder. A well-known climber had tried to climb straight up at this point and had fallen off, luckily without hurting himself. It looked a nasty place, but it seemed to me that, instead of climbing upwards, it might be possible to traverse out to the left, above the overhang. This would lead to a narrow slab, which ran up to the skyline and out of sight. It was impossible to guess what happened after that.

The traverse was Very Severe. There was one sloping hold where my rubbers would not grip at all, so at last I took them off and managed to get across in my stockinged feet.

I found myself on a tiny grass ledge, looking rather hopelessly up at the grim face above. I had crossed on to a higher part of the cliff and was already about 100 feet above the bottom, with the overhang below me. I felt very small and isolated.

I started up the narrow slab. It was far more difficult than it had looked, and wickedly rotten. I threw down every other hold. A thin ribbon of grass ran all the way up on the right, looking like a long and ragged caterpillar. I thought that even this might be safer than the rock and plunged into it. It wasn't at all a friendly kind of caterpillar; it began to peel off and slide down. I left this moving staircase very hurriedly, and took to the rocks again. I climbed on the extreme edge, where it seemed to be a little firmer. Below my left foot the rocks dropped, sheer and unclimbable, for 200 feet.

MacPhee called up that I had run out nearly all of the 120-foot line. There was no stance in sight, so I had to stand about uncomfortably while he tied on another 100-foot length. I went on and on, with things looking more and more hopeless. I wondered whether I should ever find a belay.

At last the climbing began to get easier, and I was able to traverse to a sheltered grassy recess on the left. There was a perfect thread belay, and MacPhee soon joined me. It was wonderful to think that no one had ever been here before. It was still more interesting to wonder whether we should ever escape.

I tried the slab immediately above, but did not date to pass a big loose block, resting on a ledge. A few years later, an optimistic climber was more daring; he succeeded in pulling the block on top of himself, gashing his hand very badly. He had to abseil down, weak and faint from loss of blood. He got back very late, and search-parties were out all night looking for him. By this time he was safely in bed. Some one had made a muddle of things.

We climbed a rib to a little stance. The big slab, for which we were aiming, was

The Great Slab, Clogwyn Du'r Arddu. Menlove Edwards leading the second ascent with 'AB' Hargreaves seconding.

away on our right. It was very steep and smooth here: the far side looked more hopeful. But could we reach it?

I got a long way across, and then stuck. The next move might be possible, by a kind of jump. It would be dangerous, but – well, a new climb was worth a risk. I looked at it a long time. It seemed to grow more and more grim. The exposure was terrifying and I was a long way from my second. I came back.

I managed to find an easier way across, at a lower level; but that meant that I still had the steep part of the slab ahead of me. The corner was a 20-foot wall of literally vertical grass. I made a mad rush at it. I had to climb up more quickly that the grass fell down. It was nasty and dangerous, but I dug in my finger-nails and toes (I was still climbing in stockings) and clutched and scrabbed until I reached the top. I don't know what MacPhee thought of all this. He is a safe and careful climber himself. But he is an ideal second. He watches you carefully and says nothing, except to point out a hold now and again. You feel that he trusts you and expect you to get up, and so you jolly well do get up. Also, he is equally famous both as an Alpinist and as a rock-climber, so that I knew I could not have had a better man to back me up.

The next pitch was still grass, but not quite so steep. The turf split from the slab and curled up. It was rather like standing on a roll of carpet – with the carpet going on unrolling. It was very difficult and unpleasant. But our reward was to come. We had two wonderful airy 100-foot pitches, right up and across the Great Slab, to its top left-hand corner. The rock was warm and very rough, and we felt profoundly happy and exhilarated. All the thrill of conquest was ours. The climbing was just Severe, but it was easy after what had gone before and we seemed to glide up without effort.

MacPhee said I deserved a kick in the pants or a potato medal, he didn't know which. Why only a potato medal I don't know; I felt I deserved more than that. But it had been a marvellous day. We had done 1,200 feet of rock-climbing, most of it in the Very Severe class.

Indeed, what a wonderful day on the crag; the first people to do two routes in a day on Clogwyn Du'r Arddu and a most impressive new route achieved, perhaps Colin's most famous first ascent. At that time the climb must have been one of the most committing leads made on British rock. Any inspection from above, as had been employed in the case of Scafell's CB, would have been out of the question and Colin had to rely totally on his own skill, experience and courage. Similarly Graham MacPhee's performance, particularly on the first long pitch was equally creditable, because due to the lack of protection he faced a huge pendulum over an awesome void had he fallen, or a hold snapped off. The condition of much of the rock and the degree of vegetation on the route must have made the ascent very frightening, and the route's initial reputation was considerable. It gradually got cleaned up during the Thirties and after the war became very popular, at one time being perhaps the most frequented route on the cliff. MacPhee later wrote in his diary: 'It was a perfect day, and we did not have an unenjoyable moment.'

The climb was duly written up in the Helyg log-book and it is thought that this was the first appearance of the term 'Cloggy', which was credited to MacPhee.

As a result of Colin's account of the first ascent of *Great Slab*, the following amusing letter appeared in the November 1930 edition of the Climbers' Club Bulletin. The distinguished visitor is of course Graham MacPhee.

SIR – May I trespass on your valuable space to protest against Mr Kirkus's treatment of Clogwyn Du'r Arddu. Not content with climbing this cliff by a route hitherto deemed impossible, for which he has my respectful admiration, he must needs add insult to injury by giving this imposing precipice a regrettable if affectionate nickname. I find in the Helyg Log-book.

'June 16th. West Buttress of Cloggy. G.G.M. and C.F.K.'.

The handwriting leaves no doubt as to the author and I am afraid that it is impossible to shift the blame on to the distinguished visitor. But, Sir, CLOGGY! The modern Welsh are notoriously casual; their language is fast being ruined by the continual clipping and slurring of final syllables. But, Sir, CLOGGY! Where will it end? Shall we have the Great Gully on Craigy? How fortunate that the cliff was not named Blydwyn Du'r Arddu!

Yours faithfully,
CAMBRENSIS.'

The next edition of the Bulletin appeared in March 1931, when the editor replied regarding this serious matter, attempting to put the record straight!

"CLOGGY"

It seems that an apology is owing to Mr Kirkus, who was not in fact responsible for this affectionate nick-name, but only writing under the instructions of the 'distinguished visitor.' This of course explains it all. No self-respecting Scot troubles to pronounce the last dozen or so letters of his mountain names and a man who calls Mhadaidh 'Varty' may well be forgiven for boggling a little over the last few letters of our Du'r Arddu. But Mr Kirkus must be more careful or we shall think of him, in the words of Kipling, as the 'Black M'Phee's infamous acquaintance.

This term is now adopted world-wide for the Black Cliff and 'AB' recalled this particular exchange with great glee:

I know about this! (laughter) The writer of the letter to the editor was a man called Paul Sinker, who was Jack Longland's brother-in-law. He was a Don at Cambridge, and a very good climber himself. The Editor was also an academic; John Hill was a Housemaster at Eton. That was a particularly good exchange of amusing chit-chat!

Another term of endearment for the cliff at the time was that of the great
'Ah Boo Boo', which is thought to be an invention of Alf Bridge and Jack
Longland.

'AB' was himself involved in the second ascent of *Great Slab*, which was
made three years later while Colin was in the Himalaya with Marco Pallis.
On this occasion 'AB' appointed himself manager of the party, with Menlove
Edwards leading. Due to the passing of three years from the first ascent, it
must have had almost as much danger and uncertainty as Colin and
MacPhee's adventure : 'AB' remembers that day and sums up Colin and
MacPhee's performance:

> Our party started off with Renie Bere, and Hewlett Edwards who was a very good
> climber. When Menlove and I were together at the top of the Green Caterpillar
> pitch (the cave stance), René at number three who was rather a hefty fellow just
> dashed on to the slab and promptly fell off over the overhang and into mid-air. I
> managed to hold him on the rope, but it was a serious situation because we
> couldn't lower him to the ground. Menlove just reached down, leant over me and,
> completely free-handed, lifted number three and pulled him back on to the slab.
> We then promptly sacked René! We continued upwards with Hewlett (Menlove's
> brother) but we had trouble keeping Menlove to the correct route. I had got an
> account of the route, written out for me by Colin, but he would insist on wanting
> to go straight up the Bow. He'd have done it as well if we hadn't stopped him – I
> called him back saying "....look we're supposed to be doing Colin's route!"
> Anyway, it's a lovely climb from then on, and what Colin and Graham did that day
> was a tremendous achievement. The whole thing was in doubt until they got to the
> top of the forty-foot corner, and heaven knows how they would have got down if
> the route had not gone. Yes, a very exciting occasion.

A friend of Colin's in the Wayfarers' Club, John Watson, later talked to
MacPhee about the ascent of *Great Slab*. MacPhee made it clear that Colin
had not even remotely hinted at the possibility of a new climb as they walked
up that morning. It would seem that the decision to climb *Great Slab* was
simply taken on the spur of the moment.

For those fortunate enough to be travelling home from Wales by car in
those days, Sunday evening was often something of a rush to make it to the
first pub in England for a pint of beer, before closing time. I like to think that
MacPhee pushed the Sunbeam hard over the Denbigh Moors and down
towards Queensferry that evening, in time for a celebration drink. They had
most surely earned it.

These days, sixty years on, the crux of *Great Slab* is generally regarded as
the initial moves on pitch one to reach the undercut slab, but modern
protection is readily available for the slightly unnerving step down. In
anything other than dry conditions the Forty-Foot Corner, where Colin

encountered the vertical wall of grass, still stops some hesitant leaders. The route is now probably unrecognisable from the first ascent and, in particular, the removal of grass and earth from pitch one, the infamous 'green caterpillar', left a clean crack that gives 100 feet of delightfully exposed climbing to the cave belay. In the author's opinion this is one of the best 'VS' pitches in Wales, although some loose rock remains to this day. Colin's initial attempt to reach the Forty-Foot Corner – which failed – became known as the Top Traverse, a bold and exposed variation first led by Robin Hodgkin in June 1937. *Great Slab* is no longer the most popular route on the crag as standards rapidly rise, but it still delights many people although the majority today seem to combine the early pitches with the crux of Menlove Edwards' *Bow-Shaped Slab* to do the *Great-Bow Combination*, one of the finest 'VS' routes in Britain.

When I think of Colin alone on the *Great Slab* on that June day more than sixty years ago, my mind is drawn to some of the other great adventures on the walls and slabs of this wonderful place: a young Joe Brown attempting *Vember* in the rain and then his great routes of the Fifties; John Streetly's delicate journey into the unknown on the *Red Slab* in 1952; Peter Crew out alone on the *Boldest* before a critical audience; the brave attempts on *Great Wall* by John Redhead and Jerry Moffatt; and more recently, the brilliance of Johnny Dawes keeping him alive on the phenomenal *Indian Face* climb. What links all these men, in their Black Cliff climbs, is their relative youth: they were all in their late teens and early Twenties – the inspiration of Wales's finest cliff, and that strange alchemy of technique, courage and ultimately desire, that creates the drive to make dangerous new climbs. Today's climbers face awesome and sustained technical difficulty, often with protection that is illusory or barely adequate. As Colin made this particular break through, he faced the prospect of no possible rescue from above, with one of the longest run-outs then attempted, on dangerous rock and copious vegetation, climbing at the highest standard of the day. Like Johnny Dawes fifty-six years later, he had to complete the lead in order to survive, and this before the advent even of simple equipment such as slings and karabiners.

The ascent of *Great Slab*, perhaps more than any other route, really established Colin as the leading rock-climber in the country and increasingly he turned his attention towards new routes. In 'Let's Go Climbing' he related just how important this aspect of the sport had become to him and how frustrating he found the day-to-day existence in the insurance office in Liverpool.

Cooped up all week in an office, I would just long for the week-end. On a photograph of some cliff I would have all the known routes marked with dotted lines. The black spaces in between fascinated me. Here was unexplored country; I longed to be the first to set foot upon it. I used to sit, pretending to work, with the drawer slightly open, so that I could see the photo inside. Then I would plan a route. Here was a chimney to start, but could I reach that little grass ledge 100 feet higher up? If I could find a way of connecting the next three ledges, then victory would be mine.

The first fine week-end I would put my theories into practice. Curiously enough, they usually worked. But it meant hours of suspense. I would go up, get stuck and have to come down again. Then I would try another way, until at last I found a route to the next ledge. Then the same thing would have to be gone through again, until finally I arrived triumphant at the top, with another climb added to the cliffs of Wales.

This image of Colin surreptitiously sneaking a glance at a crag photograph, in the drab surroundings of a post-Dickensian office, perhaps on a wet and miserable mid-week afternoon, has struck a chord with many climbers over the years. Here he articulates exactly what so many felt and still do feel, when, being hemmed in by the need to work, one's mind drifts to the delights of sunshine on steep clean rock and the next burst of freedom away from the office or factory. It is quite timeless.

Flushed with his success on *Great Slab*, Colin was back at Helyg the following weekend. This time he was without MacPhee who had driven up to Glasgow that Saturday to get married (stopping off en-route to climb *Eliminate B* on Dow Crag with A. T. Hargreaves!) On Sunday June 22nd Colin went round to the Llanberis Pass with J. B. Dodd to take another look at the Nose of Dinas Mot. These were still very much the early days of exploration in 'The Pass', but this bold rock feature had attracted climbers' attentions for some years, albeit with limited success. As outlined previously, Colin had already taken a good look at a possible route on the central part of the Nose in March, and was clearly aware of the likelihood of an exciting new route directly up the Nose itself. The line had been obvious for many years and had been attempted by such notables as the Abraham brothers, Archer Thomson and Geoffrey Winthrop Young, but probably all had been stopped by a hard move on the initial wall, leading to the obvious central groove, a dominant feature of the Nose. As in the March attempt, Colin soon disposed of the initial wall and set off directly up the groove. The top of this proved to be damp and greasy, but he pushed on, solved the problem of the bold hand-traverse out to the right and climbed up to the foot of the final corner-crack. This was defeated by means of a shoulder provided by Dodd, and Colin led the cracks in socks because of the prevailing wet conditions, not surprisingly he cut his feet quite badly in the process. His cairn of blood-stained socks lashed to a small tree remained at the top of the route as a welcome for subsequent leaders for some years! Colin and Dodd had certainly encountered some considerable problems, but obviously enjoyed the climb, as Colin later wrote in the Climbers' Club Journal:

> The whole climb is very exposed and increases uniformly both in difficulty and steepness as height is gained, until the final sixty-foot crack is actually overhanging in one plane. The rock is perfect and vegetation almost non-existent, except for the moss on the last twenty feet. Also the whole face dries with extreme rapidity: the first ascent was made only half an hour after the rain had stopped, following a night of torrential downpour. The time taken – from four to five hours – should long remain a record.

Colin's initial description of the climb, published in the Climbers' Club Journal, is both informative and amusing – particularly so are his comments regarding the final pitches, which constitute the major difficulties of the route. The final corner is the modern crux, but initially Colin suggested the use of a shoulder.

> (7) 40 feet. From the left-hand end of the long ledge rises a vertical corner with a flake of rock on its right. The leader will probably need a shoulder to reach a handhold at the foot of the flake. The crack between the right-hand edge of the flake and the main wall is then entered with difficulty by a lay-back movement, and is ascended with considerable effort by a series of fist-jams painfully reminiscent of the Helyg Boulder. After about twenty feet of this a slight foothold on the right wall enables a step to be made across the flake to the groove on the left, where a good (though greasy) chockstone handhold will be found if the climber happens to feel in the right spot. The remaining ten feet to a little perch and belay are strenuous but less severe. This stance is so uncomfortable that the leader would probably be well advised to put a loop round the belay and thread his rope, rather than bring up his hapless second. However, with the aid of a piece of stiff wire, a loop could be put round a chockstone in the crack, which would make the stance quite good, as the belay would then be above instead of below. Otherwise the second will probably demand loops for his feet – hence the spare rope advised.
>
> (8) 20 feet. The start of the greasy crack on the left is extremely awkward, but good chockstones soon come to hand, after which some delicate bridging enables an exit to be made on the right, without handling the fringe of turf. (Cairn and small tree, which will doubtless grow into a splendid belay. Also bloodstained socks in vicinity).
>
> Important Note – A ladder would make the final crack suitable for others than a few rock gymnasts.
>
> C. F. K.

Without doubt the *Nose Direct* on Dinas Mot is one of Colin's finest memorials, an almost perfect route on perfect rock, and a serious contender for the title of the best middle-grade route in Wales. These days the crux is generally agreed to be the starting moves on the final crack, where the shoulder was employed on the first ascent. The shoulder was disposed of on the second ascent, but you still see it used sometimes to this day, as the alternative gymnastic moves are much harder than anything else on the climb. The climb builds up in difficulty quite delightfully, the delicate entry to the long groove, the superb groove itself, the exciting hand-traverse, and finally the testing top cracks. The result is 250 feet of superb VS climbing in a tremendous position – needless to say it remains very popular, and in summer there is nearly always a team of climbers in action somewhere on the route. In later years Colin used it as a descent route when climbing on the crag!

'AB' made the second ascent of the *Nose Direct* a year later with Alf Bridge.

> This was done on the very day that Colin and Menlove climbed *Chimney Route* on Clogwyn Du'r Arddu. That day I climbed *Pigott's Route* with Alf Bridge, the four of us having walked up together. Anyway, they went off to do *Chimney Route* – I think they wanted to see how they got on together, while Alf and I made what was probably the sixth ascent of *Pigott's*, and finished before them. We could see them just completing their climb, but had it in mind to go and do the Nose on Dinas Mot. Anyway I led the thing, one of my second ascents, and a very fine climb it was too. Menlove and Colin followed us up it about an hour later. Colin's bloody socks were there for a long time! The climb suited me well, as I could wriggle up that last crack, but there were a lot of jagged edges.

It had certainly been quite a month for Colin, for in the space of five weekends he had produced important first ascents on Scafell's East Buttress, Clogwyn Du'r Arddu and the Nose of Dinas Mot – all at the top standard of the day – and he was clearly in brilliant form. Spare a thought though for 'AB', who was still recovering from the damage sustained to his hands in the accident on Dow Crag at Easter. But for those injuries, probably he would have accompanied Colin on these exciting new climbs. As already indicated however, 'AB' later made amends by being involved in the second ascents of *Mickledore Groove*, *Great Slab* and the *Nose Direct*.

The details of *Great Slab* and the *Nose Direct* were written up in detail by Colin in the Helyg log-book. His usual habit was to record new routes in great detail, in order to provide subsequent leaders with all the information they might require. This attention to detail was usually not without some humour, as a reminder that climbing rocks was after all a recreation, and meant to be enjoyed. There can be little doubt that at the end of June 1930, Colin, at the age of twenty, was fully established as the leading rock-climber in Wales, and probably in the whole of the British Isles. In the context of British rock climbing as a whole, these three new climbs were to be of very great significance and served to demonstrate his ability to take the highest technical standards of the day to the most forbidding and unlikely locations, and to produce routes of great quality and charm. These particular routes; *Mickledore Grooves*, *Great Slab* and the *Nose Direct* are brilliant products of the period and were the result of a highly developed combination of physical fitness, mental judgement and daring. A climber who cruises up the great pre-war routes with modern protection can have little idea of the mental and physical stresses posed by the early ascents of such climbs. Falls were usually punishable by serious injury or even death, and to innovate at the top level required great ability and considerable courage.

By a wholly appropriate historical accident, the next entry in the Helyg log-book after Colin's descriptions of *Great Slab* and the *Nose Direct* concerned the first visit to the Hut of another outstanding young climber from Liverpool. Menlove Edwards arrived at Helyg with his brothers Hewlett and Stephen on the evening of the following Thursday (June 26th), for a short stay.

Later in the summer of 1930, Colin joined a Wayfarers' Club party led by Marco Pallis in a short visit to the Pennine Alps and Arolla. Little is now known about this trip, other than the fact that it was Colin's first trip abroad, as he makes plain in his comments on the novelty of travel to the Alps in 'Let's Go Climbing':

> There is nothing to compare with the thrill of your first visit to the Alps, especially if you have never been abroad before. Even the customs seem exciting – but only the first time. Then there is the Channel crossing and the interest of finding out whether you are a good sailor. I overhead one old tar saying to an oldish lady – she must have come from Ireland, because her face was green: "Why, Mum! if it wasn't for seasickness there wouldn't be any fun in a sailor's life."
>
> Dieppe just before dawn – a ghostly fairy harbour in the pale half-light. The boat-train by the water's edge; the French porters; the sleepy shuffle through the customs. It is all the more wonderful because it is the prelude to the long-dreamed-of Alps. Then Paris – and the endless train journey – until you get your first view of the Alps.
>
> They look small at first, these Alps, but it is marvellous to be seeing the snows at last, hot and sticky as you are in the stuffy carriage. Bigger and bigger they grow, for many hours, until finally you are actually in the midst of them.

Colin and Marco enjoyed a fairly undistinguished visit to the Alps, making a couple of minor ascents at Arolla and climbing the south-east ridge of the Zinalrothorn at Zermatt. Marco was notorious for travelling slowly in the mountains and for enjoying the overall experience rather than being ambitious to achieve major routes. Jack Longland remembered meeting Colin and Marco on this particular trip:

....moving very slowly, and seeming particularly to enjoy bivouacking!

Jack Longland and his party were in the process of establishing a series of food dumps, in preparation for an attempt on a long traverse of the Zermatt skyline, from the Nadelgrat (Lenzspitze, Dom etc.) round to the Weisshorn, via the Monte Rosa, the Matterhorn and the Dent Blanche! Jack recalled:

We never got round to doing it all, and I assume that a lot of the food we dumped is still there to this day!

Although this was essentially a modest two-week trip for Colin, it probably served to whet his appetite for, and interest in, bigger mountains, and it must have been a valuable experience at that stage of his life. Prior to the last war it was unusual for those climbers without long holidays and/or high incomes to be able to make it out to the Alps. Most British Alpine climbers at the time were either university students, or established professional men, with the time and means at their disposal to make such a trip. With his perceptions thus widened, no doubt Colin found going back to the Insurance Office particularly traumatic, as is often the case when returning from the Alps in one's youth. The seed had been sown for the future, however, and he would soon yearn to return to the greater ranges, both in Europe and farther afield.

4 ". . . Du'r Arddu is Colin's Cliff."
Jack Longland *(illus. rear end-paper)*

Before moving on to the events of 1931, perhaps Colin's most important year of exploration on Welsh rock, it is appropriate to try to describe what rock-climbing was like at the end of the 1920s and early 1930s and just how much it differed from the sophisticated nature of the sport today – in terms of clothing, equipment and, perhaps most importantly, attitude. In general, even by the 1930s, the equipment available to rock-climbers was really no better than that of thirty or forty years previously, except perhaps that gym shoes (or rubbers, as they were known) were being more widely used on the harder routes. In fact, Colin was reputed to wrap elastic bands around the toes of his to improve their performance! Running belays were virtually non-existent and stances were only safe where a chockstone or rock-spike occurred. Parts of many crags, notably Clogwyn Du'r Arddu, were still heavily covered in vegetation, and loose rock abounded in many places that today are clean and sound. The great majority of climbers still wore heavy nailed boots which required a sophisticated technique at the top level; 'AB' humorously recalled footwear of the period:

> I knew Robert Lawrie, who at that time was a bootmaker and repairer in the Lancashire town of Burnley. When I first met him he was making climbing boots, great heavy things that were almost everlasting! I got him to make me a pair of climbing shoes, beautiful little things with tiny little tricouni nails and a metal stiffener. He came up to my office to take my foot measurements and produced these little forerunners of the present-day boots. I would carry these things up to the crag, I never walked in them, and they were absolutely excellent particularly on the rocks of Lliwedd. When Colin saw them, I got Lawrie to make him some as well and he used them for years afterwards. We'd have a great pair of clinkering fell-crushers to walk up in and then these lovely shoes to climb in. If it was still too hard, then we'd simply climb in socks.

Typical clothing of the time included old tweed jackets, discarded suits, corduroy breeches and woollen balaclavas, all of which became saturated and heavy when it rained. Ropes were still made of hemp, heavy in weight, very difficult to handle when wet, and without very great strength, particularly in the case of line – a thinner rope used on the longer run-outs. Snap-links (or karabiners) had not yet appeared, while the use of pitons was still widely frowned upon, although they did become more common over the next few years.

73

This examination of the clothing and equipment of the period is important, because although many of the routes pioneered by Colin and his contemporaries seem very reasonable to today's climbers – readily equipped no doubt with sticky boots, wires, tapes, Friends and so on – in their day they were very formidable undertakings. The maxim of the time 'The leader must not fall' was adhered to because of the known shortcomings of the equipment in use, but nonetheless people did fall, and serious, often fatal, accidents did occur fairly frequently. The psychological and indeed physical stresses of establishing new routes at the then top level must have been considerable and today's climbers, who cruise up the *Nose Direct* or the early Cloggy routes, would do well to remember the struggles of those who first ventured into these unknown places. Such climbing was not, at that time, without criticism – it was thought to be downright dangerous and unjustifiable by certain elements of the climbing fraternity.

In weather terms, 1931 was not a particularly good year and there was a great deal of rain in the mountains from January to August, which would not have helped serious exploration on the higher crags. Nonetheless, it was to be a most important year for Welsh climbing, for not only did it witness a number of Colin's finest first ascents on a variety of crags, but it also saw the emergence of a brilliant climbing talent in John Menlove Edwards who, together with Colin, was to dominate the next decade on Welsh rock.

Although some years junior to Colin in climbing terms – Menlove had only started climbing the previous year – by the spring of 1931 his awesome strength and talent for the sport were becoming increasingly apparent and were quickly recognised by 'AB':

As it happened, Menlove's beginning as a climber – his first two or three years – coincided with my own little heyday, and I did quite a lot with him during that time.

We first met at Helsby when he was a Liverpool University student and was rapidly accomplishing all the harder climbs lately done by Kirkus and Hicks. At that time I had just come to live in the Lake District and I invited him to join me for a weekend there, so that he could see what the bigger crags were like. He came and the first day among other things we did Tophet Wall Direct, which in those days ranked quite high. When I suggested that he should put rubbers on, he said, "Oh no, these will do", pointing to his almost brand new pair of boots studded with things like marbles. Nevertheless, to my surprise, he followed up quite easily.

The next day we went to Pillar and I thought I would take him down a peg or two, nails and all, by performing Walker's Gully. But as it happened, it was wet when we got to the top pitch – always a hard place for me – and I dangled on the thread two or three times and was unable to get up. So being the gaffer I said, "Sorry boys, now we've got to go down". (Like many another party.)

But Menlove said, "Let me have a go", and when I agreed to this, he promptly shot up quite easily. I have always remembered this as something quite remarkable, considering it was just about his first climb of any consequence. What a novice!

It is almost certain that Colin first met Menlove either at Helyg, or at Helsby where the latter now spent much of his free time working on his climbing technique. By all accounts, Colin and 'AB' offered Menlove much friendly encouragement and were quick to acknowledge his quite obvious ability. Although never particularly close friends, Colin and Menlove established considerable respect for each other's abilities and Menlove did climb occasionally with both Colin and his brother Guy. In 'Menlove', Jim Perrin touches on this stage in Menlove's development as a climber:

> Colin Kirkus was helpful to him at this time and his tutelage and attention gave Menlove much confidence. At later dates, he always spoke gratefully of Kirkus and the two were to be brought more closely together by several shared adventures and by Menlove's association with Kirkus's young cousin Wilfrid Noyce. For the moment it is worthwhile considering the very rapid boost which the nature of climbing at Helsby and the friendly encouragement of Kirkus must have given to Menlove's climbing, making his entry into the sport all the more immediate and dramatic.

This meeting of these two characters was to be highly significant in the development of climbing in Wales and certainly for this writer much of their personalities' resonance, albeit greatly contrasted, remains indelibly stamped on the hills and crags of much of Snowdonia; a reminder of a more relaxed and innocent period, but one where the pioneering of new rock-climbs was an often highly dangerous activity. In many respects, 1931 was to be Colin's finest all-round season on the crag, while Menlove in the joyous first-flush of his passion for rock, probably never again climbed with the intensity that was to emerge during that summer of rather indifferent weather in the hills.

The early part of 1931 saw Colin's climbing activities take the now familiar pattern of Sundays at Helsby, or weekend trips to Helyg or to the Robertson Lamb Hut in Langdale. Towards the end of January, a typical trip was made to Wales with Graham MacPhee, when they stayed at the Rucksack Club hut, Tal-y-braich, together with H. V. Hughes, who was to climb with MacPhee a great deal that particular year. MacPhee recorded that it was a particularly cold weekend and that they each slept under fourteen blankets! On the Saturday (January 23rd) MacPhee drove them over to Cwm Silyn – the rocky westernmost outpost of Snowdonia, where the entire western flank of Craig yr Ogof is taken up by the magnificent

Great Slab. Here Colin led them up an 'exposed and windy but enjoyable climb'. Considering the harsh weather and time of year, almost certainly what they climbed was the *Ordinary Route*, or possibly the *Direct Route* on the Great Slab. These climbs dated from the mid-Twenties and from the early exploration of an area at that time considered to be remote and rather removed from the mainstream of Welsh climbing. Colin was to return to the Great Slab later that year and make two first ascents of considerable quality. Probably the seeds of those two routes were sown on this bitterly cold January day. It may have also have been on this day that Colin added the lower part of the *Direct Route* on the Great Slab, which is thought to have been first climbed by him.

The following day, the three of them left Tal-y-braich early on another bitterly cold morning and MacPhee and Hughes let Colin lead them up one of the slab routes on Little Tryfan and then *Gashed Crag* on the South Buttress of Tryfan itself. As they gained height the holds became increasingly icy and a tricky descent of Tryfan followed as they made their way back to the car for MacPhee to speed them back to Liverpool with the heater full on!

A month later, on Saturday February 22nd, Colin and MacPhee spent a day in Wales. MacPhee was up and about by 3.30 am and drove round to Croxteth Grove to pick up Colin for an early morning dash down to Pen-y-Pass. Conditions were distinctly wintry but, undeterred, MacPhee attempted to drive up the Miners Path to Llyn Llydaw! MacPhee takes up the story himself:

> Had difficulty getting the car through snowdrifts, twice nearly going over the edge, but I had to go on in order to turn round. Spent an hour shovelling, then from the lake we made for the long gully on the East face of Snowdon, enjoying quite a nice climb and reaching the summit at 3 pm.

On the way back down, at the infamous zigzags above Glaslyn, Colin and MacPhee rescued a party who had fallen due to the hard snow conditions and injured themselves, a Mr and Mrs Wright and their friend Dick Irwin. MacPhee recalled in his diary that:

> We had to cut steps all the way down for them and due to the delays only just made it back for the last ferry over to Liverpool. A long day!

Colin refers to this particular rescue in 'Let's Go Climbing!' and a few weeks later the Wrights and Irwin, now fully recovered from their injuries, treated Colin and MacPhee to a 'Celebration Dinner' at the Station Cafe by way of thanks for the help given on the hill.

The Snowdon summit hotel in winter.   *Photo C. F. Kirkus (AC coll.)*

Colin spent the Easter week-end in North Wales in rather indifferent weather conditions, MacPhee having gone north to Ben Nevis. A regular feature of Welsh climbing at the time was the Easter parties at the Pen-y-Pass Hotel, hosted by Geoffrey Winthrop Young, a distinguished figure in mountaineering circles. They were attended by a wide range of people: distinguished academics, students, the foremost climbers of the time, even cabinet ministers. Young had his critics but he was genuinely interested in the progress of young climbers and held out a warm affection to them, often bringing together people who might not otherwise have met. 'AB' was a regular attender at these Easter gatherings but does not recall Colin being invited to them, apart from calling in on one or two occasions. I think there might be some significance in this, for as previously indicated, Colin found the sometimes rather elitist academic atmosphere at Helyg daunting and not really to his taste. At least one distinguished figure of the period was kind enough to throw some light on to this situation and explained to me that in some respects Colin was viewed as something of an enigma, a mystery to some of the University-based Helyg regulars. There was little doubt that he was the subject of genuine admiration for his talent, ability and considerable stamina and physical toughness. However, in some quarters Colin was viewed as '....just a little boring, too quiet and rather lacking in conversation'. This is probably not difficult to explain. The contrast between college life in the heady Oxbridge atmosphere of that time, safely divorced from the world's increasing financial and political problems, and that of a junior clerk in a provincial insurance office would, of course, have been considerable, and common interests, aside from climbing, would have been relatively few. 'AB's view on this matter was that Colin was a delightful companion, who made a pleasant change from '...the constant yapping of under-graduates!'. By this time, Colin had already formed enduring friendships with men of the character and calibre of Marco Pallis, 'AB' himself and Graham MacPhee and this says a great deal for the personal qualities of a young climber not yet twenty-one years old. In later years Colin was to drift gradually away from the Helyg scene and base his climbing activities at Idwal Youth Hostel. Perhaps, despite his spectacular successes on the crags of North Wales, he retained something of an insecurity about the place, based upon his somewhat humble occupation and relatively modest salary.

One major change in Colin's life occurred at the beginning of May, when A. B. Hargreaves left Liverpool to live and work in Barrow-in-Furness, close to the mountains and crags of the Lake District. Here 'AB' established a highly successful career in the laundry business and has remained in the area to this day, now living un Ulverston. This move on the part of 'AB' was significant in that 'AB' climbed increasingly with Maurice Linnell and Alf Bridge, who in turn began to turn their attentions towards the crags of Wales, where Colin also got to know them. Together they were to form a tremendous team, with Alf Bridge in particular becoming one of Colin's closest friends. Colin had first been introduced to Bridge and Linnell by 'AB' two years previously and they had spent an enjoyable weekend together at Idwal. Bridge and Linnell were already established as one of the best teams operating on British rock, with the tough, physically powerful Bridge the ideal foil for the mercurial climbing talents of the highly gifted Linnell, who was perhaps Colin's only equal on rock prior to the rapid emergence that summer of the brilliant Menlove Edwards.

Alf Bridge was eight years older than Colin and came from Longsight in Manchester. He had first come to prominence as a climber and bogtrotter in the Peak District, where he quickly acquired a reputation as a formidable walker. Around 1925, together with Eddie Holliday, he helped to form the Bogtrotters Club, which set out to emulate the great feats on the High Peak moors of Eustace Thomas, Fred Heardman and Harry Gilliat; by 1927 Alf was President of this tough group. A genuine 'hard man' long before the

Alf Bridge, 1949.   *Photo Peter Harding*

term became fashionable, trips such as the double Marsden-Edale, the Derwent Watershed and the Colne-Rowsley walks were regular week-end events for Alf at a time when they would have been far from commonplace. Alf was quick to realise the advantages of lightweight footwear for his walks (although the Marsden-Edale in 4-5 hours is hardly a walk!). He was also a talented rock-climber and soon acquired a big reputation on gritstone before moving on to the crags of the Lake District and North Wales. A typical weekend for Alf at this time was to finish work at lunch-time on Saturday and then to catch a train to Marsden. From here he would jog down to Edale (twenty-two miles over Black Hill, Bleaklow and Kinder Scout) carrying climbing gear, bivouac or camp for the night, then climb all day Sunday on the Edges before returning to Manchester late that evening.

Maurice Linnell, was quite simply one of the undisputed geniuses of British rock-climbing – in the tradition of Herford, Kelly, Kirkus and Brown through to Boysen, Fawcett and Dawes. Born in Stockport exactly one year before Colin in June 1909, Maurice's family moved to Skelsmergh near Kendal when he was ten and the boy immediately fell under the spell of the wild Cumbrian countryside. In due course, he became Head Boy at Stramongate School at Kendal, where he helped to form a school climbing club. On leaving school he went to Manchester University to study chemistry. Here he gained an honours degree and also became a founder member of the Manchester University Mountaineering Club, being first its treasurer and later secretary and Vice-President. His activities within the MUMC and the Rucksack Club rapidly gained for him a formidable reputation as a bold cragsman. On gritstone he was part of a hard Manchester-based group which included A. E. Chisman, A. T. Hargreaves, Roy Horseman and Herbert Hartley: together they established a number of notable test pieces at Laddow, Stanage and Widdop. After teaming up with Alf Bridge, Maurice rapidly acquired a name on the crags of the Lake District and such was the devotion of these two men to climbing that at one period they notched up seventy consecutive weekends out on the crag together. Together with Bridge, Linnell repeated most of the hard problems of the day before searching out new lines of his own and at Whitsuntide 1931 this pair completed the 24-pitch girdle of Pillar Rock, their first major new climb. A. B. Hargreaves was also involved on the second day of this epic ascent and recalled a trait of Maurice's with some affection:

> He had I remember well, a most endearing chuckle when in argument and he also had a memorable habit of taking off his steel-rimmed glasses in the middle of a difficult pitch to wipe off the moisture while holding on with the other hand.

In 'High Peak', Eric Byne included a vivid and evocative description of Maurice Linnell, after he and Clifford Moyer had shared a bivouac with Maurice at Stanage one week-end.

> Crouched over a pan of soup in Robin Hood's Cave, Linnell recounted tales of Pigott, Morley Wood, Heardman and Eustace Thomas. As he talked his shock of black hair tilted forward over his lantern-jawed face and his eyes peered down at the two lads through his spectacles.

Not least of Linnell's qualities as a rock-climber, and one he shared with Colin, was his considerable boldness on the crag. They also shared a taste for solo climbing. This often caused great concern to his companions, who feared for his safety. Indeed, Jack Longland volunteered the view that, "....quite frankly, Maurice used to frighten the life out of me sometimes". Nonetheless, Maurice Linnell's subsequent solo ascents of the first pitch of Cloggy's *Curving Crack* and the hard *Bayonet-Shaped Crack* on Scafell were clear indications of a truly gifted talent. 'AB's assessment of these two key characters in Colin's life is particularly relevant.

> In 1931 I moved up to Barrow and this rather removed me from my close climbing association with Colin. It did, however, bring me into closer contact with Alf and Maurice, who were then very active in the Lake District. Alf was what might be described as an avuncular type, being rather older than the rest of us and

Maurice Linnell, June 1930

he certainly had this relationship with Maurice whom he greatly helped. The four of us (myself, Colin, Alf and Maurice) soon made a very good quartet with similar ambitions and we had some great fun! From having been "Uncle" to Maurice, Alf quickly took up that relationship with Colin. The two got on very well and Alf quickly saw in him what was already apparent to everyone else – a great climber. He was of great assistance to Colin and they climbed together a great deal.

In addition to this, Colin also became very friendly with Maurice and as they had both already done great things they formed a formidable partnership particularly on Clogwyn Du'r Arddu. I wouldn't say that they were competitive, although there was a certain amount of rivalry there naturally. Sadly this may have contributed later to the disastrous accident on Ben Nevis when Maurice was killed. One important difference between them was that Maurice had transport, a very rare thing in those days for a young climber, whereas Colin did not. The two of them used to buzz about like maniacs on Maurice's motorcycle quite a lot! They were however very different in character – Colin was very unassuming and gentle by nature, probably never made an enemy in his life. He simply loved climbing, knew he was a quite remarkable exponent of it and was just happy to go on doing new climbs with whoever happened to be handy. Maurice, however, was far more ambitious and driven, determined perhaps, to make a great name. I would stress though that neither of them was pushy in that respect, they were both modest men. What I do particularly remember about Maurice was that he was a very ambitious and intense person who did not like to be thwarted by failure to get up something. Colin tended to be far more philosophical. If he didn't succeed – it didn't bother him. There were also other differences; Maurice was a graduate with a career ahead of him to which climbing was or might have been helpful. Colin really had no such prospect ahead of him with the Royal Insurance, where his climbing achievements might not have meant very much.

Writing in the Rucksack Club Journal several years later, Alf Bridge recalled this period and his clear affection for these key characters of the time:

> I have had the privilege of being with Messrs. Longland, Waller, Kirkus and A. B. Hargreaves and can look back on days spent from Helyg with the Climbers' Club men as the happiest I could possibly wish for.

Meanwhile, the indifferent weather of that year persisted, with more than one visit to North Wales being totally washed out. However, at the end of May, Colin had a successful and significant week-end in Wales, staying at Helyg with Graham MacPhee. Perhaps mindful of their visit the previous January, on the Saturday (May 30th), MacPhee again drove them down to Nantlle for the pleasant walk into Cwm Silyn and its Great Slab. The weather that day was poor, with constant drizzle soaking them thoroughly by mid-afternoon. They settled for a stroll up the *Original Route* on the Amphitheatre Buttress, a huge sprawling mass of rock and vegetation to the left of the Great Slab. MacPhee described this as 'a rotten, loose moderate', and the remainder of the afternoon was spent reconnoitring a new line up the centre of the Great Slab itself, before the drizzle turned to constant rain and they were glad to hurry back down to the car and the prospect of a hot meal at Helyg.

The Sunday morning dawned dry and after breakfast they set off back to Cwm Silyn, where, under a threatening sky, Colin made an excellent lead of a delightfully delicate climb up the middle of the Great Slab. This turned out to be a superb new route of Very Severe standard, with a particularly fine top pitch. *Kirkus's Route* offers a series of fine pitches, sustained at a pleasant 4c standard and has become something of a classic of the area. It was the completion of this exciting new route that really stimulated interest in this beautifully situated crag with its fine outlook over the southern part of Snowdonia. Typically, Colin and MacPhee took separate finishes to the route with MacPhee's being closer to the accepted modern finish, first recorded in 1952 by Ted Wrangham and George Band when they climbed the rather artificial line of *Central Variant*.

Two other new routes were to follow on Cwm Silyn's Great Slab later that year, but on this particular dank grey Sunday Colin and MacPhee picked out the very best line on the crag and produced a great route of considerable charm. After the war, Vin Ridgeway and, a decade later, Baz Ingle and Rodney Wilson, produced harder direct variations on the original route, but these did not surpass it in quality, only in technical difficulty. After completing their climb, Colin and MacPhee fled back to the car well satisfied, as the heavens opened yet again. MacPhee recorded in his diary: 'The nineteenth wet Sunday in a row. Ankle still giving trouble.'

Encouraged by this fine new route, the two were back in Wales the following week-end, again staying at Helyg. On the Sunday morning Colin and MacPhee, together with A. M. Robinson, walked up to Ffynnon Llugwy and over the ridge on the shoulder of Carnedd Llewelyn to a crag Colin had often visited in his youth, Craig yr Ysfa. Hidden away in the depths of the Carneddau, Craig yr Ysfa is an extensive crag but one neglected for many years after the initial pioneers had left behind some classic old-fashioned routes. On this particular occasion, Colin led his companions up a new route which followed the back wall of the Amphitheatre between *B Gully* and *C Gully*, to which they gave the rather uninspired name the *Amphitheatre Rib*. It was originally graded Very Difficult and is described in the current guide-book as a sound, pleasant Difficult route of 260 feet. In 'Let's Go Climbing!', Colin refers to this climb in the chapter on First Ascents and expresses his delight in climbing good rocks of any standard:

> You can still find places in this country where no one has ever been before. But probably many people will have tried so you will need to be a pretty good climber to reach them. But this does not necessarily follow; I found a good new climb on Craig yr Ysfa, the *Amphitheatre Rib*, that was no more than very difficult. Thousands of climbers had passed it without really noticing it; most of the people who visit Craig yr Ysfa do either the *Great Gully* or the *Amphitheatre Buttress*.

Guy Kirkus remembers an enjoyable mass ascent of this particular route by a crocodile of climbers from Helyg some weeks later. Their purpose was to 'garden' the route and clean off extraneous material. Boulders and vegetation crashed down into the solitude of the cwm below, as the party gleefully made its way to the top with most members covered in soil and grass!

As the summer progressed, Graham MacPhee was to be found increasingly climbing rock routes on Ben Nevis as he began to undertake guide-book work for the S.M.C., usually in the company of A. T. Hargreaves or H. V. Hughes.

On Wednesday June 17th, taking advantage of a lull in the weather while staying at the CIC Hut on Ben Nevis, Hargreaves led MacPhee and Hughes up a new route on the imposing Carn Dearg Buttress which they called *Route I*, 'to avoid any risk of the obsolete eponymous nomenclature which still persists sometimes!' The weather closed in again, but two days later they forced another new climb, Direct Route, on Observatory Buttress battling through sleet and snow to the top. A week later MacPhee and Hughes added a further route on the north wall of Carn Dearg.

The week-end of June 20th/21st saw Colin cycling down to Helyg in welcome summer sunshine. On the Saturday, in the absence of MacPhee, Colin teamed up again with A. M. Robinson and made for the Main Cliff of Glyder Fach. Here he forced a new route of 120 feet up the crack and groove line on the right-hand side of the Pillar Face, just to the left of the celebrated *Lot's Groove*. It gave a particularly pleasant climb, now graded Hard Severe, with some technical difficulty low down and on perfect rock. In the 1937 Guide to Glyder Fach, Colin described it:

> ....the most reasonable of the three 'Very Severes' on the cliff. The whole climb is nearly vertical and consequently very exposed. The rock is clean and sound and the stances are small, but the belays are very good. The ascent provides groove, crack and slab climbing and is less strenuous than one might expect. The difficulty is fairly great, but by no means excessive and the climb is thoroughly satisfying from the point of view both of situation and technique. Standard: Very Severe. Rubbers.

Colin called the route *Lot's Wife* and submitted the following delightful account, which is a little gem to the Climbers' Club Journal:

> Lot's Wife proves to be much more reasonable than her austere spouse. Woman-like, at first, she coyly repels all advances, but once the necessary steps of introduction have been accomplished she becomes more amiable. Her acquaintance was sought long ago, but it was thought better to subdue the husband before taking any liberties with the wife.

Colin made his way next day, alone, back to Craig yr Ysfa, no doubt recalling the visit of a fortnight before. As described at the beginning of this book, that midsummer's day, Sunday June 21st, Colin made the solo first ascent of the *Pinnacle Wall*, a lovely climb that has become a Welsh classic. *Pinnacle Wall* combines delightful climbing on sound, rough rock in a magnificent position above the Amphitheatre Wall with an outlook of great beauty. This is a climb that I defy any climber not to enjoy, with the delightful contrast between the delicacy required to traverse the quartz ledge and the groove and slab work above in a superb position. If you've never done *Pinnacle Wall*, I urge you to go and enjoy one of the real treats of Welsh climbing; when combined with Tony Moulam's *Mur y Niwl* of 1952 up the

Amphitheatre Wall, it gives one of the finest middle-grade outings in the British mountains. Here in full, is Colin's description of the route, which appeared in the Climbers' Club Journal later that year:

> Looking across the Amphitheatre of Craig yr Ysfa the west wall is seen to be horizontally divided by a wide bilberry terrace, above which is a curiously straight quartz ledge some eighty feet long. The route gains the bilberry terrace from the left and traverses right, until an obvious staircase leads to the right-hand edge of the quartz ledge, which is followed to a little grassy nook at its left-hand extremity. The corner above is then climbed and is followed by a slab and crack to a little pinnacle on the right, whence the summit is gained. The climb starts from D Gully, just above the first little cave pitch, where an obvious corner leads to the bilberry terrace.
>
> First ascent, June 21st, 1931. C. F. K.
>
> Very Severe and exposed; rubbers or stockinged feet; 100 feet of rope.
>
> (1) 30 feet. Climb grassy corner with some difficulty, the top portion being overcome by a lay back movement. (Belay ten feet below bilberry terrace.) The terrace is then traversed to the right to an obvious line of weakness in the wall above. (Belay on left.)
>
> (2) 40 feet. A rock staircase with a grassy landing leads to a stance and belay.
>
> (3) 90 feet. A ten-foot wall on the left is climbed to the quartz ledge, which is found to slope along and outwards at an angle of about twenty-five degrees. It provides a pleasing aerial pathway for about seventy feet, when an awkward step has to be made across a gap to the grassy nook at the foot of the final wall. (There is only a very sketchy belay here, but something could no doubt be arranged in the crevasse on the other side of the gap.)
>
> (4) 65 feet. The groove above is climbed on small holds with some severe movements about thirty feet up, after which a diagonal crack on the right provides handholds, until a traverse can be made to a patch of grass on the right. (Belay, but poor stance – under the circumstances probably not worth using.) The diagonal crack is regained and followed on marvellously rough rock to the base of a twelve-foot pinnacle. (Sitting-stance and belay round pinnacle, which appears to be quite secure.)
>
> (5) 35 feet. The crack is continued to the top of the pinnacle, whence a thrillingly airy step is made on to the slab on the left. The slab is then climbed up its very exposed right-hand edge to the rocky platform at the top. (Cairn).
>
> C. F. K.

What a thrilling climb that must have been for him, alone on that superb wall with an outlook as fine as any in Wales. Imagine his feelings on the breath-holding traverse of the quartz slab if it was at all wet, or the thrill on grasping the top of the pinnacle itself and then working up the easy slab above out of the shadows below. In time *Pinnacle Wall* became very popular and more than any other climb, to quote Clark and Pyatt in 'Mountaineering in Britain', '...brought new life to an old crag which had enjoyed little popularity for more than thirty years.'

In the current Carneddau guide-book, Les Holliwell rightly describes Colin's *Pinnacle Wall* as 'perhaps the outstanding example of his bold competence'. Colin did attempt to make a direct start to the climb, but being alone did not press home the attack and returned to make another attempt a year later with A. B. Hargreaves.

At the beginning of August, Colin was back at Helyg in the rumbustious company of 'AB', down from Cumbria for a holiday, and Alf Bridge. On the Sunday (August 2nd) they travelled down to Nantlle for the walk into Cwm Silyn and its Great Slab. In the course of the afternoon they looked at the area above and to the right of the Great Slab itself, and found a devious but pleasant Severe route of 400 feet which they called the *Upper Slab Climb*. This climb was notable for a very exposed top pitch high above the screes. 'AB' later returned to make the second ascent of this climb, in the company of Menlove Edwards:

> I had the honour of having Menlove as my second, and the psychological strain of that was considerable! You could feel him thinking impatiently, "What's that silly old bugger putting in all that time for, why doesn't he get a move on?" Menlove was a very casual second, but nonetheless would have clicked into action had I slipped off. Yes, psychologically he was a bad second! [laughter]

A month before Colin's lead of the *Upper Slab Climb*, Menlove had added the excellent *Outside Edge Route* to Cwm Silyn's Great Slab, and it was really these two routes plus Colin's route up the Great Slab that established the popularity of climbing in Cwm Silyn, a really delightful area away from the crowds of mainstream Welsh climbing. These climbs are still a pleasure to this day and are rarely crowded.

During that summer of 1931, following his University examinations, Menlove Edwards spent much of his free time at Helyg and was rapidly developing into a climber of the highest calibre both on the sandstone of Helsby and on the volcanic rock of Snowdonia. At the end of July, Menlove was staying at Helyg with his brother Hewlett and a friend, Doctor Alan Sutcliffe-Kerr. Menlove led a very difficult problem on the Milestone Buttress (Direct Finish to *Wall Climb* – a harsh crack problem) and followed this up with the first ascent of *Chasm Rib* on Glyder Fach and the second ascent of Colin's Great Slab climb at Cwm Silyn, adding a new finish of his own. Hewlett departed, and Colin arrived at Helyg on the Sunday night with Alf Bridge and 'AB', having just completed the *Upper Slab Climb* at Cwm Silyn. Colin and Menlove were already well known to each other from climbing at Helsby, and now the time was right for them to team up for an important first ascent in North Wales. On the Monday morning, Colin, Menlove, Alf Bridge and 'AB' made their way over to Clogwyn Du'r Arddu where Colin's *Great Slab* of the previous year still lay unrepeated. Alf Bridge teamed up with 'AB' to make an early repeat of Pigott's East Buttress route, while Colin and Menlove reconnoitred a new chimney/groove line on the East Buttress, some way to the right of Pigott's. In his obituary of Menlove in the Climbers' Club Journal, 'AB' has this to say:

> I have often wondered what happened (when) Kirkus and Menlove joined together for ..... *Chimney Route* on Clogwyn Du'r Arddu. That must have been a most interesting party – a complete contrast of styles and temperaments, with Kirkus (rather the senior) suffering a most embarrassing efficient and thrusting second. No wonder that between them they forced the 'rickety innards'.

The place they investigated that day was one that had already been attempted by E. E. Roberts and Frank Smythe as early as 1921, but that attempt had ended after one pitch. The ascent of the climb by Colin and Menlove turned out to be an epic struggle in the wet, with much grass and loose rock thrown in for good measure. The climb rapidly acquired the reputation as being the hardest on the cliff, considered to be more difficult and at least as arduous as the *Great Slab* route. 'The Black Cliff[1] contains the following description of the ascent:

> An overhang near the top almost defeated them; Edwards, secured by a piton on the slab below, gave a shoulder to Kirkus, who then moved up into loops on some loose flakes while the Rucksack stalwarts, no doubt approving of these tactics oscillated encouragingly between the ground and the Green Gallery above. The flakes, known as the Rickety Innards, are still there, as alarming as ever. The climb was thought to be harder than *Great Slab* and at least as serious. This may seem strange with hindsight, but it serves to illustrate the difficulties of pioneering on loose and vegetated rock, compared with the technical standard of the final product.
> There is always a discrepancy between the difficulty of the first ascent and the eventual standard of a climb. It seems that this discrepancy was much greater for these early ascents than for harder modern routes on clean rock. Hargreaves remembers doing the fifth or sixth ascent of Chimney and finding it a fearsome place, full of grass and loose rock, much harder than Pigott's.

In his own description of the climb, Menlove commented on the piton used with some amusement:

> The rock is excellent, bar the obvious rickety innards of the last overhang. There is no impurity except the piton, and that will be found quite susceptible of removal by even the weakest purist.

1 'The Black Cliff' by Crew/Soper/Wilson (Kaye Ward 1971)

The piton in fact only lasted until 1933, when it was removed by Maurice Linnell who repeated the route with Fred Pigott. The modern grade of *Chimney Route* is Very Severe (4c) in its cleaned-up state, but like the nearby *Pigott's Climb*, it rapidly becomes far more difficult in poor conditions and is then quite an undertaking. The initial pitches, often enlivened by leaders having epics on the harder routes on either side, are now usually combined with the superb third pitch of Joe Brown's 1951 route *Diglyph*, in order to avoid the infamous 'Rickety Innards' pitch which itself has shed much loose rock and is still considered to be rather dangerous. A variation pitch, avoiding the 'Rickety Innards', was added by Nully Kretschmer and called the *Crooked Finish*. The *Continuation Chimney*, an obvious feature at the top of the route, was climbed by Colin with Graham MacPhee later that month. Though not over popular today, *Chimney Route* is very enjoyable, particularly with the modern finish, and keeps company with fine steep routes on either side – *Diglyph* (Joe Brown's first new route on the cliff) and the elegant *Sweeper*, added in 1975 by Rowland Edwards. A. B. Hargreaves recalls that particular day on Cloggy:

> On that particular day I also led the second ascent of Colin's *Direct Route* on Dinas Mot. While Colin and Menlove battled up *Chimney Route*, I climbed Pigott's with Alf Bridge. We had all walked up to the cliff together, and I think Colin and Menlove were keen to see how they got on together so they went off to try this new line. Alf and I made what I think was the sixth ascent of Pigott's and we finished quite quickly and watched Colin and Menlove complete their climb. Alf and I had had it in mind for some time to repeat the *Direct Route* and so we walked over to Dinas Mot and I led the climb, one of my best second ascents! Menlove and Colin followed us up the route about an hour later.

After they had finished the climb, Colin had to return to Liverpool, while the other three made their way back to Helyg. That night a rescue was mounted for a climber who had fallen on Craig yr Ysfa. 'AB' remembered that night with glee:

> Colin had departed earlier, but the rest of us set off from Helyg armed with food, blankets and God knows what! We got to the Amphitheatre where we found a dead body, and there was a number of people involved trying to help. We got back to the valley about three in the morning and we had taken with us the brandy flask from the Helyg first-aid kit. On the way back down, we had a local shepherd with us and he discovered that we had the brandy with us and scoffed the whole lot in one go! It clobbered him and he was tottering about all over the place. What a night that was!

After the success on *Chimney Route*, which gave Colin an unprecedented knowledge of Clogwyn Du'r Arddu, he returned to the great cliff some four weeks later with Graham MacPhee, who was particularly fit after a good holiday rock-climbing in Scotland. On the morning of Sunday August 30th, MacPhee drove round to pick Colin up at 7 am, and by 11.30 they were unpacking their sacks at the foot of Cloggy. Colin had one or two new lines in mind, but on this particular day took a little while to get going, as MacPhee recorded in his diary:

> We nosed about for about an hour looking for a new climb, and finally decided on a crack to the right. CFK seemed reluctant for once and needed some encouragement, but ultimately we finished the climb in about 2½ hours (65 minutes for the second pitch!) and it was Very Severe and quite exposed. Then we did a Direct Finish to Colin's *Chimney Climb*, not so severe, 100 ft, and came down to the tarn for a slight sunbathe. There were clouds coming in by this time, so after an hour we left at 6.45 pm .... a marvellous day.

A marvellous day indeed, two new climbs in a day on Clogwyn Du'r Arddu, and in all likelihood no one else there as well. Their investigations along the base of the East Buttress that morning produced the climb now known as the *Pedestal Crack*. Above it, they continued with the *Continuation Chimney*, which now forms the top pitch of *Chimney Route*. It is likely that *Pedestal Crack* had caught Colin's eye for some time, as the combination of the line of this route and what later became *Curving Crack* was already known to climbers as 'The Wishbone'. The climb itself begins with a rather scrappy little pitch up a rib to the right, which brings you to the base of the crack proper. Above this Colin climbed a well-defined crack line, steeply at first (the second pitch referred to by MacPhee) before it gradually widened and the angle fell back as the Eastern Terrace was approached. Technically, the steep section of the crack on the second pitch was probably the hardest climbing Colin had so far pioneered on the cliff.

That same weekend Menlove Edwards was climbing in the Lake District with other Climbers' Club friends including Marco Pallis and Bill Stallybrass. Menlove had been climbing almost daily for the past two months and at the age of twenty-one was perhaps in the best form of his life, which resulted in an extraordinary performance. He succeeded in leading *Central Buttress* on Scafell Crag, without using aid at the chockstone to climb the Flake Crack. This was achieved by very bold laybacking, and was a considerable achievement which established Menlove at the forefront of the sport. Immediately prior to Menlove's ascent, the climb had been completed by Alf Bridge, Maurice Linnell and A. B. Hargreaves in the customary manner. Alf had attempted to lead the climb without aid himself, as he later recalled in the Rucksack Club Journal:

It is no secret that it was my cherished ambition to lead the Flake Crack of Scafell without combined tactics. For twelve months or more Linnell and I had waited for good conditions to make the attempt and after numerous more or less hilarious nights spent on the fells in the hope of snatching it from the weather, at long last the chance came in August. A. B. Hargreaves was also in the do and I was very glad of his presence as it certainly strengthened the morale of the party. We slept out at Hollow Stones that very perfect night of August 28th and as I lay in my bag I saw the moon slowly creep up until the whole of the face was showing almost as clear as day. I confess I felt very windy as I realised that in a few hours I should be on my greatest do, but sleep soon came and I woke up in fighting form. After a good 'brekker' amongst surroundings which seemed in keeping with the game in hand we started for the foot of the climb. It was decided to climb to the foot of the flake solo and this we proceeded to do. I felt very confident that I could make my lead straight through, and I would not even hear of a thread belay at the chockstone. For the rest I have very little to say. I threw myself into a layback when I reached the chockstone, confidently braced my muscles for the last few feet, and then moved. Perhaps Hargreaves, who saw the whole of my movements, could explain what happened better than I can. All I know is that my feet just shot off the wall and I made a hopeful grab for the top of the chockstone. There I made a happy landing and hung by my left hand, absolutely shot. That short drop had done quite a lot. I tried again but it had weakened my arm muscles, strained an old rugger leg muscle and caused me to lose my guts. No words of mine can express my disappointment. I was beat. A few quick turns round the chockstone with my line and I rested. Linnell then came and climbed over me and then Hargreaves. My turn came and I joined them at the top of the Flake with a great deal of help. I then finished my lead to the top of the crag but on the way I passed by the foot of the Bayonet-shaped Crack with the greatest of reluctance and resolved to return again to make it go and thus make a more direct finish to Central Buttress.

I should now like to mention other events which followed my failure on the Flake Crack. Edwards (Climbers' Club) was leading a party up the climb only a pitch or two behind ours and consequently saw my happy landing. I think I suggested that he also should have a try at it clean, and, with his permission, I left a loop for a thread at the chockstone. He threaded his rope through this loop and then made his magnificent lead up the Flake. In my den at home I have the rope which Edwards used and I often look at it and remember the day when I was the first to shake his hand and congratulate him. Well done Edwards! I can only say that I tried very hard and perhaps, who knows, I felt the same disappointment that those very great climbers Herford and Frankland experienced when they made their efforts to lead straight through!

It says a great deal for Menlove's spirit and confidence that he succeeded in this enterprise, having seen Bridge fail to make the lead free. Alf Bridge was widely regarded at the time, as physically one of the strongest climbers on the scene and it is significant that the inexperienced Edwards should feel capable of stepping in where Alf had been rebuffed. Thus was Menlove's reputation as a rock-climber established. Bill Stallybrass recalled that day:

John Watson on The Flake, 'CB', in 1935.   *Photo Bob Frost*

It was a marvellous lead by Menlove and it was also the only time that I met Maurice Linnell. I liked him immensely.

Word of Menlove's fine performance on Scafell soon reached Colin, probably in his regular post-weekend 'phone call to 'AB', or from Alf Bridge. He responded quickly and on the Monday wrote to Menlove to congratulate him:

31 Aug 1931

Dear Edwards,

Congratulations on CB. It was a most marvellous achievement to lead the Flake Crack direct. Herford did it on a rope without, but even he failed to lead it throughout. I have sometimes thought of it, but I expect I would have funked the beastly thing when I got under it. To do it straight off without exploration was a most marvellous feat. Three cheers for the Climbers' Club!

I did the continuation of our Clogwyn Du'r Arddu climb on Sunday with MacPhee. It was straight-forward chimney climbing, not very hard – nothing like the rest of the climb in difficulty. The nasty-looking block we saw was loose as the devil but we managed to back up outside it without much trouble. The pitch above is an amusing 70 ft chimney, deep-cut, dead safe, and not more than mild VD.

We also did another short new climb, about 200 ft, near right-hand end of E. Buttress. Had some fun with it.

Could you tell me how you did the Flake Crack? Did you layback all the way from below the chockstones, or could you get on the chockstones without?

Yours ever
C. F. Kirkus

This letter from Colin to Menlove is highly significant, as it demonstrates quite clearly why he was held in affectionate esteem by his contemporaries. Any insight the reader might seek into the type of man Colin had become by the age of twenty-one is contained in a document that appeared in both books written about Menlove Edwards, 'Samson'* and 'Menlove'. In 'Menlove' Jim Perrin sums up the incident very neatly:

What a kindly and appreciative character this letter reveals on the part of Kirkus! There is no arrogance or competitive edge to it, merely heartfelt congratulation, a request for information and a modest account of his own activity – which here includes, incidentally, the ascent of *Pedestal Crack*, probably the most technically difficult of his Clogwyn Du'r Arddu routes. It is the letter of a man unthreatened by competition because he climbs for the simple pleasures to be derived from the sport. Menlove obviously treasured it, for it is one of the very few papers of this nature which pass down through his estate.

For myself, as much as anything, it was the reading of this simple note, written in such a brotherly fashion, that opened up my interest in Colin

*'Samson' by Geoffrey Sutton and Wilfrid Noyce (privately published 1960)

Kirkus. It is not difficult to picture him at his office desk that Monday morning, perhaps having just spoken to 'AB' on the telephone, scribbling the note in his distinctive spidery handwriting while pretending to work, so as to get it posted that lunch-time. Sixty years on, it tells us so much about the man and his honest regard for Menlove, who had indeed climbed brilliantly that Sunday. When I discussed the letter with Colin's brother Guy, he was delighted by the content but also amused by the overall tone:

> Ah, "Dear Edwards"! How formal we all were in those far-off days.

A couple of weekends later, Colin was back in North Wales, as the weather continued to improve into the autumn. On the Sunday (September 13th) he teamed up with his companion from the first ascent of *Mickledore Grooves*, Ivan Waller, and the two of them motored round to the cliffs of Dinas Mot on the south side of the Llanberis Pass. The day was to be a significant one, for not only did it witness the second ascent of Menlove's fine new climb *Western Slabs*, but it also saw the establishment of one of Colin's finest routes. Ivan Waller takes up the story:

> We started off by doing the *Direct Route*, both leading through and when we got to the top I said, "Let's go down again Colin". He looked a bit taken aback, but he said "Alright" so we set about reversing the route back down to the ground.

Colin and Ivan then set off up the line of Menlove's *Western Slabs*, which had been put up some five weeks previously. Climbing with Sandy Edge and Andrew D'Aeth, Menlove had found the climb difficult and had been forced to finish it alone. It is a very open route on the right-hand side of Dinas Mot's Nose and for some reason Colin was unable to complete the second pitch and retreated to Ivan Waller's belay ledge. Undeterred, he then turned his attention to the unclimbed and impressive slabby rib to the left and proceeded to climb it boldly without protection. It gave a highly exposed and, for the period, very delicate pitch which led, in just over 100 feet of Very Severe climbing back to *Western Slabs*. Ivan Waller, a very competent climber himself, had considerable difficulty seconding the pitch:

> To be frank [laughter], I was pretty cross with Colin, because I thought he was taking things far too near the limit! It was, however, a superb lead on his part.

As this was taking place, Jack Longland was attempting to lead a rope up *Western Slabs* and had a ringside view of the proceedings. He recalled with mirth how Ivan continued to curse Colin liberally and with maximum good humour, as he made his own way up the long pitch on the rib with quite a tight rope above him! Writing in the Climbers' Club Journal, Jack Longland recalled the day, and Colin's performance:

I remember being lucky enough once to be climbing parallel with him, only a few feet away, over quite a distance, on Dinas Mot – Colin, of course, working out a new route while I was trying to get up one that had already been done. Not knowing his ways so well then, I was very worried about the time he was taking; the rope behind him got longer and longer and I did not see how he could possibly maintain stamina and courage enough to finish off a pitch which showed no easing off of standard towards the top. It took me some time to realise that he was safe precisely because he was slow; that a stretch of rock presenting such a continuous succession of intricate riddles of balance and adjustment and forethought, only could be led for the first time by a man possessing the endurance, technique, coolness and sober judgement of possibilities which characterised Colin's climbing.

Colin and Ivan named their new climb *West Rib*; it was very modern in concept with a long unprotected pitch up a forbidding area of unclimbed rock – perhaps Colin's most difficult first ascent in Wales. Even today, the rib pitch offers very little in the way of reliable protection, is very exposed and gives delicate and very sustained climbing. A very demanding mantelshelf some thirty feet up the pitch must have frightened more than a few leaders over the years, particularly prior to the availability of sticky-soled boots and reliable nut protection. It is fair to say that a fall by Colin on the upper part of the rib would almost certainly have resulted in a fatality. In the 1966 Llanberis South guide-book, Peter Crew described *West Rib* as, '....a technical masterpiece, well ahead of its time'. Praise indeed from one of the technical masters of the Sixties. One can picture Colin on the rib pitch, wearing his old navy-blue pullover and flapping his hands behind him to warm them up: tip-toeing up the rock, in his cheap black Woolworths' rubbers, a slow but steady progress by this young man of twenty-one to complete one of the finest pre-war climbs in North Wales. Colin's bold new climb was not equalled in Wales until 1938 and the first ascent of the superb *Diagonal* on the same crag by the gifted Arthur Birtwistle and it retained a substantial reputation for many years. Modern protection methods have helped to reduce the seriousness of *Diagonal*, but *West Rib* still retains its feeling of isolation and is a bold and committing climb, a true masterpiece at the very top level of the day. Those who 'cruise' it today should remember Colin's tenuous journey up the rib, his black pumps slipping occasionally and a heavy hemp rope behind him, with not a running belay to be seen and the likelihood of an exit at the top in doubt all the way. The modern grade of the climb is Hard Very Severe (5a) but there are some people who consider it to be Extreme (E1).

It was at this time that Colin spent a few days with 'AB' at the Robertson

Lamb Hut in Langdale. Whilst there, they enjoyed a particularly good day, leaving early one morning and walking over to Pillar Rock. Here they climbed *Walker's Gully* and *North West Climb*, before returning to the hut, having been out for more than fourteen hours. 'AB' recalled that particular day with great amusement:

> I had at that time a large wart on the side of my face, a magnificent affair with whiskers growing out of it! (laughter). The doctor had warned me not to knock it or to cause it to bleed. Anyway, on Walker's gully I hit it, and there was blood everywhere – all over me, the rope, and the rock. Colin was of course most impressed and highly amused by the whole episode!

In October, the improved weather continued and Colin paid a number of trips to Wales to round off the season. On Sunday, October 11th, he and MacPhee motored down to Pen-y-Pass for the day and wandered up to the fine old traditional buttresses of Lliwedd. Colin led MacPhee up *Reades Climb* (Direct Route) to the Bowling Green and then up *Central Gully*. They then made an attempt on a new route on the cliff, the details of which have been lost, but were rebuffed. Nevertheless, they seem to have enjoyed themselves, as MacPhee described it as '....a perfect day'. Two weeks later they returned to Wales on the Saturday afternoon, staying at Dol Peris. Sunday, October 25th dawned bright and sunny, but it was frosty and very cold. MacPhee described the day in his diary:

> Up to Cloggy, where we took photos and then started on a new climb. The rock was perfectly dry, but **very** cold. I got absolutely chilled at the stances, particularly the last one where I stood for nearly two hours, but finally CFK got up. It was a real snorter. My 280 feet of line got jammed down below and I had to cut that bit off and abandon it. We got it again at the foot, about 4.30 pm. We had started the climb at 11 and finished at 4 and having no food we hurried down to Llanberis.

The climb they put up that day, is now known as *Bridge Groove*, graded for many years as Very Severe, but upgraded in the current guide-book to Extremely Severe (E1). It is described thus: 'The entry to the right-hand groove is steep and poorly protected.' This route on Cloggy's Middle Rock must have been quite a lead on that cold autumn morning and, reading between the lines of MacPhee's account, gave them quite a struggle. This route is one of very few climbs in Snowdonia and the Lake District from the pre-war period that still warrants an Extremely Severe grading. *Bridge Groove* never became particularly popular and is still regarded as steep, awkward and poorly protected. Colin's two-hour push up the final section would have been complicated by loose rock and filthy vegetation in the groove, not to mention the customary lack of protection. For some reason, it was assumed that Alf Bridge accompanied Colin on this particular climb, but Graham MacPhee's diary puts the record straight. At some point in that 1931 season Colin also added a minor route to the extreme right-hand end of the East Buttress, which became known as *Terrace Crack*, as it led in 160 feet to the lower part of the Eastern Terrace. Although quite pleasant, the route never became very popular and today is rather overshadowed by some very hard neighbouring routes. However, by the end of 1931, seven major routes had been established on the great cliff. Colin had made early repeats of the first two (Pigott's and Longland's) while the remaining five were of his own creation. This extraordinary process was to continue the following year, with the addition of three more new routes, before anyone else got in on the act. This domination of the place by one character was not to be equalled for twenty years until the extraordinary exploration of the cliff by Joe Brown in the 1950s.

Despite being barely twenty-one years old, Colin was now established as the finest rock-climber in the country, with a spectacular list of first ascents throughout the crags of North Wales. He had by this time been working at the offices of the Royal Insurance for four years and had matured into a slimly-built man of medium height; at 5 feet 9 inches and weighing less than ten stone, he was ideally built for rock-climbing. This lean but powerful build, allied to the low pulse rate and the stamina of a good cross-country runner, made him potentially an excellent all-round mountaineer. On his regular visits to the hills, Colin was usually clad in the motley collections of old sweaters, rugby shirts, old jackets and flannel trousers that was the norm for the period (although like all good climbers he was choosy about his footwear), but he dressed smartly for the office in a dark suit with a collar and tie. Within the Climbers' Club he was noted for his neat appearance, enhanced no doubt by the odd occasion when he travelled directly to Helyg or the Robertson Lamb Hut from the office and had not been home to change. As was very much the custom of the period, Colin enjoyed a smoke and from around this time started using an elegant cigarette holder, which served to contrast sharply with the normal fairly shabby attire worn on the hill and the crag by most people. Maurice Linnell's quote that 'this year's office suit is next year's climbing attire' summed up most people's attitude to the matter! Unmarried and living at home with his parents, Colin had few major responsibilities at this stage of his life and was able to enjoy a fairly carefree existence, taking every opportunity to reach the crags of Helsby,

North Wales or the Lake District. Although the push-bike was still sometimes brought into use, increasingly Colin was able to obtain regular lifts to the hills, particularly when climbing with Graham MacPhee, and was never to learn to drive or to own a car of his own.

1931 was an important year in climbing terms; aside from Colin's continuing success on the crags of North Wales, Menlove Edwards emerged that summer as a formidable force with great determination allied to exceptional physical strength. In the Lake District, Maurice Linnell continued to impress with exciting new climbs on Pillar Rock and on Scafell. In a broader setting, that summer saw the first ascent by the Schmidt brothers of the North Face of the Matterhorn, a major climb that after the war was to delight (and excite!) several generations of British alpinists. In the Himalaya, the big event that year was the outstanding success of the British Expedition to the Garhwal, and the ascent of Kamet (25,447 ft) – at that time the highest mountain climbed. The expedition reached the summit on June 21st, the day Colin climbed *Pinnacle Wall*. Moves were slowly getting under way to send another British expedition to attempt to climb Mount Everest. No further attempt had been made to send a British Expedition to the mountain following the traumatic events of 1924 when Mallory and Irvine were lost, going for the summit. However, the time seemed right to review the situation: finance was available and certainly there was a whole new generation of able young climbers available. Approaches were made via the Indian Government to the Dalai Lama, who, though still unhappy about incidents during the 1924 expedition, finally granted permission for an all-British Expedition in the summer of 1933. Would there be a place for Colin, or indeed any of his friends on such a great adventure?

In the upper echelons of the mountaineering world in Britain, much of 1932 was to be spent in various preparations for a forthcoming expedition to Mount Everest. The fine success of Frank Smythe's Kamet Expedition had given rise to considerable optimism in this particular direction; perhaps with hindsight a misplaced viewpoint when one considers the considerable difference in the height of the respective mountains. However, Mount Everest once again captured the public's imagination and, as the year wore on, became an increasingly important factor in the climbing world. As the year opened, however, Colin was unlikely to have been too concerned with such broad matters: he continued to get out climbing regularly, locally at Irby Quarry or Helsby, farther afield at Helyg or to the Robertson Lamb Hut. The daily round of work in the Insurance Office continued, as did the regular socialising with Marco Pallis and Graham MacPhee. Colin's regular contact with Alf Bridge and Maurice Linnell, itself really a function of 'AB's move north, had also brought him into contact with a particularly talented group of climbers in the Rucksack Club, who were doing great things on Derbyshire gritstone. It looked as if 1932 could be an exciting time. Kamet had been climbed and a return to Everest was widely mooted; MacPhee was in the vanguard of a new resurgence of exploration in the Scottish mountains; and British climbers were moving into unguided climbing in the Alps. In effect a whole new set of ideas of what could be achieved was being examined by an increasingly large and talented group of people – in a way, very similar to what happened in British climbing again in the 1970s.

With regard to Colin's mid-week visits to MacPhee's place, Guy Kirkus recalled an amusing sidelight. Colin was invited for dinner with MacPhee and his young wife on a regular basis, usually with Marco Pallis. After dinner, the lads would while away the evening chatting, looking at photographs, examining MacPhee's impressive collection of maps of Scotland (he was already an enthusiastic Munroist) or getting down to the serious business of boot nailing. The whole issue of nail patterns and relative merits of tricounis or clinkers were important issues to climbers of that era (not everyone had the cavalier attitude of Menlove Edwards, to whom footwear on climbs was of little matter). A whole evening, usually round at MacPhee's flat, might be spent getting the boots sorted out for a forthcoming trip and this would on occasions cause MacPhee to break open a bottle of malt whisky, of which he was something of a connoisseur. Guy remembered that Colin's resistance to alcohol was never very high and that he was not particularly fond of Scotch. However, he would take a dram or two with his friend MacPhee and often this would result in him tottering home across Sefton Park in the small hours, boots under his arm, slightly the worse for drink but no doubt stimulated and excited by more plans hatched for the future, or for the next weekend in the hills. No doubt Colin would be more than a little bleary-eyed on the tram down to central Liverpool later that morning!

Immediately before Easter 1932, Colin travelled down to Wales one Saturday with MacPhee and they spent the night at Dol Peris. The Sunday was spent battling round the Snowdon Horseshoe in strong winds, with the hills covered in a great deal of snow. It served as good preparation for the annual winter trip to Fort William at Easter, the following weekend. MacPhee was to stay at the C.I.C. Hut with an S.M.C. party, while Colin attended a club meet at Fort William itself.

According to the Mountaineering Journal, twenty-seven Wayfarers attended the meet: M. Pallis, A. Pallis, A. Messinesi, G. Williams, J. M. Edwards, R. Nicolson, R. B. Dutton-Walker and friend, M. Williamson, F. E. Hicks, R. Spencer, M. Brown, W. Garland, C. Bicknell, P. Bicknell, A. Stewardson, F. Spencer-Chapman, H. Balfour, A. W. Bridge, M. Linnell, J. L. Longland, A. P. Sinker, Ivan Waller, A. B. Hargreaves, C. F. Kirkus, E. W. Hodge, and C. K. Brunning.

> During the week-end, which was mainly fine, most of the local climbs were polished off. J. L. Longland made a brilliant ascent of the Tower Ridge, followed by nine others, and an equally brilliant ascent of the North-East Buttress. Most of the gullies went and a good deal of ridge walking was done. Pallis and party emigrated to Skye for a couple of days and Claude Bicknell and others finished up on the Glencoe Ridge. As on previous occasions the party enjoyed the hospitality of the MacPhersons at the Waverley Hotel, except those hardy souls who slept on the Ben, to wit, Kirkus, Chapman, Waller, Bridge and Linnell. Kirkus excelled himself by scorning the luxury of a tent and sleeping outside the Observatory, rising at five to amble up and down the North-East face before commencing any really serious climbing.
>
> It is worthwhile recording the feats of the various cars which were used, one even succeeding in traversing the Mamores. Owing to the state of the roads, if they can be called such, the sporty low-slung cars suffered rather badly. However, most of them made very good time through the night, despite one missing the route and almost traversing Scotland twice. Hodge arrived three days late owing to oil trouble.

Colin, Maurice Linnell and Alf Bridge clearly had an enjoyable weekend, while Jack Longland's performances on the Ben served notice of the excellent all-round mountaineering ability he was to display on Everest the following year.

Towards the end of April (23rd/24th) Colin travelled up to the Lake District with MacPhee for a Fell and Rock meet based on Coniston and Dow Crag. MacPhee also brought along his wife and they booked into 'The Sun', while Colin found lodgings with the 'venerable Mrs Grant'. On Sunday morning Colin and MacPhee walked up to Dow Crag in a particularly cold wind. Here Colin attempted to lead them up *Murray's Direct* on 'B' Buttress, but failed on the rather fierce 'Tiger Traverse' on the first pitch. This was followed by a spirited attempt on *Eliminate C* as snow began to fall and they were finally driven off the crag by a vicious hailstorm. They returned to Coniston by walking over Coniston Old Man as the weather gradually cleared. A fortnight later the pair travelled down to Wales on May 7th, driving down from Liverpool on a particularly beautiful evening to spend the night at Tal-y-braich. On Sunday morning, they walked over to

Glyder Fach Main cliff and had a good day; Colin leading up *East Gully*, *Direct Route*, down *Slab Route* then finishing the day with *Alpha*, all in boots. Prior to doing *Alpha*, they had a good look at *Square Chimney* (Laycock and Herford's classic route of 1912) but to quote MacPhee:

> Kirkus did not like it, as it was full of snow and ice so we did Alpha instead. It started to rain heavily so we called it a day and returned to Liverpool.

With the summer fast approaching Colin increased the regularity of his training visits to Helsby, cycling over at the week-end when not in the mountains and sometimes in mid-week after work, in the time-honoured tradition of northern climbers. On June 14th, Colin wrote to Alf Bridge, who was at that time on Skye, describing a typical Helsby trip of the time. Alf had always been highly impressed by Colin's considerable stamina and endurance, as well as his unique climbing form. In his letter Colin recalled:

> I cycled to Helsby on Sunday by myself. I did twenty miles there in eighty-five minutes (including a half-mile walk over the footbridge at Runcorn) did 42 climbs, and got back in eighty-eight minutes – all between 2.15 pm and 9.25 pm. I lost 4lbs over that show, but my finger strength should be good after 1,500 feet of Helsby climbing.

Colin's fingers were soon to be put to the test! On June 15th (a Wednesday) he teamed up with Maurice Linnell and on Maurice's motor-cycle they whistled down to Llanberis to walk up to Clogwyn Du'r Arddu. They appear to have returned to examine the remaining possibilities on the East Buttress, where the existing routes of Pigott's, Chimney and Pedestal were the only breaches in the defences of this magnificent area of rock. In the event, they re-investigated the direct start to *Pedestal Crack* (which Colin had attempted with MacPhee the previous August). At the time Kirkus and Linnell probably formed the strongest partnership yet to emerge on British rock – truly the Brown and Whillans of the pre-war era. The pitch they produced that day was a particularly good one, providing Colin with what was one of the hardest leads that he made on the Black Cliff. The direct start to the Pedestal gave a very steep 50-foot pitch up a crack/groove line that still warrants a 5a grading in the current guide-book. In dry conditions (not over-common) which Colin and Maurice encountered on this occasion, the pitch gives a very fine piece of climbing indeed, utilising hand-jamming and bridging techniques, and it is unlikely that Colin found any protection on it. As late as the early 1950s, the pitch was still regarded as 'Extremely Severe'. Today, the pitch is much tamed by modern protection but has a feel and steepness more in keeping with the post-war era than that of the early 1930s.

Colin returned to Clogwyn Du'r Arddu a few days later, in the company of Maurice Linnell, Alf Bridge, Marco Pallis, A. B. Hargreaves and W. S. Dyson and camped below the cliff. This visit was notable for Marco's attempts to persuade them all on to a health diet of lentils and olives! Colin was particularly fond of camping below the great cliff, next to the dark atmospheric Llyn and years later fondly recalled such nights in 'Let's Go Climbing!':

> I have camped many nights by Clogwyn Du'r Arddu, that grandest of Welsh cliffs. It is wonderful seeing the moonlight on the crags; they look huge and ghostly and every detail stands out in the silvery light. We used to pitch our tent right beneath the rocks and the top looked like a jagged ridge of pinnacles, towering up into the sky. We felt ready for anything after such a night – even a new climb on 'Cloggy'.

On the Sunday morning, June 19th, the party awoke to particularly promising weather and Alf Bridge and 'AB' set off to make an early repeat of Pigott's East Buttress route, which still retained a big reputation five years after the first ascent; this particular ascent was AB's third or fourth time up the route! In the meantime, Colin, Maurice and Marco examined the central groove line on the Middle Rock, immediately to the right of the East Buttress. The line they climbed, immediately next to Colin's 1931 route *Bridge Groove*, gave a reasonable 200-foot climb of Very Severe grade split into two pitches. At one point, a six inch nail was brought into use as aid for a bit of genuine steeplejacking. They called the route *Birthday Crack* – that weekend being Colin's twenty-second and Maurice's twenty-third birthdays.

Later in the day, the whole team started to inspect the deep-cut curving line of chimney cracks to the left of the *Pedestal Crack* and Colin made protracted efforts to climb the initial groove but to no avail. In 'Let's Go Climbing!' he tells the story himself:

> We could not get up the bottom portion, which was a kind of smooth chimney, overhanging in places. A. W. Bridge, Alan Hargreaves and I spent the best part of a day giving each other shoulders in most perilous positions. Alf Bridge is a brilliant climber and enormously strong; his arms have saved him more than once on a desperate lead. He wedged himself 50 feet above the ground and we took it in turns to try and climb over him. He kept up a constant stream of encouragement. "I've got you; you're all right. I'll hold your feet and push you up and you can make a jump for that hold. Of course I can hold you; I could stay here for weeks."
>
> But it was all no use; there were no reasonable holds on the overhang. Alan was the lightest of the three and Alf was really most anxious to try and throw him up. Alan did not seem to think it a very good idea.
>
> We had given it up as a bad job when we heard a shout from above. We looked

up and there was Maurice Linnell at the top of our pitch. He had climbed a crack on the other side. It was such a ferocious looking crack – very narrow and overhanging for most of its 40 feet – that we hadn't even tried it. We rushed up and found it much easier than it had looked, though very strenuous. Maurice very generously insisted on my leading. He said that it was my climb, since I had first thought of looking at it. He was a very fine climber and could tackle anything that was within my powers, so it was a most unselfish action. It was typical of him.

As a friend of both Colin and Maurice 'AB' recalled this famous incident with some amusement:

> This episode did show Maurice's disinclination to be at the tail end of the party! While Colin was struggling with the obvious start, later done by Jack Longland I think, Maurice characteristically spotted an alternative round the corner and showed his face at the top of the first section! But then, also characteristically, he surrendered the lead to Colin who completed the climb. They were of course very good friends.

It was indeed a very bold and confident piece of climbing by Linnell and it opened the way to a really classic route. The initial corner-crack is quite vertical and particularly strenuous if laybacked, which is what Linnell did without knowing if there was a feasible exit at the top. Today, this crack is quite a soft option at VS 4c if hand-jammed, but over the years many leaders have fallen off it laybacking. Writing in 1950, the great Arthur Birtwistle had this to say of it:

> On the first pitch of *Curving Crack* on Clogwyn Du'r Arddu more than one climber has been unable to make up his mind and has alternated in the middle between going up and coming down, until the matter was settled by Mother Nature.

From the top of the first pitch, Colin returned to the front and led the remaining 170 feet to the top. The remainder of the climb commences with a shallow and quite tricky chimney, often greasy and unpleasant, further crack-work and then a traverse out to the right, to finish up the arête in a fine position. The Helyg poker was used a great deal for cleaning out the crack and the whole party then swarmed up it, initially calling the route Curving Chimney. Today *Curving Crack* is a very pleasant climb of its grade and a Welsh classic. For many years, it was probably the most popular route on the East Buttress and Colin included a photograph of the first pitch in 'Let's Go Climbing!' The story goes that because of this photograph, *Curving Crack* was the first route on the cliff climbed by a young Joe Brown in 1949 and later by an even younger Don Whillans, themselves both destined to write their names in the history of the place. It is said that you never forget your first route on Cloggy and over the years *Curving Crack* was a popular choice for many people, myself included. The original start that defeated Colin was climbed the following year by Jack Longland. However, it lacked the quality of Linnell's opening pitch and never became popular, being rather neglected to this day.

Following the ascent of *Curving Crack*, two interesting incidents occurred that give a flavour of the time. 'AB' was packing his rucksack and was about to add the Helyg poker to his load when Alf Bridge, who was phenomenally strong, bent it in half and handed it back to him:

> There you are Alan, it will fit into your sack now!

As this was going on Alf heard a sharp cry ......'Alf! Give me assistance.' Colin, wearing nailed boots, had soloed some way up a very steep crack line to the left of *Curving Crack*. He had got himself badly committed on the very steep wall to the left of the crack, could move neither up nor down and was on the verge of parting company with the rock. Secured by 'AB', Alf quickly scaled the crack below Colin, who was then able to use Alf's shoulder to regain the crack line and to retreat in good order. 'AB' recalled this incident:

> Colin had in fact got a long way up the crack and we were lucky to get him down quite easily. He was forever launching forth like this!

Colin later made a further attempt on this crack line, in the company of Alf Bridge, on a bitter cold wintery day. Alf later wrote:

> We were in boots and the sole of one of Colin's boots had come adrift from the upper and he had tied the two parts together with string!

It is not known how far up the crack Colin managed to get, but when it was finally vanquished in 1937 by the Manchester climber Arthur Birtwistle, the *Drainpipe Crack* was regarded as one of the hardest pitches in the country and was very sustained. It now forms the first pitch of Joe Brown's 1951 masterpiece *Vember*, and the initial moves are particularly strenuous and committing. It was an enterprising attempt by Colin, but one from which he was perhaps lucky to escape unscathed!

That night, flushed with success on Clogwyn Du'r Arddu, the party retired in high spirits to Helyg and Colin remained there for the following week. Menlove was also at Helyg at that time, but despite continuing dry weather Colin could not persuade him out on to the crags. It is tempting to muse on what they might have got up to together that week, as Colin was clearly climbing as well as at any point in his life, but sadly it was not to be. At the end of the week, Alf Bridge returned from Manchester and on Sunday

June 26th, Colin and Alf returned to Clogwyn Du'r Arddu in the company of
the celebrated Rucksack Club duo of Fred Pigott and Morley Wood,
together with the noted bogtrotter and mountaineer Eustace Thomas, who
had come along to take photographs. A formidable character of the period,
Thomas was the first Briton to climb all the Alpine 4000-metre peaks,
though he employed guides for his ascents. The result of their efforts that
day was the first repeat of *Curving Crack* and later a new route, as Morley
Wood recounted in the Rucksack Club Journal:

> As is well known, during 1932 the Liverpool and Manchester leopards have made
> several new routes on the East buttress, and during one week-end in July A.S.P.,
> E.T., and myself were taken to see them.
>
> It was a fine day after a rainy night, and the rocks were barely fit for rubbers.
> Kirkus, E.T. and I watched Bridge and Pigott start the new Pinnacle Route. It is
> always fine to see a craftsman on his job, and Bridge's lead up the forty-foot crack
> will always remain in my mind as a magnificent exhibition of climbing technique.
> He climbed with perfect certainty, obviously finding and using just the right holds,
> though telling us all the time how badly he was shaping and how much better
> Linnell had done it the week before.
>
> Kirkus took us up the Eastern Terrace to the Green Gallery, where E.T. and
> his cinema stayed. From the point where the first route reaches the gallery, two
> slabby walls lead to the foot of a very definite crack leading to the summit of the
> crag. The first wall is steep, short and wet; the second is longer and has a very
> awkward movement near the top. It was at this point that Kirkus removed a large
> black slug from an essential hand-hold and threw it at his futile second –
> accurately.
>
> We had taken so long over the two walls that Bridge and Pigott had reached the
> Gallery, so they tied on to us. The crack runs for some two hundred feet, is
> generally useful for hand or foot, graced with belays or threads at infrequent
> intervals, but without any very outstanding character or incident.
>
> Kirkus, climbing in stocking feet, unearthed a number of holds and belays. I
> was in rubbers, which were mostly greasy, and I was often glad of the rope. I
> certainly found the climb severe, though I doubt it it will eventually be classified as
> such. Certainly it is not comparable in difficulty with the routes below the Gallery.
> It provides a good finish to those routes, for the Green Gallery is scarcely a
> dignified exit to the climbs; and I personally was very pleased to be with Kirkus
> when he laid the ghost of the 'impossible final wall' of Clogwyn Du'r Arddu.

The new route pioneered by Colin and described here by Morley Wood,
was of course The Direct Finish to the East Buttress. In the current guide-
book it is described as 'A delightful pitch...' and is graded Hard Severe (4b);
it keeps company with some very hard modern routes on this particularly
exposed part of the cliff. Although Colin was only a few days past his twenty-
second birthday, this was destined to be his last major new route in Wales

and was the conclusion of a quite magnificent period of exploration on Clogwyn Du'r Arddu that was not to be equalled for twenty years. It seems strangely appropriate that Colin should have been on the cliff that day with Fred Pigott and Morley Wood, themselves both directly involved in the first two ascents on the cliff, prior to Colin's eight new routes. Colin knew this notable pair of cragsmen quite well and had a great regard for Pigott's exceptional ability. 'AB' also knew Pigott and Wood and recalled an amusing meeting with them in the Lake District:

> I once had the very great honour to lead these two great figures up a route in the Lake District. I met them in Borrowdale one afternoon and they said to me, "What's this about a new Kelly route on Pillar that's supposed to be impossible for a short man? You'd better come along and lead us up it!" So we walked over to Pillar together and I led them up *Grooved Wall*!

Sadly, only a year after this ascent on Clogwyn Du'r Arddu with Colin, Morley Wood was to die, while still only in his forties. A much-liked character of the period and a notable explorer in the Peak, Wales, the Lake District and Scotland, he was sadly missed, particularly within his beloved Rucksack Club.

Writing some years later, Fred Pigott recalled watching Colin climb at this time:

> He had the power of stopping and apparently resting, on tiny holds whilst he surveyed the next few moves; he would often tie on about twenty feet from the end of the rope and climb with the loose end dangling below him and would cut bits off from time to time to use as anchoring threads. Living in Liverpool Kirkus spent much time climbing at Helsby and brought a matured technique to these longer problems.

Colin returned to Wales the following weekend with Graham MacPhee, driving down from Liverpool at lunch-time on Saturday (July 2nd). They spent the afternoon and early evening enjoying the *Direct Route* on Dinas Mot, MacPhee noting that the final pitches were particularly strenuous. On the Sunday morning they walked up to Clogwyn Du'r Arddu, but the weather turned particularly unpleasant and they ended up by walking up Snowdon in heavy rain and got soaked to the skin – only drying off in the car on the way back to Liverpool.

Colin was back at Helyg a fortnight later and stayed for the week. In the course of this period in late July, he succeeded in putting up three new routes in the Ogwen valley accompanied by Andrew D'Aeth, a friend of Menlove Edwards. D'Aeth was a good climber himself, having the previous year repeated Ted Hick's *Rowan Tree Slabs* with Menlove, a formidable and prestigious route of the period. On Wednesday July 20th, Colin and D'Aeth walked from Helyg up to Cwm Cywion on the northern slopes of Y Garn above the Nant Ffrancon and produced the first notable route on what is known as the Pinnacle Crag. This fine cliff gives some surprisingly good climbing, but has never become popular, perhaps due to the steep approach from the valley. On this particular day, Colin climbed the big open corner that is the main feature of the cliff. This gave a 200-foot route, with a 100-foot Severe pitch followed by a 90-foot pitch that is still graded VS 4c. Unfortunately, the rope jammed and D'Aeth was unable to complete the climb, to which they gave the rather uninspired name *The Crack*. Colin was clearly quite taken with the place, as they were to return twice that week! The following day, they climbed the 250-foot gulley in the centre of the cliff, part of which had been climbed by Steeple and Barlow in 1915. Today the route is graded Very Difficult and the guide-book remarks that it is '....vegetated and entertaining as tradition dictates'. Their third visit to the cliff was made two days later on Saturday July 23rd, when they climbed a 200-foot Severe route up steep ground between *The Crack* and the central gulley. They called the climb *Little Woodhead*, now regarded as a pleasant little route in this out-of-the-way setting. Colin and D'Aeth traversed in from *The Crack*, but an independent start was added in 1943. In some ways, these three routes are typical of Colin's love of high mountain settings and hark back to his early lonely wanderings in the Welsh hills.

It was during this summer that Colin and 'AB' paid a visit to Craig yr Ysfa in the Carneddau and established a new route on the Lower Amphitheatre Wall. This is one of the most impressive rock walls in Wales, now notable for a number of hard routes in a beautifully remote setting. The route they made, *The Crack*, although short and on the edge of the face, was the earliest attempt to climb this fine wall and was a fine effort for the time. It was originally regarded as the Direct Start to Pinnacle Wall and gives a good 90-foot pitch (now graded VS 4c), notable for an awkward start and usually greasy conditions. The traverse that they encountered now appears to be somewhat easier, but the climb rapidly acquired a reputation for difficulty and it was certainly an impressive place to go and explore at that time. 'AB' described their activities that day in a splendid article 'Craig yr Ysfa Memory' which appeared in the Climbers' Club Journal in 1944. I make no apologies for including the bulk of it here as 'AB's account seems to capture the spirit of the times quite delightfully, the generally playful attitude of the young climbers, their delight in the magnificent place itself and of course the enjoyment of some excellent food!

Reading the most excellent Craig yr Ysfa Guide, published in the 1943 Journal, brought back to me a number of sudden, clear-cut memories, particularly of an old adventure, one of many experienced during the period 1927-1934 when I had the good fortune to be in at some of the major proceedings of the Welsh revival in the matter of rock climbing.

The Guide says "Pinnacle Wall, Direct Start – C. F. Kirkus and A. B. Hargreaves – 1932" and describes this item as "Standard VI" (which, being put back into the old nomenclature means, I understand, "very severe"). Well, it certainly was very "VI".

As I was constrained to "retire" from serious climbing a couple of years after that I think it would probably be the last time I climbed on Craig yr Ysfa and the day dug itself into my memory, not only because this new thing was done but because of a little bit of "fun and games" – as a happening "not according to plan" used then to be called. I had always had fun on my occasional visits to the place because they were usually to do the Great Gully, which is hardly a small man's climb. For instance, I remember, very early on, being introduced to the place by those maestros of a previous generation, J. M. Davidson and W. R. Reade. I believe my language, when trying to back up the Big Pitch with one ear on one wall and my toes scratting on the other wall, was considered shocking – and there was also some little trouble over my going to ground in a hole under the Capstone and refusing to move until towed out on the rope – though I believe I got a bit of my own back on that nice little penultimate pitch. Later on, when I had acquired cunning and the habit of not taking much notice of how six-footers did things, I used to go up the right-hand crack of this Cave Pitch, most interesting, certainly "stiff", as per Guide! I also remember a winter ascent when our party of three got so wet and cold that we had to walk all the way back to Helyg *roped*, the knots having somehow got seized....

But this day with Colin was much "funnier". The previous year he had made the *Pinnacle Wall* climb – solo – and he proposed that we should go there to do it (a) so that he could get my opinion for classification purposes, and (b) ((a) turned out to be only a blind) so that he could have a go at a little thing he had tried the day he did the climb and which he thought might go if he had a bit of moral support... I suppose I ought to have detected that there was something out of the ordinary in the lad's mind because he not only piled a lot more food than usual into the sack (that is, about a war-time week's ration of body-builders and energisers) but also a little bag which jingled, and the Helyg poker. This latter was quite a normal item of our equipment in winter because funds did not run to ice axes – but we did not usually borrow it in summer time – though the hearth brush was sometimes requisitioned then. Well, it was a nice fine day, not too hot, and we talked a lot on the way over about Clogwyn Du'r Arddu, and gardening, and about Menlove and *his* gardening activities on Idwal East Wall (blast him!), and about a certain young woman who had recently changed ownership – and about the *Pinnacle Wall*, of course, but no information was given me about the "little thing" we were going to try. We began by doing the *Amphitheathre Rib* (very good climb) just to warm up, and from there I had pointed out to me the run of the *Pinnacle Wall* climb ("It's a pity one has to go right along that Bilberry Terrace to get on it instead of straight up the corner") and then my attention was drawn to the wall below the said Bilberry Terrace ("What about that crack, that would straighten it out a bit, wouldn't it?"). I was cocky enough to second this proposal but I did jib at Colin trying to do the thing unseen, because it looked a perfectly horrible place and I insisted that we commence operations by my going to the top of the crack and fetching him up it on a rope. This turned out to have been a wise move; it took about an hour, several pulls and a lot of Colin's energy to get him up. He then reported that it would probably go if thoroughly gardened (he had already removed quite a lot of stuff) so I was sent down with the poker and spent another hour preparing the pitch for the lead. Then Colin led it, having very great difficulty, especially at the start and the finish (which would have been quite impossible as it was before it was cleaned up). I remember very well the "poor belay" near the top – and the difficult traverse out to finish; that was about the hardest bit. It was just the sort of pitch to justify Menlove's famous description – "very annoying". We were both pretty exhausted after this and were glad to fall to on the sardines wrapped in sliced tongue, and the jam sandwiches laced with Nestle's milk; we also opened a tin of bully which, with Carlsbad plums, was to constitute a final *bonne bouche*... But before we had got to that stage the aforesaid little bag was produced and I was surprised and rather shocked to see that it contained a little hammer and couple of flat pitons. I say shocked because we two were generally agreed that steeplejack's ironmongery was out of place on crags, British crags at any rate, *unless* there was something that could not possibly be led safely without such aids and which, if it could be done, would result in the completion of a climb – such as on the *Overhanging Wall* climb on the East Buttress of Scafell, made by Linnell and my namesake. Anyway, this was the first time to my knowledge that C.F.K. had thought of using the things and the place where he thought they might be required was directly above us where we sat on the Bilberry Terrace at the top of the Direct Start crack. This was a nasty-looking V groove of perhaps 30 feet, approximately perpendicular to start with and definitely overhanging at the top where it gave on to the Quartz Ledge of the *Pinnacle Wall* climb. I again proposed to go round to the top of the pitch and drop a rope so that Colin could try it that way first, but he said he had already been some way up it when he had done the *Pinnacle Wall* climb and he thought it would certainly go if he could get a piton fixed below the top overhang; also, time was getting on, so he decided to try it "clean". With some difficulty my leader got himself lodged in a sort of saint's niche about 20-25 feet up and then proceeded to fix the piton in a crack at the back. This was not so easy because he had to hold himself into the niche with one hand while hammering the piton with the other. However, he eventually got it in to his satisfaction, then he ran the rope through the ring and climbed down for a rest. We both pulled hard on the rope and the piton was O.K.'d as firm. Then Colin went at the pitch. His idea was to use the rope running through the piton to hold him in (à la Leo Maduschka, *vide* British

Mountaineering Journal of about that time) while he leaned back and reached upwards for the holds which he hoped existed above the overhang. He tried once – and came back into the niche – he tried again (harder) with me holding the rope taut – and then – (a loud "ping" and a "whirr") – the piton was out and Colin was in mid-air... Fortunately, although the Bilberry Terrace from which we were operating was quite broad at that point, I had a belay, though rather a small one, and was able to get some rope in during his gracefully parabolic descent, because he landed on his stomach at the very edge of the Terrace and just as the rope came tight on him he bounced over the top of the Direct Start crack... The brakes held, but only after I had been dragged several feet with the belay rope (line) stretching like elastic. I can still see his legs waving in the air... But although the leader was saved (it was a fairly soft landing) – at the usual cost in second man's hand-skin – a disaster had occurred; the bully tin had got kicked overboard during the proceedings so we had to eat the Carlsbad plums neat.

We did *not* do the *Pinnacle Wall* climb (ordinary way) just to preserve our nerve, according to the old prescription, although we did try – dithering down – the Quartz Ledge into the corner and then back, even more ditheringly – in fact, as the sun fell we crept slightly up one of the Amphitheatre gulleys (roped – short run outs) and slunk, chastened, down to Helyg where nothing was said about the day's doings – in fact I don't think even the Direct Start was logged.

As I did not try the pitch myself I cannot say whether or not it seemed climbable, with or without artificial aid, but it does seem worth commending it to the attention of post-war "tigers" because if it would "go" the combination of it with the Direct Start and the upper and difficult part of the original Pinnacle Wall climb, would obviously form a superb route worthy to rank with the best on Clogwyn Du'r Arddu.

Colin and 'AB's exploits that afternoon was quite possibly one of the first examples of pitons being used for tension climbing in the British mountains. This point was touched upon by Clark & Pyatt*:

The view that the use of these metal spikes, which were driven into cracks in the rock, was totally unjustifiable, was by this time in process of modification. The whole question of "ironmongery" was still the subject of perennial discussion, but a growing number of climbers believed that its use was justified only when it helped to safeguard a mountaineer without making possible that which would otherwise have been impossible. Many continental climbers thought differently, and the view of one of them, Leo Maduschka, were expounded in the first number of the Mountaineering Journal, a magazine published in Liverpool in June 1932. Maduschka advocated, as did many of his continental contemporaries, the use of pitons not only as safeguards but as physical aids on a climb. A piton could, for instance, be driven into a crack at a climber's head level, or even higher; the rope from the waist could be threaded through a karabiner attached to this or through a ring in the piton, then taken down to the second who, by holding the rope tight,

*'Mountaineering in Britain' (Phoenix House – 1957)

An Idwal group with Maurice Linnell top left and Colin fourth from right at back.   *Photo unknown*

could physically keep a climber in to the rock, freeing both the latter's hands for the difficult work to be tackled or for the insertion of another piton higher up. It was this method, an innocent harbinger of things to come, but rather shocking in 1932, which Kirkus tried on Craig yr Ysfa.

When I talked with 'AB' about this particular episode, he replied with great mirth:

> Oh, that day was a good laugh! Colin really wasn't at all mechanically minded, and I suppose he thought he ought to know about these blasted piton things! And anyhow, it soon came out and he fell off [roars of laughter].

In reality, the matter was not viewed too seriously by Colin and 'AB'. It was simply an opportunity to try out what were new and radical ideas in a secluded spot. The tenuous balance between artificial aids and free-climbing has always been a most important ingredient of British climbing and indeed still is as we move into the 'bolt age' on several crags. Colin developed his own sensible views on the subject over a number of years, and later published them in an essay in the Wayfarers Club Journal in 1939.

Around this time, Colin, 'AB', Maurice Linnell, Alf Bridge and others of their group began to spend time with a mostly Liverpool/ Manchester-based group that had developed around the recently opened Idwal Cottage Youth Hostel. The 'scene' at the hostel was subsequently to form the background for Elizabeth Coxhead's famous novel 'One Green Bottle', and the hostel itself rapidly became an important additional focus for climbing in and around the Ogwen valley. By way of digression, Elizabeth Coxhead is credited with a delightful comment on climbing:

> A sport is advanced by the handful of people who do it brilliantly, but it is kept sweet and sane by the great numbers of the mediocre, who do it for fun.

This wonderfully sane outlook on the whole slightly ridiculous business of climbing, might have been written by Colin himself and was echoed by the contents of his book 'Let's Go Climbing!'

Someone who recalled Colin and his friends at Idwal was Berta Andrews, now in her eighties and a senior member of the Pinnacle Club. As Berta Gough, she frequented the hostel for a number of years with her best friend Connie Alexander, who was the first warden at Idwal Cottage and a close friend of Colin. Berta remembered:

> Colin was a member of the Climbers' Club which had a centre at a farm close by and he used to come to Idwal quite a bit; he was, of course, only in his early twenties. When the members had left the hostel at 10 a.m. he would take Connie and me out and teach us to climb on Tryfan, the Devil's Kitchen etc. We always had to be back by 4 p.m. and he was very kind and patient with us and taught us how to climb properly.

In the years to come, Colin was to continue his connections with the group at the hostel and was destined to spend much of his own time teaching others the basic skills of mountaincraft. Both Berta Gough and 'AB' provided photographs of Colin with friends at the hostel and there will be more about the role of Idwal Cottage Hostel in Colin's life in due course. 'AB' recalled, with his usual glee, a visit to the hostel around this time with Colin:

> One of my early visits to the hostel was made when I'd just got hold of my first car. I travelled down with a girl-friend and Colin in the back. I had with me a large bottle of whisky, strictly against the hostel rules, of course, but it got shared around amongst the hostelers over dinner – everybody got some! Later we were all enjoying a game of sardines, when an eminent figure arrived at the hostel, a senior officer from the Liverpool Y.H.A. He observed the whisky bottle, now empty, still on the dinner table and brusquely enquired of Connie the warden, what it was doing there! Quickly she replied that they used it as a candle holder!

Throughout that summer, Colin continued to climb and train particularly hard, along with Alf Bridge, as both clearly had the forthcoming Everest expedition in mind. It was the view of many North Wales regulars that Colin would almost certainly be considered for the team and he continued to cycle or even on occasions walk, to and from Helyg most weekends, to build up his already considerable stamina. Guy Kirkus recalled one occasion in particular, when Colin walked home to Liverpool after a particularly hot weekend in Wales and was reduced to drinking rain water out of puddles *en route*. 'AB' also recalled this incident and remarked that it was an example of Colin pushing himself too hard and almost succumbing to sunstroke and doing himself real harm. There was no doubt that both Colin and Alf had a great desire to be included in the Everest team; indeed Colin had grown up on the epic stories of the 1924 Expedition, embodied in the books by Norton[1] and Younghusband[2] that he had read in the school library. On September 6th 1932, he wrote to Alf:

> The weekend before last, I cycled to Capel Curig and walked over Pen Helyg, Carnedd Llewelyn, Glyder Fawr, Crib Goch, Crib y Ddysgl, Y Wyddfa and back along the road to Capel in just under twenty-four hours. I am trying to get really fit to be with you on your Llandudno Junction – Beddgelert Welsh 3000s show. I'm afraid I may be considered too young, but we must manage to go together. Everest! What a life's ambition and in a few weeks, or perhaps a few days, we shall know whether it is to be realised. It must be!

It is pertinent at this stage to examine just how important this forthcoming expedition was to the mountaineering establishment of that time. Walt Unsworth's book 'Everest' (Allen Lane – 1977) covers this aspect particularly well, looking at the various issues involved and bringing to light the complex nature of national pride and competitiveness involved, even in the early Thirties. The historic epic of 1924 when Norton reached an altitude of 8580 metres on the mountain and Mallory and Irvine were lost going for the summit, were still quite fresh in the memory. In addition, some incidents connected with the 1924 expedition, in particular the affair of the dancing lamas, still rankled with the authorities in Tibet. It is relevant to quote Walt Unsworth on this aspect:

> It looked as though the Tibetans had long memories and were neither willing to forget nor to forgive. In desperation the Committee mooted the idea of going through Nepal instead of Tibet, but General Bruce warned them that Dyhrenfurth's recent expedition to Kangchenjunga had upset the Nepalese and made them more intransigent than ever.
>
> Nevertheless, seven years had passed since the last expedition and critics were beginning to complain that the Committee was not pressing the case strongly enough. This was true enough – but these were the same men who had their knuckles rapped by the India Office in 1924 and they had no intention of getting them rapped again.

[1] Lt. Col. E. F. Norton 'The Fight for Everest: 1924' (London 1925)

[2] Sir F. E. Younghusband 'The Epic of Mount Everest' (London 1926)

Had they only known it, they had at their disposal a very powerful argument; that of chauvinism. Younghusband had unwittingly touched on it at the first meeting of the new Committee when he made a reference to the ghosts of Mallory and Irvine which he hoped might soften the hearts of the India Office and Sikkim: "Attention should be called to the fact that this country should have a priority in view among other things that her countrymen lay at or near the top."

Younghusband's statement did not go unnoticed in the India Office. The fact was that Britain's monopoly of Mount Everest was being threatened. Suggestions were coming from the United States that the next British expedition should contain an American, Terris Moore, or alternatively that there should be an American expedition led by Page Stelle and including a British climber – preferably Odell, who was well known in American climbing circles. Rumour also had it that the Swiss climber Dyhrenfurth intended to press for a chance too.

More disturbing than these, however, was the growing strength of German high-altitude expeditions, both in the Andes and Himalaya. Paul Bauer was about to make his second attempt on the mighty Kangchenjunga, third highest mountain in the world, and if he succeeded it would put the Germans in a very strong position indeed to claim the right to attempt Everest. It would have been politically impossible for the Indian Government to have denied them; the rest of the world would have seen a refusal as cynical imperialism and it would certainly have stoked the already smouldering German nationalism. It would have been perfidious Albion once again up to her tricks, even if she was disguised with a sari.

Certainly there was the growing concern that Mount Everest, ostensibly a 'British' mountain (just as Kangchenjunga was identified as a 'German' mountain) might soon fall to a non-British expedition and all haste was made to secure a quick return to the mountain following the reconstruction of the Everest Committee in March 1931, referred to previously. In the event, the Indian Government began to put pressure on Tibet, despite the relative timidity of the Everest Committee, and permission was finally granted for an all-British Expedition in the summer of 1933. To quote Walt Unsworth again:

> The Dalai Lama put the position delicately, granting "reluctant permission in deference to the wishes of the British Government in order that the friendly relations may not be ruptured."
>
> Hardly the warmest of welcomes. A codicil stipulated that all members of the expedition must be British.
>
> For the Everest Committee it was a dream suddenly come true, relieving them of the growing criticism. For the Government it was a model exercise in keeping foreigners in their place without really trying.

Next came the question of leadership of the Expedition, complicated by the fact that many of the key figures of 1924 were not getting any younger, and by the increasing British ability being shown in hard guideless climbing in the Western Alps. On this basis Frank Smythe was an obvious candidate, with impressive Alpine seasons in 1927 and 1928 and his fine ascent of Kamet (25,447 ft.) in 1931, (the first mountain over 25,000 ft. to be climbed). However, for a number of reasons, not least his professional approach regarding writing and lecturing, Smythe was overlooked for the leadership and this fell to Hugh Ruttledge, an ex-Commissioner from the Indian Civil Service, already in his late forties. In no real respect an established mountaineer, Ruttledge was well known to the Committee members and was in fact nominated by General Bruce. Ruttledge, in effect, acquired a most difficult job and one unsuited to his modest, self-effacing character. In overall terms, the old order of the Alpine Club and the Royal Geographical Society still held sway and this was to emerge as the team was gradually put together. Certainly there was no lack of interest and applicants came from all manner of backgrounds.

Hugh Ruttledge recorded in 'Everest 1933':

> The composition of the party for Mount Everest required, of course, the most earnest consideration. Here a free hand was given me, on the principle that the man who is to be responsible for a team should choose it. An application file was opened, the contents of which are ample evidence that the spirit of adventure is still very much alive in England. In it are represented the Navy, the Army, the Civil Services, University professors, undergraduates, schoolmasters, men of science, pugilists, a barber, a steeplejack and last, but not least, schoolboys. Many of them had never been on a mountain in their lives and had no idea of what a big Himalayan climb means. However, it was pleasant to realise that such keenness existed. The Tibetan Government had stipulated that the European personnel of the expedition must be British. We could not, therefore, include any of the fine mountaineers of the Continent and of America. But there was no lack of trained talent in Great Britain and the Dominions, especially in the school of young guideless climbers which had grown up during the last twenty years.

In all likelihood, the most relevant consideration in team selection, which took place in the early autumn of 1932, was the great success the previous year of Frank Smythe's expedition to Kamet. Of that team, no less than seven (Smythe himself, Shipton, Birnie, Greene plus Lewa, Nima Tendrup and Pasang Bhotia) were selected for Everest and, on the basis of the success of Smythe's expedition, it could be argued that they had earned their places. With several climbing places already filled, it was clear that there were only a few places left. One of these went to Jack Longland, who had established a fine reputation as a rock-climber, as well as in the field of Scottish winter climbing and unguided Alpine climbing. Longland in turn pressed for

Colin's inclusion in the team. In 'Everest', Walt Unsworth commented on the great social prestige attached to the expedition, and the methods adopted for selection:

> Socially, there was little to distinguish the members of the 1933 expedition from those of its predecessors. The climbers came from the same class that had traditionally provided the membership of the Alpine Club for three quarters of a century; the well-to-do middle classes, with a background of Oxbridge and a decent sprinkling of Army officers and Government officials. Ruttledge recalled that applications to join the expeditions were received from 'pugilists, a barber and a steeplejack' – thereby implicitly inviting his readers to scoff at such notions as preposterous.
>
> It is doubtful whether the Committee even knew there existed a body of climbers whose horizons were the bleak moors around Sheffield rather than the Georgian porticos of South Audley Street and probably ignorance rather than snobbery kept small the corpus from which selection was made. In any case no working-class climber could afford to take the time off to go to the Himalaya. So the gulfs were practical as much as social.

One point that did emerge from the conversations and correspondence with those who knew Colin at all well was the recollection of his very real disappointment at not being selected for Everest, both in 1933 and in 1936. It is important to examine a little more of the background here to further clarify the situation. The ill-fated 1924 expedition had been almost something out of a Victorian drama, an epic tale that belonged to a different era. By the early 1930s, a whole new attitude towards high-altitude climbing had emerged, one of great (albeit somewhat misplaced) confidence further bolstered by the success on Kamet. Certainly there was considerable prestige and kudos attached to the whole venture and lobbying was rife as 'AB' recalled:

> There was a lot of lobbying for selection on the 1933 Everest show. And a lot of people were lobbying for Kirkus to go. He himself would *never* have dreamt of lobbying, he was not that kind of animal. Colin would have been content to be chosen, and would have done well in my opinion. A lot of people pushed for him perhaps too hard, in particular Colin's good friend Alf Bridge. Alf meant well, but I feel he might have been a little tactless and consequently counter-productive. It was no good trying to bully the Alpine Club into selecting X or Y, and certainly there was tremendous competition for places and all sorts of people lobbied for. I don't think Colin would have got up Everest that side at that time, but I think he would have been a most valuable member of the party. He would have fitted in beautifully as a co-operative member and not as a star.

When I discussed the question of the 1933 Everest expedition with the late Marco Pallis he was in no doubt about Colin's suitability and the injustice of his non-inclusion:

Colin should have been one of the first they selected, but it was snobbishness that kept him out in those days. I can't imagine anyone not getting along with him – he was not at all quarrelsome or offensive. Similarly, Colin would never have spoken of "conquering" or "vanquishing" Everest. Such an idea would have been unthinkable to him.

In 'Menlove' Jim Perrin pulls no punches, and approaches the issue of selection directly when discussing Colin's cousin Wilfred Noyce:

> Grace and effectiveness are two ends of a socio-sporting spectrum still operative to a degree in England today (consider the selection of many England cricket teams). In mountaineering, here lies the reason for Kirkus's exclusion from the 1933 Ruttledge expedition to Everest. Kirkus desperately wanted to go and, although relatively inexperienced, was keenly interested in Alpine and greater-ranges mountaineering. His record in the Alps was not by any means so poor as was suggested at the time. On his first Alpine season he had, admittedly, only done "a few undistinguished climbs with Marco Pallis, carried out at Marco's usual snail-like pace", but on later trips with speedier partners he had performed well and his single trip to the Himalaya proved extremely successful. But, despite Jack Longland's counsel that he should have been included, he was excluded on the grounds of his inexperience. Yet in 1924, the Oxford rowing blue Sandy Irvine had been chosen for Everest, despite his Alpine experience encompassing no more than a few very easy peaks in the Bernese Oberland.
>
> That a class-bias existed in the mountaineering establishment is unarguable. Its distinctions were fine-drawn; the northern office worker Kirkus was beyond the pale; the Charterhouse and Cambridge colonial who was his cousin perfectly acceptable.

Certainly, with the benefit of hindsight, it is tempting to adhere to the view that the exclusion of Colin and indeed Alf Bridge (Ruttledge's 'steeplejack') and Maurice Linnell was itself a class-ridden conspiracy designed to keep 'rough northern climbers' out of the team. Although there might be an element of truth here, the reality was probably more complex and subtle. A revealing insight into contemporary attitudes regarding team selection, comes from 'Kamet Conquered'[1] by Frank Smythe himself:

> Himalayan mountaineering depends upon unselfish team-work and unselfish team-work depends upon having a team of men who are temperamentally in phase. Your friend in civilisation may become your enemy on a mountain; his very snore assumes a new and repellent note; his tricks at the mess table, the sound of his mastication, the scarcely concealed triumph with which he appropriates the choicest tit-bits, the absurd manner in which he walks, even the cut of his clothes and the colour of the patch on the seat of his trousers, may induce an irritation and loathing almost beyond endurance. None of these things may matter at sea-level and why they should matter on a mountain is a problem more within the

[1] 'Kamet Conquered' (Hodder & Stoughton 1932)

scope of physiologists and psychologists than the writer of this volume. But the whole success of an expedition depends upon them not mattering.

The ideal team is one that includes different interests, paradoxical though this may sound. It is a profound truth that men sharing identical interests seldom get on well together in the wilds. If they do it is as much of a miracle as a happy marriage. Wide divergences of opinions that count for so much. I cannot conceive a team of mountaineers composed exclusively of doctors, barristers, or politicians.

Notwithstanding the sentiments outlined by Smythe, on the basis of current form and fitness Colin, Alf Bridge and Maurice Linnell were then the equal of any climber in Britain. There were probably few tougher and fitter regular climbers available. However, what they did all lack was serious and extensive experience outside Britain on big mountains. At this point, Colin had only had the one visit to the Alps – the 1930 trip with Marco Pallis. In addition, by the prevailing attitudes of the time, he was regarded as rather young for high altitude work and a number of Alpine Club members probably had a better broader claim to inclusion. By the summer of 1935 however, Colin's claim to a place on an Everest expedition was to be far stronger. At this earlier stage of his life, it is almost certain that Colin's lack of alpine experience was to be a crucial factor in his exclusion from the team. Commenting on this aspect, Jack Longland summed it up thus:

All very different from today, when young lads seem to go straight from the gritstone quarries to the great faces of the Himalaya.

Following Colin's omission from the final party for Everest, Alf Bridge wrote angrily to the Alpine Club, outraged at the decision to omit his friend and suggesting that '...perhaps the members expected Everest to be climbed from the playing fields of Eton'. Guy Kirkus recalled that Colin was highly embarrassed by this episode, but there is little doubt that Alf's heart was in the right place and that he shared Colin's great disappointment. Certainly, it is interesting to ponder on what might have been, particularly in the light of Jack Longland's excellent performance on the 1933 Expedition.

Fortunately, Colin's disappointment was to be short-lived, as Marco Pallis was planning a Himalaya trip of his own for the summer of 1933 – a small-scale expedition to the Kumaon, largely made up of Wayfarers, and a place was soon found for Colin. Elsewhere on the British climbing scene, 1932 was notable for the continuing development of Menlove Edwards as an explorer, with hard new routes in Wales (*Procrastination Cracks* and *Grey Slab* on Glyder Fawr). Writing of Colin and Menlove at this time, Geoffrey Winthrop Young commented:

...seeing Kirkus as slow and inevitable as the hands of a clock upon a holdless slab and Menlove Edwards, serpentine and powerful as an Anaconda coiling up loose or wet overhangs, I had the conviction that human adhesiveness in movement could go no further.

That year also witnessed the start of Maurice Linnell's campaign on the East Buttress of Scafell, with the brilliant lead of *Great Eastern*. In retrospect, however, perhaps the most significant event that year in the British hills was the Kinder Trespass which took place in April, followed by the subsequent trial and imprisonment of Benny Rothman and his friends. This event was to be a watershed in the developing struggle for access to the wild places, that would culminate in the establishment of the National Parks after the war.

As for Colin, perhaps his greatest days in Wales were already past, though at the time he was not to know that. Certainly however, 1933 promised adventure in plenty, if the Royal Insurance could be persuaded to grant him extended leave to visit the Himalaya with the rest of Marco Pallis's team.

The year ended on a nice note for Colin with a long weekend in Wales. A. B. Hargreaves had by this time become very friendly with the famous Lakeland painter Heaton Cooper, and spent many days on the hill with him. 'AB' discovered that Heaton had never been to North Wales and persuaded him to come down to Helyg for New Year. 'AB' takes up the story:

> It certainly was a memorable trip with Heaton, and we had Colin with us as well. It was a long journey down to Wales and a cool one as my car at the time was an open MG (laughter!). We stopped off at Ruthin to sleep; myself in the car while the other two went off into a nearby graveyard, though I think they actually slept in the church porch. I felt sure that Colin and Heaton would get on because they had very similar natures, I doubt if either of them ever made an actual enemy. The following day I think we climbed on Tryfan and Heaton painted a splendid study of Y Garn with the Rivals and the Lleyn Peninsula behind, from the summit. I think he got the shape of Y Garn beautifully and it is one of the very few paintings he has done of Snowdonia.

The painting of Y Garn that resulted from this particular trip is now owned by 'AB' himself and is a quite delightful study of the mountain on a cold, clear morning. Talking to Heaton Cooper himself, he recalled the day on Tryfan with 'AB' and Colin and particularly remembered Colin's kindness and patience in the face of his own somewhat faltering steps on that cold morning almost sixty years ago. As they sat near to Adam and Eve on the summit of the mountain, Heaton got to work with his brushes and paints and produced a picture of great beauty and a lasting reminder for 'AB' of a good day on the hill with two good friends.

5 Himalayan Interlude

We turn now to Colin's Himalayan trip of 1933, and the best introduction is in his own words:

How would you feel if you got the chance to visit the greatest mountain range in the world – the Himalaya – to climb peaks that had never been climbed before? Naturally I was nearly mad with excitement when I was asked to join the Gangotri Glacier Expedition in 1933.

Prior to the protracted deliberations over the composition of the 1933 Everest expedition, Colin had been involved in the early plans of Marco Pallis, to lead a Wayfarers Club expedition to a virtually unexplored region of the Himalaya. A great deal of detailed planning was carried out and, in particular, specialist equipment was provided by Robert Lawrie from his new premises in London. Much of this equipment was tested in the Alps in the summers of 1931 and 1932 and Colin and Marco tested sleeping bags in conditions of extreme cold both in Snowdonia and in Scotland. Colin recalled one of these occasions in 'Let's Go Climbing'. It is an interesting passage that reveals much of the joy and humour Colin found in the hills:

One of my most interesting bivouacs was on Snowdon. It was the coldest day of that winter, though it was well on into March. After getting out of the car, my ears were completely numb before I had walked fifty yards along the road.

We set out about nine o'clock at night. The ground was frozen hard, and it was bitterly cold. We walked briskly, and soon got warm.

We were really going out to test some new sleeping-bags, specially designed for the Himalaya. We also wanted to see whether we could build a snow-house or igloo, after the Eskimo fashion.

Above Glaslyn the snow was deep and fairly hard. It was quite tense work, cutting steps in the darkness and cloud, with the gale swirling the snow violently into our faces. We also had the Alpine danger of crevasses, for there are some disused copper-mines above Glaslyn that often get completely bridged by snow.

There was an absolute blizzard raging when we arrived on the ridge between Y Wyddfa and Crib y Ddysgl. There were 18 degress of frost. In an experimental mood I put my tongue on to my ice-axe and nearly got it frozen on.

We worked feverishly, cutting blocks out of the hard snow to build our house. I am afraid it would not have passed a town planning director; it blew down almost as fast as we built it up, sometimes faster. Perhaps it was like some of the "desirable modern residences – all conven., h. and c." – which won't stand a wind until they have the support of the wallpaper.

All we managed to do was to build a low-semi-circular wall, rather like a sheep-shelter. I was last in bed, and I ran round and round the encampment in an effort

A high winter camp.   *Photo C. F. Kirkus (AC coll.)*

to keep warm. Little particles of ice were being whipped stingingly into my face; the wind was shrieking and howling, and the snow and cloud were being driven along in a smoky fury. My clothes were frozen stiff as boards and covered with hoar-frost.

With numb fingers I took off my boots and squirmed into the bag. My boots came in with me, clogged with snow as they were. I knew how impossible it was to put on frozen boots in the morning.

The opening over the face fastened up with press-fasteners. In a later pattern we used zips. I had to warm my fingers several times before I could get the whole thing done up. I found it hard to breathe at first and thought I was going to suffocate; I felt as if I were in a coffin. The sensation soon passed; actually it was quite easy to breathe through the down.

I "dined" inside my bag, with the aid of a torch. All the food was frozen solid and seemed to have completely lost its taste. I was enjoying a slab of cake; I shone the light on it and it turned out to be corned beef.

Our bags had shiny black waterproof covers. These were very effective for a single night, but unfortunately they made the bags wet by condensation, so that they could not be used for a second night without first being dried.

We slept well and kept beautifully warm. It gives you an eerie feeling when you put out your head in the early morning.

Everything looks white and unreal and cheerless after the snugness of your bed. The air always feels damp at first, however hard it may be freezing. Your first thought is that a thaw has set in. Then the cold strikes home, and you pop your head in again.

We laced up our boots with cold and fumbling fingers. Our camp site, seen in the daylight, looked the very last word in desolation. We hurriedly stuffed the bags in our rucksacks, together with a good deal of snow, and made our way towards Crib y Ddysgl.

The blizzard was still blowing as strongly as ever and I got one of my eyes frozen up, and had to break the ice on the lashes before I could open it.

We used the ropes over Crib Goch and descended to a very welcome breakfast at Pen-y-Pass.

Marco Pallis's intention was to attempt peaks around the virtually unexplored Gangotri glacier until the rains arrived, and then to cross the Ganges Satlej watershed to a district beyond the monsoon's influence, and passing through Poo, attempt the ascent of the fine peak of Riwo Pargyul. The desire of the party was to try to demonstrate that it was possible to climb mountains of this scale (20,000 feet plus) without vast number of porters and 'a general martial spirit' to quote Ted Hicks; in effect to climb in much the same way as one would in the European Alps. The expedition was largely financed by Marco, and there is little doubt that he was keen to give Colin his chance in the Himalaya.

The climbing party consisted of Marco Pallis himself, his close friend and climbing companion Richard Nicholson, Dr. Charles Warren who was destined to go to Everest in 1935, 1936 and 1938, Ted Hicks, and Colin. While these last two were very much the rock-climbing 'tigers' of the party, all five had Alpine experience of some kind although none of them had been to the Himalaya before. In effect it was a party of friends embarking on a great adventure, with between them considerable scholastic, linguistic and climbing ability. Colin's friends were delighted that he would be going out to the Himalaya after all. One night over a pint, Alf Bridge playfully chided him: 'Now Colin, don't go putting your foot in it out there in the Himalaya. Remember the Dalai Lama isn't a Tibetan newspaper, he's the God-king of Tibet!'. In addition to contacts established by Marco himself, much help was forthcoming from the famous Himalayan explorer, Tom Longstaff, who was then President of the Climbers' Club. Help was also available from Colin's uncle, Frank Noyce (the father of Wilf Noyce) who was in the diplomatic service. At the time a Himalayan trip was a very considerable undertaking into largely unknown territory, and any assistance at all must have been welcome. At that stage of Himalayan exploration virtually all climbing had been done with the use of vast support resources in terms of porters to carry all the necessary equipment and supplies. Nonetheless Marco's party was encouraged by the views of Tom Longstaff and a few other visionaries who were convinced that the lightweight approach was the way forward. (This was to be demonstrated further by the magnificent achievements of Eric Shipton and Bill Tilman throughout the 1930s. Incidentally this famed duo visited the Gangotri glacier the following year, during their reconnaissance of the Nanda Devi region.) Certainly before the party set off, there was no shortage of Jeremiahs only too eager to write off the expedition's chances of success, and to point out that peaks of this size were not climbable by their proposed method of approach. There is no doubt that Marco and his party were adopting a thoroughly modern approach, particularly praiseworthy in view of their lack of high mountain experience.

The area chosen for their initial attention was the Gangotri glacier, located to the west of the Garhwal Himalaya (and its now famous peaks such as Nanda Devi, Changabang and Dunagiri). It is the largest glacier in that particular region and is the source of the Bhagirathi River, the main tributary of the River Ganges. To the north-west is the magnificent peak of Shivling. The Gangotri region has three summits of over 7,000 metres, two of which were climbed soon after the war, while the third, Badrinath II, is still unclimbed. From the road-head to base camp, was a distance of over 120 miles and it was proposed to employ the minimum number of porters to carry supplies and equipment, in order to maintain as great a degree of self-sufficiency as was possible, and to keep costs down.

Talking to Marco Pallis and Richard Nicholson fifty-three years later, they recalled with amusement the great deal of hard work in which Colin was fully involved, that went into the preparations for the expedition. In particular they remembered the excitement that they all experienced at the prospect of such an adventure, not least of which was that of a twenty-eight day sea voyage to Calcutta. The expedition generated a great deal of interest in Liverpool itself, and some limited sponsorship was forthcoming from the Liverpool Post, for which Colin wrote a number of articles and reports both during and after the expedition. An indication of Colin's growing status in the sport, and perhaps that of the Wayfarers' Club itself, was the fact that the Royal Insurance Company agreed to let Colin have leave of absence from his job to attend the Gangotri stage of the expedition – an enlightened attitude by an employer, not common at that time. In the busy period prior to departure, Marco remembered seeing Colin virtually daily:

> He would come around to my house almost every night to continue the work on the expedition, and was always cheerful and helpful. I do remember one occasion however when Colin was feeling particularly under the weather and was unable to contribute very much that evening. He was feeling the effects of the series of injections we all had to go through.

Despite the increasing pressures of preparation for the forthcoming expedition, Colin continued to climb whenever he could in order to maintain a good level of fitness. On February 2nd he was in North Wales for the weekend, and did the second of only two new rock routes he climbed with Menlove Edwards, that of *Nebuchadnezzar's Crawl*, on Dinas Cromlech in the Llanberis Pass. In 'Menlove' Jim Perrin refers to the ascent, and Menlove's own summing up of it:

> This route, on Dinas Cromlech, was the second and last new line he pioneered with Kirkus and was one of the poorest of Menlove's career. Its quality is so low that it has virtually been written out of the modern guidebook, but Menlove and Kirkus seem to have found it entertaining enough:
> "It would be tedious to describe in detail the types of turf to look for en route. The name is Nebuchadnezzar's Crawl; Neb's Crawl for short. It will be remembered that, during a period of mental aberration, this old gentleman went on his belly seven years with the beasts of the field, size not specified, and his face he buried in the grass. There was an amusing incident on the Crawl when we got into a corner and then got out again."

Certainly Neb's Crawl is not a distinguished route (it is graded Difficult in the current Llanberis Pass guide-book and is not often climbed, being vegetated to this day.) However the two climbers seem to have enjoyed a good day out together before returning to Helyg. By this time Menlove was already very interested in these steep vegetated cliffs on the north side of the Pass, and certainly their potential must have been obvious enough to Colin. The gradual development of the cliffs on both sides of the Pass, within which Colin's early explorations on Dinas Mot are notable, was to continue throughout the 1930s and into the post-war era. Sadly Colin was never to climb two of the finest pre-war routes in the Pass, namely *Main Wall* on Cyrn Las pioneered by Roberts and Cooke in 1935, and the splendid *Diagonal* on Dinas Mot climbed by Arthur Birtwistle in 1938. Both routes were well within Colin's capabilities, but it seems most likely that neither received a second ascent until well into the 1940s.

Some weeks after the ascent of Neb's Crawl, Colin attended a most important event when, on March 18th, the formal opening of the enlarged Climbers' Club hut at Helyg took place. Some thirty-four members of the club, including the President Tom Longstaff, then gathered at the Pen-y-Gwyrd for a 'Reformation' banquet and among them were Colin and friends such as Menlove, A. B. Hargreaves and Bill Stallybrass. There was even some rock-climbing done over the weekend and during the after-dinner speeches Tom Longstaff spoke of his climbing experiences in India, and

Tom Longstaff on Cul Mor.   *Photo courtesy of Mrs Sally Amos*

wished the forthcoming Gangotri expedition every success. Colin was a great admirer of Longstaff, and readily acknowledged the great help that he gave Marco Pallis and his companions prior to their departure. Years later in his biography[1] Tom Longstaff remembered climbing with Colin, and mentions his own admiration for the young man's obvious skills and ability.

Finally the preparations for the expedition were completed, and the day for embarkation from Liverpool docks arrived – April 1st (the significance of the date was not lost on the party!). The journey to Calcutta was to be in a ship of the Harrison Line, the Custodian, which was a cargo ship, and the five climbers were to be the only passengers on board, thus making for a most interesting voyage.

The sea voyage did in fact last until April 30th, when they finally docked at Calcutta having journeyed past impressive views of Gibraltar and the Atlas Mountains. Colin's fascination with life at sea (no doubt shared by the others in the party) was well conveyed in this quote from 'Let's Go Climbing'.

> The genial Captain O'Connor amused us with a host of stories. He told us that monkeys could speak if they wanted, but they were afraid that they would be made to work if they did. We did a great deal of sunbathing. Marco walked about the hot iron decks barefoot, to get his feet hardened, and one of the Lascars asked him sympathetically if he hadn't got any shoes.

[1]'This My Voyage' (John Murray – 1950)

The Gangotri expedition was well documented in an article Ted Hicks wrote for the Climbers' Club Journal in 1934, and on their return from the trip the members undertook a number of public lectures. Colin wrote an article for the Wayfarers' Club Journal, and this later formed a chapter of Marco Pallis's book 'Peaks and Lamas'.[1] This gave an account of the 1933 trip, and a subsequent journey in 1936 to the Sikkim and Ladakh regions of the Himalaya. Colin's own diary of the expedition, which he kept from May 10th until his return to Mussoori on July 21st, has been kindly lent by Guy Kirkus to aid the writing of this book. This quite charming document, hand-written in an exercise book, gives an invaluable insight into a young man's perceptions of so many totally new and exciting experiences together with candid descriptions of some of the hardships of travel and of climbing on the world's greatest mountains.

The expedition members enjoyed excellent weather throughout the voyage, and after an initial period of resting (following a chaotic period prior to departure) parts of the ship were sought out to provide 'rock-climbs', and other exercise sought to maintain fitness. In addition, much effort went into the study of languages, in particular Hindustani. This was hard work for Colin and Charles Warren as the other three members were quite accomplished in Hindustani, and even in the very difficult Tibetan. In the words of Marco Pallis:

> For us so occupied, four weeks slipped by all too quickly, and it was with mixed feelings that we saw the mangrove-fringed coast near the mouth of the Hoogli slowly loom into sight and knew that it was the last time we should hear the cheery voice of Captain O'Connor summoning us to his cabin, at the end of the day's work, to join him in a 'sundowner'. But there was a thrill in the thought that this turbid waterway, with its jute factories and barges, its feather palms and slimy mud flats, suited to the fiestas of crocodiles, was a mouth of the self-same Ganges which we were about to follow all the way to its source, goal of many pilgrims, where it issued from the glacier ice.

Only one day was spent in Calcutta, before the party made their way to Howra terminus to commence the 600-mile train journey across the Indian sub-continent to Dehra Dun. The train journey took the best part of two days, and was full of hazard for the Englishman abroad, as humorously described by Marco Pallis!

> One of the minor peculiarities of an Indian tour is the sheer hopelessness which attends any search for a drinkable cup of tea, although this is the land which contains Darjeeling and Ceylon. Neither prayers nor threats will make the Indian

[1]'Peaks and Lamas' (Cassell – 1939)

servant on the railways or in hotels believe that every Englishman does not like his tea 'ystrang' that is to say of such a consistency that I could easily have written this book by filling my fountain-pen from the teapot.

From the railhead at Dehra Dun the party made their way to Mussoori, where the road ends. They spent a whole week there, based in an hotel and preparing loads for their porters – a last respite before the approach march itself. Marco described the view that greeted them one morning:

> The sun rose in a clear sky and for a brief hour or two the matchless panorama of the Gangotri peaks was uncovered. Our goal stood outspread before us; catching that first glimpse of the land of our dreams, what a passionate eagerness welled up in us to set out, leaving all tedious last-minute organisation to run itself. We longed to start, not the day after the day after tomorrow, but in that very instant, along the winding tracks that cross seventy miles of forested foothills to the base of the snowy ranges. Whoever has had experience of a get-away into the Himalaya must be familiar with this impatience.

Prior to 1933 few expeditions had set forth from Mussoori and therefore a fair amount of time was required to make the necessary arrangements, not least of which was the selection of an expedition cook (high among Colin's priorities). At last, on the morning of May 10th, they finally set off with their 70 porters, with warnings that the path of their route had been carried away in many places by avalanches.

Marco Pallis wisely encouraged the whole party to carry loads, partly in order gradually to build up their fitness and partly to win the respect of the porters with whom they were soon on very good terms. The crucial question of appointing a reliable cook was resolved by the hiring of a porter, Maidar Singh, who seemed more intelligent and adaptable than the rest – he was to be an unqualified successs, much to Colin's relief! The initial trek from Mussoori to Harsil, scheduled to take some nine days, began on a beautiful morning complete with fine mountain views to the north. In 'Let's Go Climbing' Colin described the early part of the trek, his first experience of such work.

> The trek was very hard work, but very interesting. It was terribly hot at first – anything up to 100 degrees in the shade (and there wasn't much shade). Our shoulders got sore from the sacks and we suffered a good deal from thirst. We had to boil all water before it was fit to drink, otherwise we might have got cholera or dysentery or some other unpleasant disease.

Certainly the combination of a heavy load, the heat, and limited food and drinking water took some getting used to, but in his diary Colin noted with delight early sightings of a scorpion and a family of amusing monkeys.

However, the overall impression, was that he found it quite hard going – something first-timers to the Himalaya would probably recognise.

> May 11th......It would have been quite an enjoyable trek but for hunger and especially thirst. I was so thirsty that I drank out of the main stream, although there were houses about. I hope it is not infected. My back and shoulders are getting very sore from the rucksack. I had a lighter load than yesterday but it seemed heavier and the stage seemed more like 30 than 11 miles. We saw several eagles and ravens. There was a storm of thunder and rain at 3 o'clock which stopped about 6.30. Good meal at 8 o'clock of soup (very dilute), tongue, potatoes and onions. Fine night but cold. Bed 9.30 p.m.

By the third and fourth days out from Mussoori the team was gradually becoming accustomed to the effort involved and now there were other occasional diversions to encourage them. A quote from Colin's diary again:

> May 12th......There were marvellous views of the big mountains today – the twin peaks of Bandarpunch really dominating the scene. Sri Kanta (20,120 ft.), Kedarnath (22,770 ft.) and Badrinath (23,190 ft.) looked amazing but terribly difficult. There were beautiful trees all round which set off the mountains most magnificently. In the opposite direction we could just see the houses of Mussoori and Landour – about 20 minutes away as the crow flies, 2½ days as man walks.

It is interesting to note the regular features of Colin's diary which are food (and almost constant hunger!), humorous incidents en-route and his fascination with the totally new forms of wildlife encountered. Examples are:

> Charles saw a snake today – believed to be a kreite, most deadly of all. Jai Datt killed it with a stone.'

> 'We have drunk a great deal of Ganges water (after filtering and boiling) and feel very holy. The water is so filthy that a gallon of it stops up the filter, which then has to be cleaned.'

> 'This is an extraordinary place at night. The crickets are deafening, there are many other kinds of strange beasts. I found two large crickets in my tent. They look like shrimps, with large frightened eyes, and jump. Also spiders, ants, beetles etc. One spider about four inches across – probably poisonous.

The march towards Harsil continued without undue incident, the team heartened and amused by Marco Pallis's efforts at speaking to the locals in Tibetan. Colin continued to remark in his diary about how hungry he usually felt but they were all gradually getting acclimatised. At one stage they had a rest day for the benefit of the porters, and Colin showed perhaps a suggestion of homesickness.

> The view from my tent might easily be in the Lake District or Scotland – ferns in the foreground, then the river and a road with fir trees on the right and tree-clad hills behind. It rained and thundered all the afternoon, which made it even more home-like.

During the well-earned day of rest, Colin was called upon to despatch an unfortunate sheep with a humane killer. He seemed impressed at how effective it was and having washed some clothes, bathed in the Ganges, filmed by Charles Warren.

> So now I am absolved of all my sins!

Later in the day Colin tried his hand at bouldering despite the heat and humidity, but was rather anxious about the possibility of snakes sleeping in some of the handholds! In many respects he seems typical of an impatient young climber on the walk-in, anxious to get to grips with the high mountains, yet fascinated by all the new sights and sensations around him. In our less innocent times, it is easy to forget what a wonderful and exciting experience it must have been for a young man of Colin's age, background and occupation to travel to such a place. Later on they experienced more sultry conditions under a cloudy sky, and were plagued by flies. Colin seemed to particularly dislike this aspect of the journey.

> The flies are an absolute curse; the floor of my tent is covered with dead ones which the live ones are devouring. There are at least thirty on one of my boots. I have given up trying to kill them and sit with a sleeping bag over my legs and a mosquito net over my head. However, I had a campaign afterwards and exterminated the flies in all the tents with "Flit", dragging out several hundred corpses on each groundsheet.

By May 18th the party was approaching the stop-over point at Harsil, but for the first time on the trip, Colin complained of being unwell, passed a bad night, and felt ill all day. Fortunately, by the time they all arrived at Harsil, Colin was fully recovered and was able to help with the various tasks that Marco Pallis had prepared for everyone. After the rigours and discomforts of the past few days, Colin seemed to be most taken with Harsil.

> I arrived alone at Harsil (8830 ft.) at 1.45 p.m. This is really a most beautiful spot. We are camped on soft turf near some trees by the river. There are hardly any flies here even in the heat of the day.

There was much work to be done at Harsil, where it was intended to spend three days in order to pay off the Mussoori coolies and to replace them by local men, better suited to the rigours of glacier travel. Colin enjoyed a day of relative rest, bathing and recovering from his illness. He expressed his fondness for many of the Mussoori porters who were being paid off – they seem to have been a good bunch of lads! The second day at Harsil was taken up with packing and odd jobs, Charles Warren holding his almost daily clinic for the locals. After an afternoon storm and a large meal of goat flesh and rice, the party was entertained.

We were treated to an exhibition of dancing by six Tibetans – three men and three women (two of them quite old). The women had some beautiful shawls; most of their clothes were old and patchy but very picturesque. It was really quite impressive – slow heavy movements with hands and feet, with a kind of solid gracefulness about it all. They sang weird but tuneful songs. Some of it was very amusing as they wore broad grins most of the time. We gave them small presents. The local Chief Lama was present – a delightful little old man with a wisp of a beard, almond eyes and a Dutch cap. There are two Lamas in Harsil which is half Hindu and half Tibetan.

Having taken on their new porters, the party set off from Harsil on May 22nd having entrusted mail and film to the departing Mussoori men. The early part of the stage followed a good path, and at one stage Colin noted an amusing sight:

> A little past Danali we saw some pilgrims carrying their wives in chairs on their heads – the height of henpecking!

Farther on the party began to enjoy dazzling views of the Gangotri peaks now only some forty miles distant but, alas, problems were developing with the porters who were far less willing than the Mussoori men and who had proceeded very slowly all day. On reaching the temple of Gangotri, the end of the pilgrim road, a break was made for sight-seeing and lunch. However, on trying to get the porters to continue, Marco Pallis was confronted with great reluctance on their part and every inch seemed to be contested until Pallis was forced to dismiss Jai Datt (the head porter) and a particularly officious ranger who between them seemed to have stirred up trouble with the porters. By this method, a strike in remote surroundings was narrowly avoided and the porters continued the march in much better spirits. By May 24th they were at around 11,000 ft and approaching the Cow's Mouth, and base camp. That particular day Colin helped a sick porter by carrying a 60 lb load:

> It was not too unmanageable, though it was very difficult to balance on steep slopes, and cut badly into my shoulders. I have felt very fit today despite the altitude, and have a most immense appetite.

That night the party was delighted by the arrival of their first mail from home – Colin got a letter posted on April 27th.

A camp was finally established at a spot just below the left moraine of the Gangotri Glacier, close to plentiful supplies of juniper wood. The majority of the porters were paid off, only four remaining behind. The location of this camp afforded wonderful views of the Satopanth peaks and a magnificent nightmare version of the Matterhorn (which is now known as Shivling).

On May 25th Colin and Ted Hicks had set off to prospect for a campsite on the glacier itself. Colin describes his reaction:

> We passed over some horrible moraines and then crossed the river with a good deal of difficulty. I had to wade it. We continued up to a long terrace of snow on the right and put on skis. Slow but not too strenuous. We took off our skis on a rocky ridge and continued on foot to a point overlooking the glacier. About 14,400 ft – the highest I have ever been. I did not feel the altitude much – only a little breathless. Yet in the Alps I am always violently sick on my first day above 12,000 ft. My throat felt dry and parched; high altitude throat is no myth apparently.

Colin and Charles Warren were the first of the party actually to occupy base camp, whilst the remainder of the equipment was carried up. By this time the night temperature had fallen to 25°F, and the climbers were aware of almost constant avalanches on the peaks around them. An initial reconnaissance of the glacier was made by Colin and Charles Warren: they ascended to 14,500 feet in a chilly wind and took due note of the relative positions of the peaks around the glacier, Colin being particularly inspired by Shivling[1] (Matterhorn Peak). Colin later used a fine photograph of this mountain in his book 'Let's Go Climbing!'. On their return to camp, Ted Hicks had arrived, but there was no sign yet of Pallis or Nicholson, who turned up later in the evening, having been up to 16/17,000 feet on an adjacent peak the day before. That night Colin recorded his impressions of the view from the glacier:

> The Matterhorn Peak is on the right-hand side of the glacier, a little farther up. We saw its far ridge today, it looks as hopeless as the rest of it. The two Satopanth peaks are very marvellous and the higher one looks just possible. The glacier itself is a maze of abominable moraine mounds interspaced with snow. The tents are in two lots, about 50 yards apart on their own islands. As soon as the sun goes down it gets bitterly cold. A wind always springs up at sundown, then dies down, rising again later in the night.

The following day, Colin spent most of his time struggling up on to the glacier with two of their porters to do some plane table surveys of the area, before descending again in strong winds.

The next day, May 30th, the weather had improved and the party again split up to explore out from the camp in various directions. Colin set off on skis to take a look at the glacier on the near side of Satopanth and, after a tiring climb over ice and a particularly foul moraine, found himself at the foot of a small peak in front of Satopanth 2.

[1]Shivling (21,467 ft) was not climbed until 1974, and the ascent was contentious, using siege tactics and much fixed rope.

Shivling.   *Photo Allen Fyffe*

I decided to make an attempt on it. Two steep slopes mostly of good snow led to some loose-looking rocks which proved to be a little tiring. Then there was an exhausting V-shaped chimney filled with soft snow, followed by a traverse along a rock ledge and across a snow slope inclined at about 50°, which I was afraid might avalanche, for there were a lot of V-shaped pieces where the top surface had slid off. However, the top surface was only an inch or two thick so there probably wasn't much danger, especially as I kept my hands on the rock for as long as possible.

I was feeling very weak and moving slowly, taking one or two breaths to each step and resting frequently. I reached the summit, a rocky ridge, at 3.35 pm and put a cairn on each of the little peaks. It is really only a minor summit of the peak in front of Satopanth and is about 17,000 ft high. I noticed that Satopanth 2 looked possible by the left-hand ridge, though difficult.

Colin had a fairly uneventful descent and then set off alone down the glacier, only reaching the camp in near darkness at 8 pm. There then followed two days of rather poor weather during which Colin suffered badly from an inflamed nose and badly cracked lips. He slowly recovered, eating a number of healthy meals while the others continued their exploration of the area.

Colin's next venture into the mountains was in the company of Ted Hicks on June 2nd. On this occasion they went a little higher than Colin's previous excursion, climbing snow-slopes with interesting rock-scrambling stretches, both more difficult than the previous ascent. They reached the summit (at almost 18,000 feet) of the peak in front of Satopanth, Colin's previous ascent being of a minor summit of this same peak. In his diary Colin commented that he felt he was acclimatising well, and that the descent was fairly straightforward apart from the long grind down the moraine:

> Coming down the mountain we had both got bad headaches, Hick's severe and continuous even after we reached base camp, mine more intermittent and less severe, disappearing half way down the mountain. We found Pallis at base camp, and had a large evening meal composed entirely of chip potatoes. I don't feel very tired, but my lips are badly burned – swollen and yellow.

After a brief rest Colin, together with Ted Hicks, set about making an attempt on a peak on the ridge to the west of the Gangotri glacier. This was to be significant for Colin because it was to be his first time above 20,000 feet. In 'Let's Go Climbing!' he only mentions in passing his later fine ascent of Satopanth II with Charles Warren; instead, and with typical modesty uses this ascent of a minor peak as an example of Himalayan exploration.

The first part of the climb was another dreadful slog up the glacier, followed by a long moraine ridge to a point at about 16,000 feet where they

Ted Hicks at altitude.   *Photo C. F. Kirkus*

were able to erect their tent. In 'Let's Go Climbing!' Colin describes the typical routine required in high altitude camping, in particular the need for plenty of water, balanced against the joys it can give:

> It was a wonderful night – so wonderful that we kept the door open. We were just opposite the great north face of the Matterhorn Peak[1] – 7,000 feet of it. We could see the two peaks now, sticking up like fearsome fangs against the evening sky. The rock went deep red, and the icy summit a delicate pink. The shadow crept up and everything was dark except for the scarlet flush where the sinking sun still touched the final ice-cap.
>
> Presently the moon rose and made the scene even more exquisitely beautiful. The snow slopes looked dream-like and ghostly where they curved down into the glacier bed, but the towering rocks still looked bold and black and strong.

The two men were understandably awed by the magnificent view from the tent, but humour was never far away. In his diary Colin records:

> Hicks and I gave a mock running commentary, every other sentence ending with the words, in slow and solemn tones: "We are lying on our stomachs on a moraine".

Colin slept only fitfully, and next morning they were away by 5 a.m. after a grim breakfast of pemmican from a thermos. They made steady progress throughout the day, despite Hicks in particular suffering badly from the effects of altitude. At one point they had to negotiate a small rock overhang, which was found to be very exhausting indeed. They finally decided to camp at around 2 p.m. having reached a point just below the main ridge of their peak at 18,800 feet. Once the tent was erected, they collapsed inside exhausted, Colin recording the pain in his diary:

> I took two soda mints and two aspirins and slept quite well. We both carried sacks weighing 30 lbs today – absolute purgatory! It had been a trying and difficult day. No-one had even attempted the mountain before, so we had no idea whether it was possible or whether we were on the best route. Yet this is the part of it that makes all the hardships worthwhile. There is all the excitement of being where no man has ever been before; there is the interest of the route-finding and the difficulty of the climbing. There is an urge that sends you on and makes you feel that no effort is too great.

Colin had to get up early next morning to thaw out his boots, which had been left uncovered in the tent. The two men had a makeshift breakfast in their sleeping bags, and then set off at 7.30 a.m. unencumbered by rucksacks, which were left in the tent. Ted Hicks was now moving well, and it was Colin's turn to suffer from the effects of altitude and the increased

1 Shivling.

lack of food. Initially they had intended to pack up their gear and descend as the weather looked threatening, but gradually it cleared and they resolved to make it to the top. Colin described that day in 'Let's Go Climbing!':

> I felt terribly weak and had to rest every few feet. Ted had to cut most of the steps, but I managed to do the last hundred feet or so to the top, in hard snow. I would cut five steps, with two breaths to every step, then rest, leaning on my axe or collapsing in the snow. Not an atom of enjoyment. We reached the summit (about 20,100 feet) at 10.30 a.m. We felt no sense of exhilaration – just thank goodness that's over. Thick cloud – snowing off and on. A snow summit, with a few stones about – also two spiders, poor devils! We hadn't the energy to build a cairn.

The two climbers quickly quit the summit, and set off down in the increasingly gloomy conditions. They safely reached Base Camp at 5.30 p.m. It is interesting to note that Colin went to 22,000 feet on two further occasions later on the expedition, but it was on this minor ascent that he suffered the most, although he displayed good powers of recovery once food and rest were available.

Despite his relative exhaustion Colin only rested at Base Camp for one day, before setting off again on June 7th with Charles Warren and Ted Hicks to make an attempt on what they then called the Great Snow Mountain, or the Great White Lump, which we now know as Kedarnath.

They set off on skis with five days' food, and made for a previously decided Advanced Base at the foot of the mountain. They arrived at this point at approximately 15,170 feet by mid-afternoon, with Colin still suffering rather. That evening they dined well on omelettes and other delicacies and delighted in the magnificent position of their camp, with Shivling to one side and Kedarnath to the other. The night was particularly cold and clear.

The second day was something of a grind for the party, consisting largely of a long snow traverse, much of it on skis, of some five miles to the right-hand ridge of the mountain. Camp I was established at 17,000 feet on snow. It is worth noting at this point that Colin and Charles were very new to the delights of skiing, both learning on this trip! In his diary Colin recorded a number of amusing tumbles by them all, as they struggled to ski with heavy sacks on.

The next day, much reduced loads were prepared, and the three men set off, as lightly encumbered as possible, to establish Camp II at around 19,400 feet on a rock point of the ridge. Colin and Charles suffered somewhat with the altitude and blazing heat, but again the camp was in a wonderful situation. Colin recorded in his diary:

I felt better after five cups of pemmican. A boiling hot day with a marvellous evening with grand cloud effects.

That night they all crammed into a small bivouac tent, and no-one passed a good night. Next morning it was decided that it was necessary to ration out the remaining food (biscuits and boiled sweets), to leave behind the skis, and to make a concerted push for the top. The continuation of the route was up interminable snow slopes which proved to be most unpleasant, and Ted Hicks in particular had a bad time that day. Colin just gritted his teeth and got on with the job in hand:

> Twenty steps, one or two breaths to each, then a rest of ten or twenty breaths, leaning on the ice-axe with head down.

By mid-afternoon they had suffered enough, and set about making a camp on the snow slope. At first they cut into a concealed crevasse, and Charles Warren almost fell into it. In the end they were forced to descend some 200 feet to find a suitable spot on some rocks, although still very exposed at around 20,000 feet. By this time shortage of food was becoming a problem, particularly to Colin, and morale fell somewhat as the weather started to close in. In the circumstances, they passed a reasonable night.

Next morning they set off at 8.30 a.m. and made reasonably good going in the tracks left the previous day, although they were all now very tired and hungry. Colin recorded in his diary:

> It was bitterly cold, and my feet got very chilled. We had to rub Hicks' feet to bring them back to life. We were going quite well, but it was a ghastly business. I had a terrible weak feeling in the stomach and legs and it made me giddy to stand up. I thought with regret of the comforts of Mussoorie and Calcutta, and Liverpool!

As the party continued upwards, the weather was taking a sharp turn for the worse, and black thunder clouds were developing from the north-west. At around midday, having reached 21,500 feet (some 800 feet from the summit) they finally agreed to turn back as it was becoming only too obvious that to continue meant becoming caught in the approaching storm. With regret they began to descend and hurried down in increasingly bad conditions. The skis were retrieved, and the descent continued to the moraine where they spent a cold, damp foodless night. Despite their disappointment Colin recalled the experience of skiing down in the teeth of the storm as being very exhilarating.

The following morning saw a reasonably ordered retreat back to Advanced Base, where the party hoped to find some food cached. Charles

Warren elected to remain at Advanced Base, while Ted Hicks and Colin continued down to Base Camp in an impressive thunderstorm. That night they were cheered by the arrival of letters from home, and enjoyed a huge meal around the camp fire. It had been a very arduous effort for all concerned, and Colin was glad to spend the next day resting at Base Camp, eating and letter writing.

After only one day of rest, Colin packed his sack and set off back to join Charles Warren at Advanced Base; it was now June 14th. The original intention was for the pair of them to carry out further survey work on the main Gangotri glacier. However, left alone at Advanced Base, Charles Warren had worked out what looked like a feasible line up the very imposing Central Satopanth peak (now known as Bhagirathi III) and this prospect seemed too exciting for he and Colin not to attempt to climb it. Charles Warren describes the peak in his article[1] in the 1934 Alpine Journal:

> The glacier side of the second Satopanth peak is composed almost entirely of bare rock. This stupendous granite wall forming the greater part of this face of the mountain is supported at its right-hand corner by a ridge which, at its uppermost extremity, merges into the main mass of rock not far below the summit. In the angle between the buttress and the rock wall a long gully seams the face. A small gap high up on the buttress at the head of this gully appeared to form a site for a bivouac on the way up. At this place we should be encamped at the foot of the first great step on the climb.

By this time, both climbers were thoroughly acclimatised and recovered from their previous exertions on Kedarnath. The following day they set off across the glacier heading for the foot of the buttress, carrying a tent, sleeping bags, cooking equipment and food for a week. This resulted once again in heavy loads in excess of 30 pounds each, but the weather looked reasonable, and the climb in prospect seemed the very antithesis of the endless snow grind they had previously endured. The rather monotonous approach up the glacier was enlivened by a diversion on to a fine rock rib that reminded Colin warmly of Wales – in particular some delicate moves up a slab near the top. By the middle of the day they had reached a suitable snow patch that would accommodate their tent, and Camp I was established at 17,500 feet after two hours of digging out snow, and building up small rocks to level the site. The weather deteriorated later in the day and an impressive storm broke across the valley as they sat in their tent. Although they had first met in 1929 on the occasion of Colin's first ascent of *Lot's Groove*, this was the first time that Charles Warren and Colin had climbed alone together. Speaking of this event some 54 years later, Charles remembered Colin as

1 'The Gangotri Glacier & Leo Pargial, 1933'

splendid company on the mountain, the two of them getting on together well. Dr Warren was later to go to Everest on three occasions (1935, 1936 and 1938) and performed with distinction. He is now a senior and much respected figure in the Alpine Club. Talking of the Satopanth climb, Charles made this comment, which is of interest:

> There is a great deal of talk nowadays about Alpine-style climbing. Well, this was really the first Alpine-style climbing expedition to mountains of this size. We literally carried all our four camps up Satopanth Peak, and did our own carrying with no porters – they all stayed down at Base Camp. Needless to say, it was an exciting climb!

The next morning saw Charles Warren and Colin up at 6 a.m. but because of the bitterly cold wind they had to wait before they were able to fold the frozen tent. The climbing was continued with the ascent of a difficult gendarme and some technical slab work, to avoid another pinnacle on the ridge. Despite increasingly difficult route-finding they continued to gain height and eventually an easy snow gully led them back to the ridge where a halt was made to brew tea. They then continued climbing into the afternoon, and found a perfect campsite at a col at 19,500 feet on a flat, slaty site at the foot of the final peak. Colin described the situation in Chapter IV of 'Peaks and Lamas':

> One could not hope to find a better spot at 19,500 feet; it was an amazing luxury not to have to camp on snow. A full vertical mile below was our Base Camp and whole dreary ribbon of the glacier. In front was the face of our mountain – 3,000 feet of the smoothest, sheerest yellow – silver rock, almost luminous against the clear blue of the sky. Behind, over the Ganges, the clouds were gathering – monsoon clouds had we but known; but who would have expected the monsoon to come three weeks early?

After spending a comfortable night at the col, they set out to turn the first step on the ridge proper. This was done by making a long traverse, then utilising a rock gully to return to the ridge above the step. Quick progress was then made up a steep snow-slope which was in very good condition, before they had to cross an area of rotten rock, including some loose overhanging blocks on the ridge. Camp was pitched early, at 1.30 p.m. and Colin described his thoughts at this point:

> We pitched Camp III on a miserable spot at about 20,900 feet. Before we actually put the tent up I wandered on alone and had a look at the next section. It was only 1.15 p.m. and I thought we might have gone on a little further but, as Warren pointed out, there was quite a possibility that we might not find another suitable site in time. It is Dr. Longstaff's golden rule of Himalayan mountaineering always to bivouac by three o'clock.

Central Satopanth Peak – now known as Bhagirathi III – showing camps.   *Photo C. F. Kirkus*

IV   III   II
21700   20900   19500

Camp I
17500

Gangotri
Glacier
15000

North   South

Charles and Colin had to dig out a snow slope with much effort, and the tent was pitched below a fearful cliff with a great snow slope below. Supper consisted of pemmican and boiled sweets, the cooking now being done on smoky solid spirit cookers. It snowed all night, and ominously at that altitude there was only 16°F of frost – a likely indication that the monsoon was just about upon them.

The morning of June 18th dawned rather grey and did indeed appear to be the beginning of the monsoon, with heavy mist and sleet obscuring the view. Certainly in those conditions both Colin and Charles Warren felt distinctly pessimistic about their chances of success. However, by 7.30 a.m. some gaps had appeared in the cloud and, following a meagre breakfast, they set off an hour later. Charles takes up the story:

> The climb up the lower rocks of the last great step was both difficult and exhausting on account of their steepness and the sprinkling of new snow. It landed us at the foot of a very disconcerting-looking corner which Kirkus surmounted by a brilliant piece of rock-climbing.

The corner was in fact vertical, the holds flat and not incut, and there was an overhang at the top – it was clearly the crux of the route, and Colin certainly found it difficult, as he recorded later in his diary:

> Then came the upper wall, a terrifying pitch where one had to go right out over an exposed corner, overhung above and below, depending upon loose blocks. At the top there was a kind of horizontal wafer of rock sticking out and I kicked off the top layer and put my whole weight on it with much trepidation. I was only just in balance as I struggled on to the stony slope above and my heart was throbbing with fright as well as with the exertion and the altitude.

Certainly this was a tour-de-force on the part of Colin, and it turned the key to the route to the summit. It was a very bold effort indeed as, with the equipment then available and bearing in mind their isolated position high on the mountain, a fall from that overhang would have had the gravest consequences for them both. Charles soon followed Colin up the pitch, and an easy slope of slates above led them to a small pinnacle on the ridge, from where a steep snow-slope led to what looked like the top. Having climbed the pinnacle by 11.30 a.m. they rested for an hour and brewed some tea. Recovered, they cut steps up the final snow-slope to the summit, which they reached in thick cloud at 1.05 p.m. The actual summit was so narrow that they could only stand there one at a time, and photograph each other. On the same day Ted Hicks and Richard Nicholson climbed another 21,000 feet peak near to the Base Camp.

The summit Charles and Colin had reached was at 22,060 feet, and after a brief rest they traversed to the other summit of the mountain some distance away at 21,991 feet. An hour later they were back at the original summit, and ready to commence their retreat. By this time it had grown considerably colder, and the weather was increasingly threatening as they set off down. Colin was feeling particularly tired by this stage and proceeded in a curious bent-up position. They regained their sacks at 2.15 p.m. and descended the pinnacle on the ridge to find a good site for Camp IV at around 21,700 feet below a large sheltering rock. It was not a pleasant night, as they had little food, and not enough fuel to melt snow for drinks. It had been a very hard day, with a high degree of nervous tension for them both, but they had pulled off a very fine ascent.

They awoke next morning with bad headaches and severe thirst, but were away in perfect weather by 8.15 a.m. Both men felt rather weak now, but at least they knew they were heading down. Colin summed it up, and indicated the only too obvious danger at this stage of a climb.

> On the ascent I had been keyed up with the urge to get to the summit; now a reaction of listlessness had set in.

They were soon back at the top of the great corner, down which they abseiled (almost losing the tent in the process) and continued down to the site of their previous Camp III. The descent from here was a mixture of poor rock and increasingly dangerous snow-slopes coupled with bad weather as the monsoon arrived. It was with some relief that they reached the col at 19,500 feet at 3 p.m. and erected the tent yet again. It had been another tough day, as Colin recorded:

> We have been moving singly all day, partly owing to the difficulty of the ground and partly owing to fatigue. We were in cloud the better part of the day. It was warm enough to sit outside the tent at 5 p.m. I am sick to death of soup and we have only five biscuits each left, to eat when we please.

During the night several inches of snow fell and the morning dawned very grey and misty, but they resolved to get down that day, leaving at 8 a.m. The route-finding was not too difficult, although by this time Charles Warren was suffering from the effects of partial snow blindness, not having used goggles the previous day. Nonetheless they were pleased to reach Advanced Base by mid-afternoon.

> We finished down the turfy slope which we had left nearly a week before. Now streams of crystal water were flowing across it and little alpine flowers were springing up all round in soul-satisfying contrast to the grimness above. There could hardly have been a more idyllic ending to our climb.

Charles elected to spend the night at Advanced Base where they were able to ease the pain from his eyes, but there was not enough food there for them both. Colin therefore continued down to Base Camp, arriving early in the evening and then enjoying a wonderful meal and endless cups of freshly brewed tea. Both he and Charles must have felt great satisfaction at having pulled off a magnificent climb in very difficult conditions, and in a situation of considerable commitment.

At the conclusion of the Gangotri stage of the expedition, Colin and Ted Hicks had to return to England – Colin to the Insurance Office and Hicks to his teaching post at Oxford. The remainder of the party set off from Harsil to make the crossing of the divide between the basins of the Ganges and the Satlej, into the country of Kunawar. Later on this journey Charles Warren and Marco Pallis succeeded in climbing the 22,210 foot Riwo Pargyul, on the Tibetan border.

From Harsil, Colin and Ted trekked down to Mussoori, setting off on July 11th and soon encountered very hot, humid conditions as they gradually lost altitude into northern India. On the third day of the trek, one of their porters returned from a nearby village with an unexpected haul of chickens, eggs, potatoes and onions. Colin was understandably delighted:

> I slew the fowl by cutting off its head with a penknife. We had it boiled in ghee – most delicious and quite tender; the best meal I have had for many weeks. Hicks burst into song!

The dreadfully humid conditions made them glad to leave the Ganges valley and a rest day was spent at Bhandarki where Colin and Ted both delighted in purchasing beautiful curled-toed native shoes (for 2 rupees a pair!) and Colin took photographs of the whole party.

> The delayed action shutter is rather good as it makes a kind of buzzing noise and the subjects can't help smiling before it actually goes off, however grim or important looking they may have tried to look at the start!

By July 20th the party was approaching Mussoori, and eating well as better local food became available. One night Colin had eaten well and slept heavily, recording in his diary what then happened:

> I dreamt that I was in Liverpool and had just got outside the house when I discovered I had a very dirty shirt on. However I tucked the ends into my trousers (they had apparently been hanging out, coolie fashion) and decided it would do. When I got on the tram I found I had no shirt on at all, which didn't seem to embarrass me much as my skin was nicely sunburnt. I was sitting next to a high official of my Company who very politely made no remark but after a while asked me if I would like a shirt, an offer which I accepted. Then I woke up!

The end of the trek and Mussoori was reached on June 21st, much to the relief of Colin and Ted who were now looking forward to some civilized comforts. Colin completed the last stage of the journey into Mussoori in a rickshaw, which he felt rounded off the trip to the utmost satisfaction! There then followed the luxury of hot baths, shaves, clean clothes and good food prior to the train journey from Dehra Dun, and the month-long sea voyage from Calcutta back to Liverpool, which was reached late in August. Colin had been away for almost five months, on what had been a most enjoyable and successful first visit to the Himalaya. In 'Let's Go Climbing!' he summarised some of his thoughts on the matter:

> I don't believe that any one, at the time, can really enjoy being high up on a Himalayan peak. There is the urge that makes you go on; there is the satisfaction you feel after a successful climb. Then there is the awe-inspiring scenery; only the climber can enjoy this to the full. He is in tune with the mountains. You feel these things and decide to climb the mountain. But high up all pleasure disappears. You push on because, when you were down in the valley, you made up your mind to push on. And when you get down again you are glad that you have not given in.
>
> I suppose that the natural human urge for adventure is at the bottom of it all. The hundreds of unclimbed peaks in the Himalaya will satisfy that urge for a long time to come.

Certainly the Gangotri stage of the expedition had yielded good results, six peaks climbed with failures on a further two. Although some disappointment was expressed that more exploring and mapping was not carried out, the performance of Colin and that of Charles Warren on Satopanth II (now Bhagirathi III) was highly impressive for the time and was almost certainly the hardest climbing attempted at altitude at that date. Of great virtue was the fact that only four porters were used at base camp and they did no carrying on the mountain. It is now felt that the achievement of Kirkus and Warren never received the recognition it deserved at the time, and wider publicity for the climb was only achieved in 1939 when Marco Pallis's book was finally published. One is left feeling that Colin would not have been disgraced had he gone to Everest, and would probably have contributed a great deal in terms of willing effort and unselfish support of others.

By the time that Colin returned to Liverpool and to climbing in North Wales, the summer was almost at a close, that of 1933 having been a particularly hot and dry one. Elsewhere in the Himalaya, Ruttledge's expedition to Everest had managed to go no higher than 28,000 feet due to savage weather conditions, although Jack Longland in particular performed with great distinction. On the domestic climbing scene it was very much a year of consolidation with repeats of some of Colin and Menlove's new routes. Of particular note were the performances of Colin's friend Maurice Linnell who made the third ascent of Clogwyn Du'r Arddu's *Great Slab* (Menlove having made the second ascent at Easter) and what was probably the second ascent of *Chimney Route* on the East Buttress. Linnell then left his own mark on the cliff, with his ascent of the delicate and serious *Narrow Slab* on the West Buttress, which he climbed in August. The previous month Linnell had also discovered the bold and intimidating *Overhanging Wall* on the East Buttress of Scafell, so it had been a very fine season for him on British Rock. For Menlove it had been a difficult year, for although he graduated from Liverpool University, his brother Hewlett died following a road accident, and much of Menlove's climbing that summer and autumn was on the damp, steep and loose cliffs around the Devil's Kitchen. However, he did make the second ascent of Colin's *Curving Crack* on Clogwyn Du'r Arddu, with 'AB' leading the route, and later visited the Alps with Graham MacPhee.

Colin did not share Menlove's taste for the Devil's Kitchen cliffs to the same degree, but ventured there on October 22nd when he and Maurice Linnell climbed an 80-foot pitch on the south cliff of Clogwyn Y Geifr, which they called *South Gully*. This area of cliff had already been looked at by Menlove who in particular had established the *South Nose Route*, *Botany Bay Climb*, *Piece by Piece Climb* and probably *Central Groove*. The pitch Colin led on this occasion was the wet left-hand corner of the South Bay (described in the current Ogwen Guidebook as......'definitely not an attractive area. It is composed of depressingly rotten ribs separating channels which are constantly awash.') and above the corner they continued up the esoteric delights of *Botany Bay Climb*. Earlier in the year Colin had also added a variation pitch (Left Crack Exit) to *Hanging Garden Gully*. This direct exit up the back of the gully is now graded severe, and is very exposed. In general Colin preferred to perform on cleaner, sounder rock than that found around the Kitchen, and he made no further additions there.

In the following year Colin's brother Guy established a very bold route in the Devil's Kitchen, having previously climbed there with Menlove. Guy's route, *Right Wall Route*, gives a very stiff 90 foot pitch up the right wall of the Kitchen to escape out by means of an exposed traverse. A climb of great atmosphere due to the presence (and noise) of the waterfall, it is usually very wet and greasy and still warrants a grade of VS(4c). In Menlove's 1936 guide to Cwm Idwal it was graded Severe, and regarded as one of the hardest single pitches on the cliff. 'The holds are smooth and the place moist and wet. Technical difficulty is perhaps greatest near the start, but nowhere greatly relents.'

Guy was no mean climber himself, and 1934 was probably his best year on rock. Unfortunately, following his bad fall at Helsby when he broke his pelvis, Guy moved to Accrington to work, and this increasingly curtailed serious activity in the mountains. Prior to his accident Guy had been approached to produce the forthcoming guide-book to Tryfan, an indication of his ability at that time. The work was carried out in due course by Menlove Edwards and Wilfrid Noyce. To this day, Guy retains a great interest in the sport, particularly in the literature and poetry of mountaineering, and takes great pride in Colin's achievements.

During the latter part of the year Colin resumed regular climbing at Helsby and returned to Wales a few times with Graham MacPhee, who himself had climbed rather infrequently that year due to recurring ankle problems. On one occasion in early November they ventured on to the cliffs of the Devil's Kitchen and climbed *Devil's Staircase* and *Hanging Garden Gully*, both in really wet conditions. Sadly, MacPhee's opinions on the day's sport were not recorded!

On their return from the Himalaya, Marco Pallis and his party, including Colin, gave a number of lectures describing their adventures and Colin produced a collection of over 100 glass slides of the trip. This wonderful photographic record of the expedition was left to Alf Bridge after Colin's death, and he in turn later presented it to the Alpine Club.

6 Tragedy and Recovery

It is likely that the success of the Himalayan trip had done much for Colin's confidence and greatly broadened his outlook towards mountaineering as a whole. Pallis's small expedition had done extremely well in what was a virtually unexplored area and Colin had made a substantial contribution to its success, with some bold climbing to his credit. Whilst Colin was in India, Maurice Linnell had enjoyed a particularly good season on British rock and by the start of 1934 was climbing as well as anyone in Britain. Colin and Maurice had begun to climb together as early as 1932 and now commenced to climb as a team on a more regular basis. By all accounts they had ambitious plans for the following summer, aided by the convenience of Maurice's motor-cycle – there was even talk of a possible trip to the Alps. This partnership, though awesomely talented, was the source of considerable misgivings amongst their friends. Both men's climbing activities were characterised by boldness and a desire to innovate, and, one might even say, by the occasional lack of restraint. To some the partnership appeared to be ill-fated. This viewpoint was to prove tragically prophetic as the events of that spring unfolded.

Colin was then climbing less frequently with Graham MacPhee, but at the beginning of March the two of them accompanied Frank Smythe, who was present as guest of honour, to the Wayfarers' Club Dinner at Preston Hall. Smythe gave a speech entitled 'Climbing on Everest' which was illustrated with impressive slides of the 1933 Expedition. After the dinner, MacPhee drove them all back to Sefton Park and Smythe stayed the night with MacPhee and his wife before returning to London. Most of MacPhee's climbing activities that year were centred on the Lake District (usually with Albert Hargreaves or George Bower) and his continuing work on the forthcoming Ben Nevis guide-book. He did, however, venture out to the Alps that summer and resumed more regular climbing with Colin the following year.

Around this time Colin made his one notable contribution to gritstone climbing, with the addition of a difficult new route at the southern end of Stanage Edge. Colin's visits to the Peak District were infrequent: based in the Liverpool area, he had quick access to North Wales or the Lake District, with the local sandstone also readily at hand. Interestingly, Colin expressed the view to Alf Bridge (reported by Alf's friend, Peter Harding) that he did not really like gritstone, although this may have been due to the fact that he climbed on it only on occasion and never really gained the specific knack of climbing this particular rock type. Nonetheless, Colin is known occasionally to have visited crags such as Laddow and Stanage in the company of Alf Bridge, Maurice Linnell and other acquaintances from the Rucksack Club. The role of gritstone climbing at this time was becoming increasingly significant, standards were rising rapidly and the great influence the northern outcrops were to have on British rock-climbing was already apparent. Talented individuals who emerged from this period were Harry Kelly, Fred Pigott, Albert Hargreaves, Alf Bridge and Maurice Linnell, and later Arthur Birtwistle, all of whom advanced the development of rock-climbing both in the Lake District and in North Wales. A very fine photograph, taken by Eric Byrom, exists of Colin climbing Harry Kelly's classic *Tower Face* at Laddow in the early 1930s. As he was a lover of mountains and wild places, I suspect that Colin would have liked Laddow, particularly its remote outlook and the fine moorland walk from Greenfield to reach the crag. By this time Laddow was past its great era of exploration, but some fine and difficult routes had been established (notably *Leaf Buttress*, *Priscilla*, *Terrace Wall* and the Cave routes) and it remained a popular haunt of Manchester-based climbers in particular. Indeed, it is likely that much of the crag was more heavily used than is the case today, when lichen is finding its way back on to many routes now not frequently ascended.

By 1929-30 the emphasis of gritstone activity in Derbyshire had shifted to the fine escarpment of Stanage Edge, above the Derwent valley. The Rucksack Club regulars were prime movers in this period of exploration on Stanage and great deeds had already been done by Albert Hargreaves, Roy Horsman and Herbert Hartley. Alf Bridge and Maurice Linnell were also active with this group and were confirmed Stanage enthusiasts. Of perhaps the greatest significance at the time was the futuristic ascent in 1930 of *Wall End Slab Direct* by the Sheffield climbers Frank Elliott, Harry Dover and Gilbert Ellis. Graded Very Severe in Eric Byne's 1951 guide-book, this bold unprotected effort of sixty years ago is now graded E2 5b, and was probably as difficult as anything achieved on British rock until 1945. It was clear by this period that there was a wealth of excellent climbing to be found on this superb edge, destined to become a Mecca of British rock-climbing.

It is intriguing to imagine Colin visiting Stanage at this time, most probably with Alf and Maurice. On a cold, early spring morning they would have walked up to the edge from Hathersage, maybe as a mist cleared gradually from the moor, so revealing the miles of rock winding away to the

north (a very impressive sight on first acquaintance as generations of climbers will testify). As they strolled along the bottom of the crag Alf would have pointed out the classic lines with an enthusiastic and proprietorial air, conveying his deep affection for the place and his pleasure in persuading his friend to visit. Unlike today, there would have been no crowds on the Edge (although Stanage was rapidly gaining in popularity well before the war) and vast areas of prime gritstone still lay untouched by the hands and feet of climbers. Possibly our party commenced their day with classics such as the *Black Slab*, the *Mississippi Buttress* or *Inverted V*, before Alf proudly pointed out his two fine routes of *Cave Innominate* and *Cave Gully Wall*. These two climbs, dating from two years previously, were very fine efforts and Alf's lead of the latter on a cold, snowy day was a *tour de force* by this often underrated climber. As they returned towards the south end, Colin's attention would have been drawn to a possible line up the right-hand side of the forty-foot high Flying Buttress. It involved a very tricky start over an overhang, followed by delicate (and for the period, very bold) climbing to the top of the crag, to produce a fierce route not upstaged by later additions nearby such as *The Unprintable*, *The Dangler* and *The Tippler*. In 'High Peak', Eric Byne and Geoff Sutton recorded the event thus:

> From his training-ground on the sandstone crag of Helsby in Cheshire came the great climber Colin Kirkus, a shy and unassuming man who found his means of expression in mountaineering. He had impressive confidence in his own abilities and never seemed in the least affected by cold or wet. These gifts coupled with extraordinary muscular endurance and insensibility, enabled him to stay on small holds for long periods and so create a new standard on the crags of North Wales. On Derbyshire gritstone he had a style that strangely enough failed to impress, giving an appearance of clumsiness that was, however, totally deceiving, for it took him up places both delicate and strenuous where no one else seemed able to go, such as his route over the bulge on the Flying Buttress. He also added *Grey Wall* and a new route on the Trinity face to the Stanage repertoire. Clad in an old navy-blue sweater, his hair tumbling down over his brow, his slight figure gave no hint of his superlative performance.

Strangely, Colin's route was not included in Eric Byne's excellent 1951 guide-book to Stanage, and first appears in the 1957 publication 'Further Developments in the Peak District' along with the hard new gritstone routes of the early Fifties. In the current (1989) Stanage guide, *Kirkus's Corner* is graded E1 5b and is described:

> Fine climbing but somewhat lacking in protection. Step from blocks at the right end of the slab and pull round the overhang, (reachy or dynamic). Step left into a shallow scoop from where a delicate leg-wobbling exit may be made.

Colin on Tower Face, Laddow.   *Photo Eric Byrom*

A bold, unnerving and rather strange climb, it was regarded as an advanced problem for its time and is thought to have been unrepeated until September 1953 when it was top-roped by Peter Biven, T. Turner, P. Hassall and Joe Brown. To quote the current guide again:

> That even Biven and Brown declined to lead it added considerably to its reputation.

Today, the route does not appear to be over-popular despite the good quality climbing it clearly offers, and still seems to deter most casual attempts to solo it (the fate of most pre-war routes on the Edge these days!). It was a very fine effort from someone who claimed no great liking for the peculiar delights of gritstone. Colin also added a new climb up the grey wall overlooking Avalanche Gully just to the right of the Flying Buttress. This wall was at one time called the Jitterbug Face (as opposed to the nearby Jitterbug Buttress) and now contains a number of variations. Colin's original route takes a pleasant and direct line up the left-hand side of the wall and is graded Very Severe 4c in the current guide. An enjoyable route of the grade, it offers quite exposed climbing in an open position. Colin is also thought to have added a variation to the routes on the Trinity Face, but the details have long been lost.

Easter[1] that year fell at the end of March and as was the custom at the time several of the major climbing clubs such as the Rucksack Club, the Wayfarers' Club, the Climbers' Club and the Midland Association of Mountaineers (M.A.M.) had organised meets in the Fort William area. The Wayfarers' meet had been organised by Carl Brunning and a number of Colin's friends, including Marco Pallis, were to attend. It seemed likely that there would be a large number of climbers in the vicinity that weekend, encouraged by good snow and ice conditions and a reasonable weather forecast. Colin had arranged to attend the meet with Maurice Linnell, but they intended to camp rather than use a hotel in Fort William. They finished work on the Thursday afternoon (Colin at the Royal Insurance in Liverpool and Maurice at the Ellis Jones & Co. laboratories at Stockport, where he was an assistant chemist) and met up in Kendal, where they loaded their equipment (including a tent, rucksacks, ice-axes and skis) on to Maurice's motor-cycle. Shortly after midnight they set off north, hoping to reach Fort William in time for breakfast. Before departing they chatted to 'AB', who was on his way down to Pen-y-Pass for the Easter weekend. 'AB' recalled:

[1]For a more detailed account of this course of events, interested readers are referred to Ian Thomson's recent book 'The Black Cloud: Mountain Misadventures from 1925-1966': The Ernest Press, 1993. I am greatly indebted to Ian for his help in preparing this section of my work.

Maurice Linnell with Colin in the side-car, Idwal, 1933.   *Photo unknown*

I have to confess that I left them with an awful foreboding of trouble to come and duly travelled down to Wales.

Colin and Maurice made good time over Shap and into the Border country. The roads were almost deserted and they sped through the night and into the dawn alongside Loch Lomond. Then came the long haul over Rannoch Moor down Glencoe and across the Ballachulish ferry until they reached Fort William mid-morning. They must have been cold and tired from such a journey but, undeterred, they loaded the gear onto their backs and set off up the hill. Their intention was to set up camp in Colin's battered old tent from the Gangotri expedition, alongside the frozen Lochan Meall an t-Suidhe. This point is quite easily reached from the tourist track from Fort William to the summit of Ben Nevis and is at an altitude of almost 1800 feet. From this campsite Colin and Maurice would have had quick and easy access to the many climbs on the northern side of the mountain. By the time they had established camp, the Friday afternoon was already well advanced and they used the opportunity to do some skiing, the rudiments of which Colin had learnt the previous summer in the Himalaya. This activity came to an end when Maurice broke one of his skis. It was dark by about 7 p.m. and after a large meal they turned in, intending to make an early start the following day.

Ominously, the Saturday morning was not particularly cold, the calm conditions overnight having given rise to a degree of temperature inversion over much of the West Highlands. It is likely that Colin and Maurice were up and about quite early, eager to get some climbing done. They set off from the campsite and contoured round the north-west shoulder of Carn Dearg and into the glen of the Allt a' Mhuilinn, to beyond the foot of Castle Ridge. Here, located between North Castle Gully and South Castle Gully is a fine rock buttress, The Castle – a major feature of this part of Ben Nevis. The buttress was first climbed by Brown, Maclay, Naismith and Thomson in 1896, and was known to provide a testing climb in winter conditions. The climb itself is about 700 feet in length and here Ian Thomson describes it in detail:

> By today's standards, the ascent of The Castle is not especially difficult but, in 1934, it was regarded as one of the more testing winter routes.
>
> In winter, the start of the climb is often made rather hard by a section of steep ice, although this pitch can be obliterated by an accumulation of snow or avalanche debris. After the initial difficulties, the route moves on to a relatively easy snow-slope which leads to a rather more demanding vague groove about halfway up the climb with a slightly steeper snow-slope beyond. The route ascends this slope, moving somewhat leftwards to avoid a direct assault on the hundred-foot rock-band which is a prominent feature of the upper part of The Castle, and towards a conspicuous block under which there is a good stance. From here, the climbing becomes considerably more difficult. A rightwards traverse from the block reaches a steep hundred-foot groove, icy in its lower section and, after flattening a little and then steepening again, snowy in its upper section. Above the top of this groove, there are two steep chimneys leading directly to the top of The Castle. The route ignores these chimneys, instead traversing rightwards below them along snow-covered ledges to a stance some fifty feet beyond the top of the groove. This is the final belay of the climb; the route continues traversing upwards to the right to a snowy bowl or recess which gives access to the cornice at the top about sixty feet above the final belay. The slabby nature of the upper section of the route makes it prone to avalanche in certain snow conditions, a fact well enough known today but not in the 1930s. On Easter Saturday 1934 there was a lot of hard snow and ice and a cornice at the top, but there was also, in places, some softer and unstable snow lying on the hard surface underneath.

It would appear that Colin and Maurice had this particular part of the mountain to themselves, and had probably commenced climbing by 8.30 a.m. They alternated the lead and moved quickly up the buttress, secured in the main by the method of belaying whereby, the rope is tied around a driven-in ice-axe, while the moving climber is safeguarded by the shoulder

Maurice Linnell at the foot of The Castle, Ben Nevis, March 31st 1934.   *Photo C. F. Kirkus*

belay method of rope management. There appear to have been no witnesses who actually saw them on the climb and characteristically they appear to have made swift progress. It is thought that they had reached a point on the slabby area close to the cornice at the top of the buttress by between 10.30 and 11.00 a.m. With Maurice belayed (almost certainly to his ice-axe driven into the snow) Colin was leading some distance above him, when the accident occurred. In a statement made to the police on being discharged from hospital Colin described what happened:

> Linnell and I were climbing the Castle and we had got over the difficult part and had almost reached the top of the cliff. At this point neither of us had any suspicion of danger. Although we had reached a comparatively easy spot, we took all precautions. We took turns at leading. I was leading and had reached the cornice, when a step I had cut in the snow collapsed and slid off the very hard snow underneath.
>
> I immediately fell down, leaning on my axe so as to try and stop myself, but I was going too fast and I went over a cliff about fifty feet lower down. That is the last thing I remember until I regained consciousness and found myself lying some 300 feet lower down. I could not remember where I was at first, so I followed the rope, which had not broken and found Linnell on the other end, some 80 feet higher up. The rope had caught over a ridge of snow so that we were suspended on different sides of it. When I reached Linnell, I found the rope had slipped up and caught round his neck.

He had a spare loop round his waist, so I put the ice-axe which I found quite close to his body through this and into the snow so as to support him while I released the rope from his neck, otherwise he would have slipped down the slope. I think he was dead then, but I was not sure at the time. He was lying on a slope of about 50 degrees, and I tried to pull him up on to a ledge but had not the strength. I ran the rope out to its full length, however, so as to serve as a guide to a search party. Then I cut the rope, as the knot was too tight to undo, and continued up to the top of the cliff, shouting for help at intervals and cutting steps with my ice-axe, which I had found sticking in the snow. When I reached the ridge, I made a small cairn on the edge of the snow to indicate the spot to the searchers.

We cannot be certain how long Colin was unconscious and his account of the events of that day has to be viewed in this context. He was to lapse in and out of consciousness during the afternoon and on the way down to the hospital and on his arrival there, was found to have serious head injuries, amongst a number of others. He and Maurice had both fallen over 250 feet and had probably struck rocks and areas of ice on their way, before being halted by the snagging of the rope. To return to Ian Thomson again:

It is not known how long Kirkus remained unconscious. However, the air temperature was about freezing level and it would have been cold for the two men lying on the snow-covered east-facing buttress; on ascending to Linnell, Kirkus found that Linnell showed no detectable signs of life, but that he was still warm and this may indicate that Kirkus's period of unconsciousness was short. Kirkus also discovered that the rope had somehow managed to become wrapped round Linnell's neck and, as it seemed to Kirkus, had apparently strangled him. It is not difficult to understand how the rope would wrap around Linnell's neck. He would have been providing Kirkus with a shoulder belay and this would have allowed the rope to catch around his neck when he fell, although it could have done so simply in the confusion of the downward plunge. In fact, Linnell was not killed by the rope. The Rucksack Club's Accident Sub-Committee's report contained the following information on the cause of death:

From the medical and other evidence it would appear that Linnell fell sheer, struck the ground with the left side of the front of his head and did not move further. The head being forced backwards by the weight of the body, the neck was broken, resulting in instantaneous death.

Ian Thomson also raises the issue of the complex and contrasting statements made to the press and authorities regarding Colin's movements after the accident, and in particular which route he took to the top of the Castle. What is known, is that after securing Maurice's body as best as he could, he made his way to the shoulder above The Castle and Castle Gullies. In his injured state and advanced shock, lapsing in and out of consciousness,

The Castle, Ben Nevis: the line of the route taken by Colin and Maurice is shown.   *Photo D. N. Williams*

and with only a broken ice-axe, this must have been a superhuman effort. Most evidence indicates that he reclimbed The Castle and negotiated the cornice alone. In the snow conditions then existing on the route it is a wonder he was not avalanched.

At approximately 1 p.m., Colin was seen attempting to descend from the shoulder of Carn Dearg towards the halfway lochan (Lochan Meall an t-Suidhe) by two climbers, Alastair Borthwick and Bill Thomson, on their way up to do a route on the mountain. The pair were about 100 feet below Colin, but clearly heard his cries for help. They quickly climbed up to Colin, where they were joined by two other climbers, Petrie and McKinnell. Despite his injuries, Colin explained to them where Maurice lay and how he had tried to build a small cairn at the spot where he breached the cornice. Gradually more people arrived, while Petrie set off for the top of the Castle. Somebody was despatched at once down to Fort William and while Colin was helped slowly down to his tent, the remainder of the party followed Petrie up the hill, alerting other parties of what had taken place. Colin was helped down to the tent by two members of the Swiss Alpine Club, Mr Slingsby and Dr. Alfred Rogers, who made him as comfortable as they could, before rounding up further assistance for a rescue attempt.

Meanwhile, higher up the mountain, a Rucksack Club party standing at the top of No. 3 Gully received word of the accident from F G Brettell who was climbing the gully with a large M.A.M. group. The Rucksack Club party consisted of George Bower, Frank Bennett, H. V. Hughes and H. Taylor. They at once made their way to the top of The Castle and in the Rucksack Club Journal described what then took place:

> Bower climbed down for about 200 feet; but, after further reconnoitring, the party decided that in the conditions then prevailing it was impracticable to descend to the body and that rescue work must proceed from below. They descended North Castle Gully until it was possible to break out onto the buttress, but were overtaken by dusk before they could reach their objective. They reached the S.M.C. Hut about 11 p.m.
>
> The next morning, the same four men, reinforced by Messrs Beck, Brettell, Henn and Mills Walker of the M.A.M. proceeded to The Castle and recovered the body, which they got down to the foot of the rocks about 6.30 that evening.

Someone else who was on the Ben that weekend was Showell Styles, who was with the M.A.M. party. Showell recalls:

> On the day of the accident on Ben Nevis, I emerged from No. 3 Gully too late to see anything of Kirkus and the subsequent stretcher party. When I got to the head of Castle Gully, (presumably South Castle Gully) Bower and others of the Rucksack Club were engaged in their abortive attempt to reach Linnell.

The next day I was with the support party at the foot of The Castle. Late in the day the body of Linnell was lowered to be received by George Lister (A.C., M.A.M.) and myself. Linnell showed no sign of his injuries though the body was as stiff as iron; his features were peaceful and had all the hues of life. We lowered him by rope-lengths to the stretcher party below and there followed a difficult carry, mostly in the dark, which involved a tricky lift over a deer fence.

And so Maurice's body was carried down to Fort William by men of his own Rucksack Club, and the Midland Association of Mountaineers.

While the protracted efforts were being made to reach Maurice Linnell, a stretcher was brought up the hillside to the tent beside the lochan where Colin was lying.

It was late in the day before the stretcher party was able to begin the descent, and transport Colin down to the safety and warmth of Fort William. Alastair Borthwick[1], who was a young climber making his first visit to the Ben that day, described the descent in the Glasgow Weekly Herald:

> Meanwhile we had returned with thirty other climbers to the tent on the mountainside which Kirkus had pitched on the previous night and in which he then lay. On a stretcher we worked in relays and carried him to the ambulance at the foot of the mountain. It was a strange and sad procession which wound its way down the mountain path by torchlight. No-one spoke much. Ice-axes clattered on the stones as climbers gave them to someone else while they took their turn at the stretcher.
>
> Kirkus was wonderful. He was jolted pretty badly, yet he did not say anything. And then it was the ambulance and hospital and it was all over.

It was eleven o'clock in the evening before the rescue team delivered Colin to the safe-keeping of the staff at the Belford Hospital in Fort William, more than twelve hours since the accident. From the early diagnosis on the hill, Colin's injuries had not appeared to be too serious although he was clearly suffering from shock and concussion. However he remained in the Belford Hospital for almost three weeks and it was several more weeks before he was able to return to work. To quote Ian Thomson:

> It is evident from the press reports of Monday, 2nd April that even on the Sunday the full extent of injuries suffered by Kirkus were not known to the public since the newspapers stated that they were less serious than originally feared. However, the real seriousness was known by the Tuesday by which time it had emerged that, in the words of "The Courier and Advertiser" of Tuesday 3rd April:
>> " . . . .his head injuries are so extensive that it will be at least ten days before he may be allowed any visitors."

Indeed, initially he was not even allowed to make a statement to the police

1 Alastair Borthwick was later to write "Always a Little Further" (published by Faber in 1939 and republished by Diadem in 1983) – the classic book about outdoor life in Scotland in the 1930's.

about the incident. His right leg was injured, his jaw was damaged, he was suffering from a degree of exposure, he had a fractured skull and was still concussed to such an extent that, according to "The Times" of Tuesday 3rd April, he continued to lapse into unconsciousness on the Monday. But the most serious damage was to his right eye which had become permanently misaligned. He was eventually discharged from Belford Hospital on Thursday 19th April, almost three weeks after the accident and this is a measure of the severity of the injuries from which he suffered.

Colin was in fact allowed one visitor on the Sunday, when his brother Guy was able to speak to him briefly. Together with a group of friends Guy had been climbing and walking on the Ben More-Stob Binnein group of hills near to Crianlarich. Guy recalled that weekend:

> We had enjoyed a day of bright sunshine on the Saturday and returned to our tents unaware of what had taken place. We saw a headline in the Sunday papers "Accident on the Ben" and I remember an awful moment when I saw a photograph of Colin on the front page. We rushed over to Fort William right away and I was able to see him. Colin's face was terribly misshapen and swollen. Typically, he was quick to make light of his own situation and was much more concerned about how my own weekend was going.

It is difficult to imagine what went through Colin's mind as he lay in his hospital bed for the first few days. He was in considerable pain and there was particular concern expressed about the damage to and around his right eye. The death of Maurice and how it came about must have been a terrible shock to him. At the age of twenty-three, it was a sudden end to the carefree innocence of his youth.

Maurice was buried on the Tuesday (April 3rd) in Glen Nevis. The small cemetery there stands close to the River Nevis and below the great bulk of the Ben and its outlier Meall an t-Suidhe, with fine views up the glen towards the Mamores.

Maurice's father and sister had arrived the day before and made arrangements for the funeral which, as requested by them, was a quiet one. A number of climbers up for the Easter weekend had remained behind and followed the cortège from the Belford Hospital, where a service was held, to the graveyard just over a mile away. It was a bright spring day, with the sun shining on the snow low on the hillsides, as the Reverend Mr. MacLean carried out a simple ceremony at the graveside. A small headstone was later erected and so was laid to rest Maurice Linnell. He was one of the most talented figures of his generation and was perhaps Colin's only equal in Britain at that time. It is tempting, as others have done in the past, to ponder on what these two men might have achieved together prior to World War

Two. Suffice it to say that the story of climbing in Britain and of British achievement in the Alps, might well have been very different, had fate not intervened that Easter weekend.

Reflecting on the accident and its aftermath, 'AB' had this to say:

> Colin took a long, long time to get over it. It knocked him back quite a lot – not only physically but mentally as well. It was very much on his conscience and he felt in some way responsible, but in those situations surely you share the risk anyway. In the mid-to-late Thirties, Colin often came to stay with us at Ulverston, but he was never quite the same man again in my opinion. It affected him very deeply, and I suppose it's important to remember that at the time of the accident, Colin was still only twenty-three.

Years later, in 'Let's Go Climbing!', Colin refers the reader to the matter of accidents and perhaps obliquely relates to his own experiences at this time:

> A fatal accident is a very terrible thing. Don't think of yourself, but think of the effect on all your relations and friends if anything were to happen to you. Or think how you would feel if you had to meet the parents of a friend who had been killed while climbing with you.

In his fine book[1] on Ben Nevis, Ken Crocket commented on what befell Colin and Maurice:

> Their accident is only one of a series of fatal episodes in this area of Ben Nevis, parties being avalanched either while approaching or while climbing The Castle or the Castle Gullies. The slabby rocks hereabouts can only just hold snow, an avalanche being easily triggered by the unwary or unlucky climber.

Following his return to Liverpool towards the end of April, Colin set about slowly regaining his mental and physical equilibrium, although it was some months before he ventured back to the mountains. Very much a solitary and rather withdrawn man, this must have been a most difficult and painful period for Colin and, in the opinion of people close to him, one that affected him deeply for the remainder of his life. Marco Pallis, Graham MacPhee and Alf Bridge appear to have been particularly staunch allies at this time. The tragedy must have particularly affected Alf, as Maurice and Colin were probably his closest friends. The verve and boldness of both men had caused more than a little concern among their friends and the question of them teaming up had been viewed with some misgivings. 'AB' enlarged on this point.

> 'They were not competitive with each other but they were both very ambitious to create new climbs and I did not think that either would be likely to restrain the other when they were on a climb getting difficult.

1 'Ben Nevis' by Ken Crocket (SMC – 1986).

Similarly, Jack Longland recalled that Maurice, in particular, showed such flair and confidence on the crags, that ' . . . he frequently scared the life out of me!'

Sadly, following Maurice's death, Colin did not escape a degree of criticism from certain elements within the climbing world. It was murmured for instance that the run-out was too long and so on. In effect, Kirkus and Linnell were the subject of the kind of criticism always levelled at those at the very forefront of the sport, should things go wrong. In addition, the superb new rock-climbs established in the early 1930s were not universally admired. There were still the traditionalists who questioned whether such climbing was at all justified. What such people failed to recognise was that climbing was changing with increasing rapidity and that Colin and Maurice, among others, had realised what was required in acquiring the necessary mental and physical strength to operate safely at the top level. By the standards of the time, both men climbed a great deal, and had further tempered their skill and nerve in the unforgiving practice of solo climbing. At their best they would have been almost as far removed from the mainstream of the sport as today's E8 activists. Risk has always existed at the forefront of climbing and always will, but sadly Colin and Maurice were unlucky enough to meet lethal snow conditions, of which today we have a better understanding. Nonetheless, Colin was a sensitive young man and any criticism after the event must have hurt him and affected his view of climbing in general.

One consequence of the death of Maurice Linnell was that Colin was invited to attend a meeting of the Rucksack Club Accident Sub-Committee later that spring. This Committee had been set up by the club to investigate serious accidents involving club members, in the hope that valuable lessons might be learned for the future. Colin was well known to many of the club's membership and willingly agreed to attend the meeting, accompanied by Marco Pallis. The matter was recorded in the Rucksack Club Journal, which published the findings of the sub-committee:

> Many of those whose evidence is available testify to the fact that snow conditions on the Saturday afternoon were showing definite signs of deterioration and it cannot be too strongly emphasised that snow on our British hills must be treated with as much care and circumspection as would be used in the Alps. At the same time it must be remembered that the two climbers were men of skill and experience. They were climbing in the early part of the day and were not led to suspect at all the soundness of the snow they encountered; so that there seems no valid reason to impugn their judgement on this head.
>
> The use by the party of such long run-outs on this climb is open to serious

criticism. It is an extension of the tactics employed perforce on modern rock climbs to circumstances under which they are neither necessary nor appropriate. When climbing steep snow the members of a party should never be so far separated if it can possibly be avoided; and it is especially desirable that they should be in close proximity when tackling the final section of the climb.

The conclusions of the Committee were:

1.   The party should have had less rope out and Linnell should have been near Kirkus just below the final steep section. In view of the manner in which the leadership was arranged the responsibility for these mistakes must be considered a joint one.

2.   There is no reason to impute to either climber any other fault either of judgement or technique.

3.   The recovery party conducted their operations in an entirely satisfactory manner and did all that was possible under most difficult circumstances.

The death of Maurice Linnell was the first taste of tragedy in Colin's young life. It profoundly affected his approach to climbing and the early flame of bold exploration was very largely extinguished. Maurice's name is now remembered as one of the unfulfilled talents of British climbing.

One further aspect of the accident that befell Colin and Maurice was that it served as an early example of elements of the Press handling a mountaineering incident particularly badly. As outlined previously, a number of reports published in the press were conflicting, inaccurate and sensationalised. This caused considerable anger, amongst friends and associates of both Colin and Maurice who were present in Fort William at the time of the accident. Carl Brunning referred to the matter in an article that appeared later that summer, in the Mountaineering Journal:

In the Rucksack Journal for 1933, P.J. Monkhouse[1] writes on the subject of the Press and mountaineering accidents. The inaccurate and sensational reports that appear have long been deplored and Monkhouse, himself a Pressman, advocates that when an accident does occur, some person should issue an authentic account.

It was agreed that this should be done and an official account giving no more and possibly less information than above was issued by me. At the time the results of this tended to be overlooked as the attention of all concerned was focused on the more unscrupulous section of the Press who made a sensational story of the accident. It was unfortunate that it should happen at a time when the Press was suffering from a dearth of news and from their point of view it must have been a god-send. Two daily papers and their associated evening papers published false and highly sensational accounts. The fact that Kirkus was a late member of a

1 Patrick Monkhouse of the Rucksack Club was on the staff of the Manchester Guardian and later became its Northern Editor. In the early 1930s he wrote the classic books "On Foot in the Peak" and "On Foot in North Wales".

Himalayan expedition and that a number of his colleagues were present gave the story a certain air of distinction and they lent a pleasant air of truth to one of their accounts by quoting it as a personal inverview with the Editor of the "Mountaineering Journal". This interview was, of course, quite fictitious.

These descriptions of the accident were apparently given to them by two freelance journalists who happened to be on the Ben at the time. Monkhouse's suggestion of correcting inaccurate accounts was adopted and the worst offender published an accurate statement the next day signed by Marco Pallis and myself.

Apart from this yellow section of the Press, the accounts published were reasonably accurate and out of some ninety-four which I have seen, eighty-three were quite reasonable and the others erred in certain points. Two stated the rope broke, which it did not, seven stated I organised a rescue party whereas I was some twenty miles from the scene of the accident on Saturday and two were completely garbled.

Allowing for the fact that most press accounts are handled by a large number of people before they are printed and are written to suit the tone of the paper, I feel that Mr Monkhouse's method is reasonably successful and if pursued a millenium may arrive when such accounts will be inserted without alteration. It is evidently inadvisable however, that they should be issued by an individual, else some of the papers will make use of that person's name, willy-nilly. They should be written out and handed to the local Press agent by some third party such as a hotel porter.

The reporting of mountaineering accidents continued to cause problems for many years and perhaps only now has it reached an acceptable level with the huge advances in communication techniques in recent years.

Colin did return to climbing later that summer, visiting Helsby again and eventually going back to the mountains of North Wales. One reason for this return was a request from Colin's sixteen-year old cousin Wilfrid Noyce, to help teach him to climb. Earlier that year Noyce had climbed with Colin's brothers Nigel and Guy, and in his book 'Mountains and Men' (Geoffrey Bles 1947) he included a most interesting account of climbing with Colin at this time:

> The next holiday was to be with Colin, now recovered from the Ben Nevis accident in which he was badly injured and Maurice Linnell killed. We stayed at Idwal Youth Hostel; the first evening I walked up to meet him on his way back from the cliffs. Lean, nervous, tattered, a cigarette in a long holder streaming smoke behind him, he said very little until he came to suggest, with a glint, the *Monolith Crack* for after supper. The crack held for a long time the reputation of being the hardest climb in North Wales. The Abrahams themselves called it more difficult than the Devil's Kitchen, if not quite so dangerous. The main pitch is a thin rift cut deep into the small Gribin rock face. The Abrahams, who were large of build, had been forced to climb it on the outside, with great difficulty. "We," said Colin, "get right in now and wriggle up". We left before dusk and roped at the foot. There followed something like this, of thoughtful monologue:

"Roped all right, this first pitch easy. Now Colin's inside and up the long crack. Looks difficult...but once inside said to be easier...and safer. My turn, pushed in, difficult. Then to get up. Whole thing smooth, "worn smooth", they say. A foot jammed across, heave up, the thing comes out. Back below, where we started, no breath, sweating piglike. Body twist, the knees grating the sides, trousers too thin. That graze will be painful, don't feel it now. Fingers scrabble; one on a ledge, get the other on, pull up, even the hair seems to stick. No matter how bloody later, let's get there now...thank God I'm up; I've been praying long enough.

The thought current bubbled out in pattering accompaniment to hasty breathing; in its exactness, impossible to recapture and unprintable. It was the same many times on following days; in the chimney behind the holly tree of Holly Tree Wall, in the final crack of the *Direct Route* on Glyder Fach. I was at the top each time, but my conscience only knew what I had expended to get there "Lovely!" I panted down at my 'conquest', and wrote an ecstatic postcard to Ffestiniog.

We finished with my first lead, Crib Goch Buttress and some more severe rubber climbs. Both experiences showed up other qualities of Colin: the power of carefully coaching his inexperienced, nervous leader, complete confidence, and the moral push to get him over the tricky patch. Crib-goch Buttress needed that, as we did it in the evening light after '*Paradise*' on Lliwedd and the Snowdon *Horseshoe*, with the tramp back to Idwal still ahead. Then on the last pitch Colin sent me, unroped, ahead to photograph him, and stayed himself quietly bilberry-eating on a ledge, with the rope dangling to 'Mr Nobody' at third man. And on the east wall of the Idwal Slabs I watched each detail of the balanced slow movement of his body and the shifting of his toes in slippery crevices. It was later that I learned of his reputed astonishing use of the big toe at tricky points; on it he was said to stand for hours spying holds. This time he bound elastic round his feet to give free play to the celebrated object, and moved forward over the slimy nobbles of Ash Tree Wall, for instance, inserting it at the convenient holes to stand and survey the next section.

On the smooth clean rock of the harder Dinas Mot Nose, I saw the same skill. Colin showed no nervousness, as he well might have done with a weak second and the Ben Nevis accident behind him. For myself it was a lesson in rhythm, in a continuous and ever upward-glancing movement that would tire less and give the greater joy. It was possible even, through imitation of Colin, to keep my own rhythm more consistent on the steeper angles; and I had for my enjoyment, as well, the pleasure that Dante was at times too cowardly to accept – that of putting firm trust in the leader, watching him wrestle with the difficulties and going down happily, if need be, with him.

Later in the holiday, Colin also led Noyce up the *Original Route* on the Holly Tree Wall at Idwal – an impressive start in the sport for a youngster at that time. It is heartening to picture Colin taking pleasure in teaching a novice to climb and no doubt Wilfred's unbridled enthusiasm must have

Graham MacPhee and H. G. Knight after their first descent of Moss Ghyll Grooves (with Lawrence Pollitt) on May 30th 1928.   *Photo L. H. Pollitt*

been therapeutic in helping him to return to the hills and crags of North Wales. Wilfrid Noyce, of course, went on to become a most distinguished mountaineer, particularly after the War when he played his part in the successful exploration and ascent of Mount Everest. He was killed climbing in the Pamirs in 1962, together with the brilliant young Scottish climber Robin Smith.

At the end of June, Graham MacPhee was once again up at the CIC hut working on the Ben Nevis guide-book. Typically, Graham's journey up there was highly unorthodox as he made what is thought to be the first solo (unsupported) ascent of Snowdon, Scafell Pike and Ben Nevis in under twenty-four hours! Late on June 19th (Colin's 24th birthday), MacPhee walked to the top of Snowdon. He left the summit at midnight and drove directly to Wasdale Head, where he was up and down Scafell Pike in two hours. From there he drove to Achintee and walked up the tourist track to the top of the Ben reaching the summit at 9.30 pm! From there he descended to the CIC hut for the night. A fine effort, given the condition of the roads almost sixty years ago, by this remarkable character. The following day MacPhee, in the company of George Williams, climbed the Castle. En route they found Maurice Linnell's ice-axe and the shaft of Colin's. MacPhee, as well as being a close friend of Colin, had known Maurice through mutual friends in the Rucksack Club and that afternoon on the Ben must have been a melancholy experience for him.

It is pertinent at this stage (summer 1934) to refer once again to the Youth Hostel at Idwal, both in terms of its substantial contribution to Welsh climbing and its significance in Colin's life then and in subsequent years. In the late-Twenties/early-Thirties, the Merseyside Y.H.A. opened a chain of hostels in North Wales and among these was the one at Idwal. The building itself was thought to be connected with the disused quarry at the rear, dormant for over fifty years, the stone of which was notable for the making of hones for cut-throat razors. Presumably with the passing of such razors the reason for the quarry's existence went also, and hence the availability of a building destined to become perhaps the most famous hostel of all – albeit greatly altered over the years. Prior to post-war alterations the western end of the building consisted of an open verandah where there were six bunk beds in two tiers of three. Here, hardy souls slept summer and winter – it was not unknown to awake with a light covering of snow on the blankets! The Y.H.A. appointed a resident warden to all its hostels and the first at Idwal, when the hostel opened in Easter 1930, was Edith Constance Alexander – always known as Connie Alexander. She came from a Liverpool family with strong connections with various charitable organisations in the city. The success of the hostel was guaranteed as the cheap but homely accommodation (15p a night for dinner, bed and breakfast!) was located in magnificent surroundings. By accident or design the Y.H.A. had acquired a rock-climbing centre almost without peer, offering quick access to the fine climbs at Idwal, Glyder Fach and on Tryfan. As the members of the Climbers' Club and the Rucksack Club were unlikely to desert their respective well-established bases, Idwal became the centre for a whole new group of climbers. At first this was largely a random group of people who had no formal connection with any of the established clubs and most of whom came from the Liverpool area. In effect the hostel might almost have been regarded as a 'poor man's Helyg'. Pre-eminent among this group of climbers was R.C. (Bob) Frost, who had emerged by the mid-1930s as a rock-climber and mountaineer of considerable talent. There will be more about Bob Frost in due course, as he was to form a fruitful climbing partnership with Colin in the period 1935-37. In the early days of the Idwal hostel, relations were somewhat strained with the proprietress of the nearby Ogwen Cottage, Mrs Jones. This was perhaps not helped by the clandestine visits of hostellers to climb on the tempting boulder which stood in Mrs Jones's garden. This was of course the same Mrs Jones who presided over Ogwen Cottage when the

George Radcliffe, Connie Alexander and Colin, Idwal 1935.   *Photo courtesy Berta Gough*

Abrahams Brothers visited at the turn of the century, and whose coal-hammer Archer Thomson borrowed to make the first ascent of the Devil's Kitchen via the frozen waterfall in March 1895! It is interesting to imagine just what the revered Mrs Jones made of her new and youthful neighbours!

As mentioned earlier, Colin and numerous other climbers of the time had got into the habit of calling in at the hostel from its earliest days. Colin, often accompanied by A.B. Hargreaves, Maurice Linnell or Alf Bridge, was particularly well-known there and became in time virtually an honorary member, although it is thought unlikely that he actually joined the Y.H.A. Nor is it likely that Colin actually stayed at Idwal prior to 1934 as Helyg usually formed his Welsh base. However, following the Ben Nevis accident Colin increasingly used the hostel and became part of the regular clientele. Maurice Linnell had been particularly well liked at the hostel, and after his death a fine photograph of him was displayed in the entrance hall for several years.

Returning to the mountains that summer, Colin initially preferred to spend much of his spare time simply relaxing in the vicinity of the hostel. He had formed a close friendship with Connie Alexander and was content to stay nearby, helping Connie with the day-to-day running of the hostel and increasingly teaching beginners the rudiments of rock-climbing and mountain craft. Someone who recalls Colin at the time is the late John Watson of the Wayfarers' Club, who was a regular visitor to Idwal from 1933 until the outbreak of the war. John was a friend of both Bob Frost and Colin and remembers that:

> Colin could be most remarkably uncommunicative and sometimes at Idwal, even in the company of like-minded people whom he knew, he would sit in prolonged silence as though he had just read Rose Maybud's book of etiquette with its injunction "Don't speak until you are spoken to!" Colin could also appear remarkably gloomy. A friend once told me that he had met Colin by chance in Liverpool and couldn't get over how miserable he looked as he walked along, as though all the cares of the world were on his shoulders. Of course, other people might have other opinions and after all most of our friendship was after the Ben Nevis accident which must have had some effect. Whatever the reason there was of course another side as there usually is. Colin could be in lively and unbuttoned mood if the situation arose, but looking back over fifty years I am sure that in later years anyway the more sombre side of his character predominated.

Travel from Liverpool to the mountains of North Wales at this time was not always a simple matter, although Colin was usually able to get a lift down with Graham MacPhee, John Watson, Bill Stallybrass or other Liverpool-based friends who had motor cars. In the past, of course, he had cycled and even walked to Helyg, and occasionally used the Crosville bus service that ran on a Friday night from Birkenhead to the Ogwen Valley, the return service being on Monday morning. Another option was to get the train from Liverpool to Bangor, then the local bus to Bethesda. From here it was possible to catch Mr Robert's local bus which ran infrequently along the Nant Francon and Ogwen Valley up to Capel Curig. John Watson made the point that despite the difficulties of getting to the Ogwen Valley, it was far easier for Colin than getting up to the Lake District. With today's sophisticated road network however the reverse is probably the case.

John recalled that even getting out of Liverpool presented its dificulties. In the early 1930s, the Mersey tunnel did not exist and the journey to Wales would start by crossing the Mersey in a flat-bottomed ferry boat accompanied by all sorts of traffic including teams of horses pulling huge carts. After that it was fairly straightforward by road, apart from a gate on the road across the Denbigh Moors which was always kept closed. On arrival at this point, a toot on the horn would produce a small child from a nearby cottage, who would open and then close the gate for a nominal fee. In those days cars were so infrequent on the road that if you came upon one that had broken down you invariably offered assistance. For most people there was not as yet a five-day working week and departure from Liverpool was not usually until mid-day on Saturday with the return home late on Sunday evening. Some climbing would be grabbed on the Saturday if possible but the main activity usually had to wait until Sunday. Often the hostel group at Idwal would adjourn to the Douglas Arms at Bethesda for a pint on Saturday night, making sure they returned before lights out. Here John describes a typical Sunday at the hostel in the mid-thirties:

> A typical day would be to go up to Glyder Fach, do something on the Alphabet Slab and then a route on the main cliff, *Chasm Route* or maybe *Oblique Buttress*. Other venues may be the Milestone or Tryfan's East Face. We had to be back at the Hostel in time for our evening meal and then it would be the drive back to Liverpool. We had one member of the group whose ambition on a Sunday evening was to get to the first pub in England before it closed. We usually managed it! Longer trips were reserved for more extended stays as at Easter when the Hostel would be crowded. Then we might travel as far as Cwm Silyn which at that time was virtually unknown and completely deserted. It remains one of my favourite places. Another virtually unvisited cliff was the Black Ladders. We went there a few times to climb some of the gullies and it was a long walk there and back!

Altogether 1934 had been an eventful and dramatic year for the Kirkus family. In addition to Colin's accident on Ben Nevis, his youngest brother Guy fell and badly fractured his pelvis whilst attempting to solo the *Flake Crack* at Helsby (referred to earlier). The long term of convalescence this accident required caused Guy to lose his job, and he subsequently moved to Accrington where he found work in the textile trade. On a happier note, that year the family settled in a semi-detached house at Acre Lane in Heswall, on the Wirral peninsula. This house, No. 36 and called 'Suncroft', remained Colin's home until he married in 1940. The house remained in the Kirkus family until the summer of 1987.

On the British climbing scene, 1934 was notable for Menlove Edwards' continuing development of new routes in North Wales, in particular the *Slow Ledge Climb* on Dinas Mot. In the Lake District F.G. Balcombe discovered a number of new routes on Great Gable including the magnificent *Engineer's Slabs*, while in Scotland, MacPhee and Bell continued their separate explorations on Ben Nevis.

On a sad note 1934 was notable not only for the loss of Maurice Linnell, but also for the death on Mont Blanc of John Hoyland. Hoyland, who was not yet twenty, was the forerunner of a talented group of Oxbridge climbers who were to make their mark in North Wales in the period prior to World War Two. That year also witnessed the ill-fated attempt by Maurice Wilson, to climb Mount Everest alone. His body was discovered the following year at 6400 metres.

As the year 1935 opened, Colin could be seen to have made a gradual recovery, physically at least, from the Ben Nevis accident of the previous Easter. As outlined earlier, many of the effects of that experience were to have long-term effects on the young man, not least in his broader attitude to climbing and the pioneering of new routes in particular. However, by the latter part of 1934 regular trips to Helsby and to North Wales had again become a regular feature of Colin's life. In particular he chose to spend increasing amounts of time in the mountains with his friends at Idwal Youth Hostel. At twenty-four and as yet unmarried, Colin continued to live at home with his parents and brother Nigel. During the week he persevered with his job as a clerk at the offices of the Royal Insurance Company in Dale Street in the heart of Liverpool. Several contemporaries have remarked on Colin's relative lack of interest in his office job, and certainly in his early days he was relatively undistinguished in this direction and something of a disappointment to the friend of his father who had helped secure him the position with the Royal. It is likely that for Colin, the considerable confines of a rather staid insurance office was simply too great a contrast to the heady pleasures of being in the mountains. Jack Longland once said of him:

> Colin Kirkus was more totally focused on his climbing than anyone I ever met to the extent that he wasn't the least interested in the job he was doing.

In a conversation with Jack Longland, he volunteered the viewpoint that the life of a full-time climber, such as we see today, be it guiding, instructing or even retailing, would have suited Colin's temperament perfectly. Unfortunately the nature of life in the 1930s for someone of Colin's class and background, together with the nature of the sport at that time, made full-time involvement of this type quite impossible. Consequently, like the majority of climbers, he set about living the double life of the demands of the office during the week and of breaking out at the weekends. This is perhaps best summed up by a fine quote credited to Alf Bridge, writing of this period:

> Every precious moment was squeezed out of our weekends – youth, vigour, ambition and the joy of living in our mountains meant so much to us.

In one respect this may help to explain Colin's high level of activity in the mountains, where the maximum of action was extracted from virtually every visit despite the vagaries of the weather. Writing of his cousin some years later, Wilfrid Noyce had this to say:

> Colin Kirkus was by profession a black-coated worker in Liverpool. His excursions to the hills, on foot or by bicycle if he could not afford the train, were life itself to him. In this he was the prototype of many since.

It is not difficult to picture Kirkus the office worker enjoying a brisk lunchtime walk along Dale Street on a winter's day, perhaps to take some fresh air at the Pier Head and to glance across the river towards the Wirrall, before returning to the office. Possibly on the way back he might look up at the Gothic façades of the office buildings in the City Centre, working out possible routes up them towards the bright sky above. No doubt the photographs of Clogwyn Du'r Arddu and other crags were still in the desk drawer for some mid-afternoon inspiration. After work it would be home on the tram in the dark, the next trip to Wales still three or four days, or even a week away.

At the end of January 1935 Colin enjoyed a typical trip of the time to North Wales, with Graham MacPhee. This was to prove a busy year in the hills for MacPhee, who was hard at work producing the forthcoming Ben Nevis guide-book for the Scottish Mountaineering Club, and was no doubt eager to keep fit. This production of what was to be a particularly fine guide-book, from a home base in Liverpool was a quite extraordinary achievement, not least in terms of of stamina. Regular round trips of 800 miles in the mid-nineteen thirties, long before the dawning of the motorway system, would have tested the resolve of anyone. Nonetheless this remarkable climber continued to travel between Liverpool and Fort William on a regular basis, rapidly adding to his extensive knowledge of the great mountain, whilst also regularly climbing in North Wales and the Lake District. Modern climbers tend to take today's rapid communications for granted and should remember that it was not always the case. Indeed car ownership among climbers at the time was, in itself, very far from being the norm.

Returning to the January weekend in North Wales, MacPhee collected Colin in Liverpool on the Saturday in his trusty Riley, and they sped rapidly to Ogwen via the newly-opened Mersey Tunnel. The two friends reached Tal-y-braich at about 6 p.m. and finding a meet of the Rucksack Club in progress adjourned to Helyg. Sunday morning dawned bright and very cold, and they made their way to Idwal where Colin led Menlove's fine *East Wall Girdle* (still graded Hard Severe and sustained in character). This was followed by a rapid ascent of the *Original Route* on the Holly Tree Wall, before making their way to the frozen summit of Glyder Fawr and then back to Helyg. After a good day out, for January, they returned rapidly to Liverpool in darkness.

In March, Colin and MacPhee paid a rare (for Colin at least) visit to the Lake District, driving up to Langdale and the Wayfarers' Club Hut (Robertson Lamb). Colin served on the Committee of the Wayfarers' Club

Gimmer Crag, with climbers on The Crack.   *Photo C. F. Kirkus (AC coll.)*

for almost the whole of the 1930s and in 1935 was a Vice-President of the Club, Menlove also being on the Committee. This particular weekend was in fact a Fell and Rock Climbing Club Meet, MacPhee being on their club committee at the time. Most people attending the meet were booked in at the New Dungeon Ghyll Hotel, and Colin and MacPhee shared the hut with Edmund Hodge who climbed with them next day. The Sunday was spent on Gimmer Crag, with a leisurely ascent of *Bracket and Slab*. Lunch was enjoyed at the top of the route, and to quote MacPhee '...we just loafed about'. The crag was of course familiar to MacPhee, who had been involved in the first ascents of such routes as *Hiatus*, *Gimmer Crack* and *Joas*.

That same month, shortly before Easter, Colin got involved in one of Menlove's maritime adventures, when the pair of them set out to row across the Irish Sea. It is interesting that their friendship extended as far as one of these undertakings, although they appear to have climbed together only infrequently. In 'Menlove', Jim Perrin records this particular episode:

> They had borrowed a small boat, and set off from Conway on the evening tide, intending to go with it through the Menai Straits. Unfortunately, a gale blew up and they spent the night in an exhausting struggle to keep the boat head on to it off Traeth Lafan. When the morning came they went back into Conwy Harbour on the wind and tide and spent the day sleeping off the adventure, glad to be alive.

While Colin returned to his friends at Idwal Cottage, Menlove rowed the boat the 50 miles back to Liverpool. The adventure was not yet over for him, for on arrival at Liverpool, a wave sucked the boat under the landing stage but Menlove escaped unhurt. It is not known whether Colin ever put to sea with Menlove again. That Easter, Colin's cousin Wilfrid Noyce was staying at Helyg and met Menlove for the first time. The two men climbed together and so began a famous climbing partnership.

Colin returned to North Wales towards the end of April, again with MacPhee, and they stayed at Dol Peris. On the Saturday (April 28th) they walked up to the great cliffs of Clogwyn Du'r Arddu on a rather chilly morning. It is possible that this was Colin's first visit to Cloggy for some considerable time, since it is unlikely that he would have gone there during the summers of 1933 and 1934, being abroad during the former year and largely recovering from injury in the latter. This particular morning saw Colin lead MacPhee up a damp *Curving Crack* on the East Buttress, MacPhee recording in his diary '...I found it very hard as my arms seemed very weak.' He had in fact spent the previous week step-cutting on Ben Nevis, and was perhaps fatigued by a combination of prolonged efforts and the journey back down to North Wales. After a break for lunch Colin attempted a new route, but MacPhee recorded that '...it would not go!' Sadly no further details are forthcoming and one wonders just where Colin attempted to make the next breach in the cliff's defences. By the summer of 1933 the most obvious places had all been tried, and the only additional major pre-war route on the cliff was to be *Sunset Crack* on the East Buttress, climbed in 1937 by Cox, Hodgkin and the Mallory sisters. This may have been where Colin investigated, or – pure conjecture now – perhaps a return to the still unclimbed *Drainpipe Crack* or just possibly an investigation of the front face of the Pinnacle – obvious enough from the Green Gallery. Although no details are left to us, it seems significant that nearly three years on from his last contribution to the cliff, Clogwyn Du'r Arddu still held great interest for Colin, but perhaps a little of the edge had gone from his desire for new routes, or it simply could have been that conditions were not conducive to completing a new route.

By this stage of the season Colin was again climbing regularly with friends based at Idwal Youth Hostel but returned to Wales with MacPhee on the weekend of May 18th/19th. MacPhee must have been getting very fit by then, and spent a great deal of time that summer climbing rock-routes on Ben Nevis. This particular weekend saw them staying at a cottage in the Nant Ffrancon, three miles below Ogwen. They walked up to the Idwal Slabs on the Saturday afternoon and climbed *Ash Tree Wall*, followed by *Lazarus* on the Holly Tree Wall. Despite the time of year, there was a great deal of snow about and they finished the day quite wet. The next day the weather had deteriorated to steady rain but, undeterred, the pair returned to Idwal for a good mountaineering day climbing *Hope*, Holly Tree Wall *Original Route* and then continuing up *Continuation Wall*, *Lava Slab* and finally the *Central Arête* of Glyder Fawr by the Direct Start.

By now most of Colin's time in North Wales was spent climbing with friends from Idwal Youth Hostel, or taking novices out for instruction. Alf Bridge once made the point that Colin had become rather disillusioned with the attitudes of some of the older members of the Climbers' Club, and it may have been this, in conjunction with the aftermath of the Ben Nevis accident, that drew him away from Helyg towards the Idwal group, and a situation that seemed to suit this stage of his life particularly well. This is not to suggest a major break from the Climbers' Club, for Colin did still sometimes stay at Helyg, as these two charming anecdotes from this period reveal. One is from David Watson who for several years was the assistant custodian of Helyg, working with Stuart Chantrell. He recalls the mid-Thirties:

Bob Frost   *Photo C. F. Kirkus (AC coll.)*

At the time that I knew Colin I was a beginner. He was a climber of great stature who behaved towards beginners with great modesty and never with condescension. I remember him as a quiet person who had a prodigious appetite and a quiet sense of humour. Struggling on the Idwal Slabs in tricouni boots, I have seen him walk past us, upright, hands in pockets finding the holds with rubbered feet. He'd wait at the top and say "Let's go on up the Holly Tree Wall." I know that I was very sad when I heard that he had been lost during the war.

A regular feature of Colin's weekend trips was the need to travel down to Wales often straight from work in his city clothes, involving travelling back in them on the Sunday night. This is remembered in this amusing recollection of Tony Smyth:

> In the 1935/36 period we used to hold Imperial College meets at Helyg and Colin was always very kind to us beginners. On one occasion when we were playing about on the Helyg boulder he came out of the hut on his way to catch the bus, or other transport. In my mind's eye I see him arrayed in a bowler hat and umbrella, but this may have been imagination; however he was dressed for the city, not for Helyg. We asked him to show us the way up one particular problem which had defeated us. Without more ado, and without even taking off his hat (bowler?), in a few quick movements he was at the top, amid the cheers of the watchers.

When considering Colin's connections with the Idwal hostel group at this time, it is necessary to introduce the key figure of R.C. (Bob) Frost. Like

Colin, Frost was a member of the Wayfarers' Club and was born on Merseyside in 1912. After leaving school he took up a position as a clerk in the offices of the City Corporation Trams Department and, like Colin, devoted his weekends to climbing. He had become interested in mountaineering in his late teens and joined the Wayfarers' Club in 1933 at the age of twenty-one. Frost soon became a regular visitor to Idwal Hostel and also climbed regularly at Helsby. He rapidly acquired a particularly polished technique as a rock-climber and took his training seriously. Fellow Wayfarer John Watson told of Frost packing a heavy rucksack and tramping up and down his parents' stairs in heavy boots to build up stamina between trips to the hills. Likewise he used to practise step-cutting in the boulder clay cliffs at Caldy in the Dee estuary. By diligent application Frost soon reached the highest standards of the day but, although he made numerous early repeats of the notable routes of the day, he made few first ascents himself. During the 1934 season he had served notice of his rapidly developing ability with two ascents of Scafell's *Central Buttress* and numerous leads of hard routes in North Wales, including some early repeats on Clogwyn Du'r Arddu.

By the mid-Thirties Colin and Frost had become firm friends and climbed increasingly together (at this time most of Colin's climbing was done with either MacPhee or Frost). In many ways Colin and Frost were very similar in temperament, and as regards ability and technique Frost was to prove by no means the junior partner. John Watson, a friend of both men, occasionally drove them down to Wales from Liverpool, and felt that one of the major considerations regarding Colin's return to climbing was the development of a good partnership with Frost, coupled with an approach made to Colin by the Climbers' Club to produce a new guide-book to Glyder Fach. By the mid-Thirties a new series of guide-books was felt to be overdue and Menlove was soon hard at work on a new guide to Idwal, which appeared in 1936. In addition to Glyder Fach, new guide-books were also scheduled for Tryfan and Lliwedd. Increasingly located at Idwal and with a supply of prospective companions at the hostel, Colin was in an ideal position to work on the nearby cliffs of Glyder Fach, Bochlwyd Buttress, the Nameless Cwm and the Gribin Facet, and set to work that summer exploring and checking the area. The result of this work was to be a guide-book of great charm, the equal of Menlove's fine work elsewhere in Wales, but very different in character and a delightful insight into the nature of climbing in North Wales at that time.

The development of his friendship and partnership with Frost was to be of great benefit to Colin and, writing of Frost, John Watson had this to say:

It is interesting to compare the abilities and technique of the two best climbers I
was ever associated with, that of Kirkus himself and Frost. I spent much more
time with Bob Frost than with Colin, and I think that in terms of pure rock-
climbing skill there was very little to choose between them. Yet Colin achieved
pre-eminence in the climbing world and Frost is barely remembered, and when
the old Idwal generation is finally gone will probably hardly be remembered at all.
So, you will not be surprised that I welcome the opportunity to bring to the
present generation some memories of a very fine climber. Both men were of
course great technicians but although Colin could sometimes appear clumsy,
Frost never seemed to. He was I think the neater climber of the two. Both had the
ability to appear comfortable in the most difficult situations. I remember that
during an ascent of Longland's Climb on Clogwyn Du'r Arddu, when both Frost
and Kirkus led a rope, I was most impressed by their confidence and ability to
change from stockings to rubbers whilst apparently standing on nothing and
holding on to nothing! And of course both men would inspire utter confidence in
those who were acting as their seconds.

From July 6th-28th Graham MacPhee's wife and children were on
holiday near Porthmadog, at Borth-y-Gest. MacPhee drove down to Wales
each weekend, bringing Colin and depositing him at Idwal. Then, Colin's
work on the Glyder Fach guide-book really got under way, and on Sunday
July 21st Colin wandered over to the Bochlwyd Buttress with Bob Frost.
This attractive little crag is situated on the walk up to Cwm Bochlwyd and
the Glyder Fach cliffs. It stands out against the hillside by the stream that
cascades down from Llyn Bochlwyd, and was very handily located for the
Idwal regulars. It remains a delightful place to climb, particularly on a
summer evening. The place had previously received attention from
B.L. Bathurst (one of the early explorers of Dinas Mot) who discovered the
Gargoyle Traverse, and from Colin's friend Ted Hicks who had led the first
ascent of the exposed *Wall Climb*.

On this particular day Colin and Frost climbed two new routes on the
right-hand side of the crag, *Two Pitch Route* and *Five Pitch Route*, both
pleasant 100-foot Severe climbs despite the rather uninspired names
afforded them! *Two Pitch Route* is regarded as pleasant, with a fine exposed
finish, while *Five Pitch Route* is a little broken but contains some enjoyable
short pitches. Worthy additions though these were, better was yet to come.
Later in the afternoon Colin was joined by another Idwal regular, Charles
Brennand, and proceeded to lead a delightful pitch to the right of the
previous two routes, up a rough slab to form a direct start to the 1927 route
Arête and Slab. The name given to this charming climb, *Marble Slab*, referred
not to the nature of the rock encountered *en-route* but to the fact that during

the ascent Colin was loudly singing 'Around the Marble Arch', a popular song of the time. It is nice to imagine a happily singing Kirkus on a climb he clearly enjoyed, to quote the comments he later made in the guide-book:

> A delightful climb of great delicacy and beauty of technique on perfect rock. If done in rubbers, a concession hardly to be grudged on such a climb, its standard might be reduced to merely Severe. Standard: Very Severe.

The climb is indeed a lovely exercise in technique, with one balancy move over an overlap on the slab – a little Kirkus gem for the connoisseur today, graded Severe.

On hearing of Colin singing on Marble Slab, Guy was highly amused:

> My God, that must have been grim, Colin had the most awful singing voice and was well out of key!

Writing later in the Glyder Fach guide of the day's exploits, Colin remarked that:

> Bochlwyd Buttress was transformed into a maze by the addition of three more climbs, the last of which was the Marble Slab.

Since 1935 only a few additions have been made to this pleasant crag, the best being the early-Sixties routes of *Bochlwyd Eliminate* and *The Wrack*, both technical products of their time.

Colin's two most regular climbing companions of this period, Frost and MacPhee, combined forces themselves on August 5th to produce a first (summer) ascent on Ben Nevis as part of MacPhee's continuing guide-book work. The climb in question was *Gardyloo Gully*, and the ascent must have been a difficult one as prior to Marshall's 1969 guide, the route was still graded Very Severe (Scottish).

By the early summer of 1935 the issue of a British return to Everest had again arisen in senior mountaineering circles. The Everest Committee resolved to send a post-monsoon reconnaissance later that year, under the leadership of Eric Shipton, with a full-scale expedition planned for the Spring of 1936. Great consideration was duly given to the composition of such an expedition, which was again to be led by Hugh Ruttledge, the core of the party being made up of Shipton, Smythe and Wyn Harris from the 1933 team. Colin was almost certainly one of a number of contenders for the remaining places, who in turn were considered by the expedition leadership. It was certainly felt by a number of Colin's contemporaries, particularly those at Idwal, that this time his inclusion was likely to be a formality. Just how Colin felt about the whole business is difficult to gauge at this distance, particularly in view of the aftermath of the Ben Nevis accident, although he did again commence weekend cycling from Liverpool to the Ogwen Valley. There was no doubt that his non-inclusion in the 1933 team had been a tremendous personal disappointment, particularly in the light of the confident manner with which that multi-talented enterprise had set off for Everest in a blaze of publicity. Now, almost three years on, with plans and expectations possibly tempered by the experiences of 1933, a somewhat more professional apporach could be expected, particularly in relation to team selection, and also in light of rapidly increasing climbing standards. At the time of selection for the 1933 expedition, Colin's major handicaps would have been his relative youth and his clear lack of notable Alpine experience. However, the very real quality of Colin's performance on Pallis's Gangotri Expedition would have left little doubt as to his ability to translate British efforts into a high altitude situation. Unfortunately the achievements of the Gangotri expedition never received the publicity they surely warranted. Articles did appear in the Journals of the Wayfarers' Club, the Alpine Club and the Climbers' Club, but Marco Pallis's book did not appear until 1939. However, one effect of the success of the Gangotri expedition was the selection of Charles Warren for the 1936 Everest team, as the Expedition Doctor.

As regards selection, it fell to Smythe and Shipton to climb with a number of people in order to assess their suitability for the forthcoming expedition, and Colin was one such contender. In early August he was one of a group of climbers who travelled to Zermatt at the invitation of Smythe. Someone who recalled that trip to Zermatt was Jim Gavin of the Alpine Club, who was himself selected for the Everest expedition:

> I did some very enjoyable climbing with Colin in August 1935. How it happened was this: I had written to Hugh Ruttledge after reading in the papers that he was to lead a new Everest expedition the following year. Hugh wrote back to me saying that Eric Shipton was trying out some climbers in the Himalaya and Frank Smythe was shortly to do the same thing in the Alps, and would be based at Zermatt. I immediately persuaded a climbing friend, Charles Nicholls, to come to Zermatt with me, and there, in the Monte Rosa Hotel, we duly met up with Smythe and his party – Colin Kirkus, Peter Oliver and Oakes-Smith, on the 9th August. Next day Smythe and his party went off somewhere, I can't remember where but it might have been the Dom-Tasch traverse, while Nicholls and I went off to do the Viereselgrat on the Dent Blanche. We all returned to the Monte Rosa hotel and Smythe asked Nicholls and me to join his party.

On the 15th August Smythe and his party of five left Zermatt in the afternoon, and set off for the Betemps Hut. The following morning they set

Zermatt group. L to R: C.R. Nicholls, J.M.L. Gavin, P. Oliver, Oakes Smith, F.S. Smythe.

Photo C.F. Kirkus

off at 4 a.m. for the Margherita, breaking new snow, enjoying an amusing climbing variation on the way. They reached the hut at midday and in the afternoon climbed the Zumsteinspitze, returning to spend the night in the unpleasantly crowded hut. The following morning (Sat. 17th) the party left the Margherita Hut at 6 a.m. and traversed Lyskamm, Castor, Pollux and the Breithorn to reach the Gandegg Inn at 8 p.m. They reached Zermatt at 11 p.m., having descended the path in darkness – a formidable day! Not surprisingly the next day was spent resting, but Monday 19th saw the party walking from Randa up to the Weisshorn Hut. The next day they climbed the Weisshorn, returning to the hut in poor weather. On arrival back at Zermatt they discovered that Aldous, Lloyd and Bicknell had arrived to swell the party. Jim Gavin takes up the story again:

On August 21st Oakes-Smith left for the Bernese Oberland, while Smythe set off with the new arrivals. Kirkus, Oliver, Nicholls and I walked up to the Hörnli Hut for the Matterhorn. The following morning we left the hut at 3.40 a.m. and lost our way immediately! However, we then made a very fast ascent of the Hörnli Ridge in perfect conditions, passing everybody. I climbed with Colin, and we reached the summit at 7.15 a.m. Sadly he then had to leave us to return to England, descending to the Hörnli Hut alone. The rest of us went down the Italian Ridge, skirting the mountain to arrive back at Zermatt that evening. I still remember what a happy time those few days were. I met Colin later at Helyg, but we didn't climb together again. He was a superb rock-climber, and of course a delightful companion.

It is a long way down the Hörnli Ridge then on to Schwarzsee and on down the endless path to Zermatt, particularly when alone and tired. Colin would have had much to think about as he descended to the valley to catch the afternoon train home. Had he done enough to justify his selection for the forthcoming expedition? It obviously meant a great deal to him and this might well be his only chance to go to Everest, still tantalisingly unclimbed.

The decision on the composition of the final party for the 1936 Exedition was not made until the late autumn, after Smythe and Shipton had compared their various findings and reported back to the Everest Committee. In the event, Colin did not receive an invitation to join the Expedition, but at least had the consolation of being in good company, for amongst those overlooked were Bill Tilman and Noel Odell. Tilman and Odell of course replied brilliantly to the Committee with their ascent the following year of Nanda Devi (25,645 ft.) in the Garhwal. This was to remain the highest mountain climbed, until the French ascent of Annapurna in 1950.

The party selected for Everest included Peter Oliver and Jim Gavin from the August trip to Zermatt. Both men had clearly performed well in the Pennine Alps, and had impressed Smythe with their ability and stamina. Peter Oliver was an army officer serving on the North-West Frontier, and had already attempted Dunagiri in the Garhwal, and made the second ascent of Trisul (23,360 ft.) together with a porter. He was to take part in both the 1936 and 1938 Everest Expeditions.

As regards his own inclusion in the 1936 Everest team, Jim Gavin modestly put forward the view that:

> I have often felt that maybe I was given Colin's place on the expedition. Possibly Frank Smythe felt that my technique on snow and ice was slightly better, but Colin was by far the best of us all on rock. I was very sorry that he was not selected, as the 1936 Expedition was a very happy one despite the weather.

Something of the background to Colin's non-selection and to the prevailing attitudes can be gleaned from this extract of a letter written by Smythe to Graham MacPhee on 22nd November 1935:

> Tomorrow the final decisions will be made about the Everest party. I'm afraid Kirkus won't receive an invitation. I'm very sorry indeed for him. I like him personally immensely and only wish he was a first choice. But when I tell you that out of the nine people I climbed with this summer only one is likely to be invited you will see what a difficult business it is. There will be three of the 1933 party

Jack Longland and Ivan Waller bouldering somewhere in Wales. (Inset: Longland in swimsuit.)

Photos courtesy Jo Longland.

and three (probably) of Shipton's party. Then of the two remaining places in the climbing party of eight, one is already filled by Hunt[1] who went to nearly 25,000 ft. in the Karakorams this year and who has an excellent service record. So you see how it is. I did not know there was any prejudice against Kirkus by people who hadn't climbed with him. Why? The only prejudice, if you can call it so, has been due to his accident and its possible effects on him. Have you observed any effects?

After discussing other matters, Smythe concludes: 'It looks like a real team this time – no scratch affair like 1933.'

One is left with the suspicion, also indicated in Harry Calvert's biography,[2] that Smythe may have formed an unfavourable opinion of Colin's ability as an all-round mountaineer. And yet, of the Everest leadership, Smythe would almost certainly have had the greatest knowledge of what had been taking place in British Climbing in the Thirties, and in particular of Colin's considerable role. Harry Calvert did volunteer the view that this may well have been an occasion when Smythe was guilty of an error of judgement.

Whatever qualities were needed to go to Everest, Colin did not appear to quite match the requirements although, notwithstanding the possible effects of the Ben Nevis accident, it is difficult not to conclude that he was rather hard done by. At the same time one should acknowledge that both Smythe and Shipton were very professional in their approach to climbing Everest and were highly ambitious to succeed this time. It is likely that they would have included Colin in the party if they had felt he could have made an important contribution.

John Watson recalled that the Idwal regulars in particular were very disappointed that Colin was not invited on the expedition. Some further insight into the attitudes of the time might be gained by a comment from Charles Warren regarding the matter:

> Because Colin was such a brilliant rock-climber, we somehow never took him seriously enough as an all-round mountaineer.

On hearing of Colin's non-selection for Everest, Alf Bridge reassured his friend over a pint.

> The trouble is Colin you're not a "good chap" who can talk about things other than climbing. As a bloke who eats, drinks and sleeps rock-climbing, you've no chance! What use would you be in a little tent at Camp 5 or 6? Instead of being able to discuss the Life and Works of Leonardo da Vinci to take your companion's mind off the howling blizzard outside, you would only be able to tell him about some dreadful route on Cloggy. You'd frighten the poor bugger to death!

1 This refers to John Hunt, who was to lead the successful 1953 Expedition. In the event, he did not take part in the 1936 attempt on Everest, failing the required medical examination.
2 'Smythe's Mountains' – (Harry Calvert – Gollancz 1985)

In reality, the day of the ordinary working man on a major Himalayan expedition was still almost twenty years away, commencing with Joe Brown's selection and brilliant success on the Kangchenjunga expedition of 1955. However, by that time another World War had passed, bringing with it the necessary social and economic changes to enable such a broadening of opportunity to be achieved. Sadly, Colin's heyday simply came too early in the development of a sport, still rather hamstrung by established attitudes and prejudices.

All things considered, 1935 had been a relatively quiet year for Colin, but elsewhere much was going on in the British climbing scene. MacPhee and Bell continued the extensive exploration of Ben Nevis, while in North Wales new routes began to appear steadily in the Llanberis Pass. Most notable this particular year were Roberts and Cooke's ascent of the magnificent *Main Wall* on Cyrn Las (which remained unrepeated for many years), Menlove's ascents of *Shadow Wall* and *Crackstone Rib* on Carreg Wastad, and the addition of the fine *Sabre Cut* to Dinas Cromlech by E. Pentir Williams and Richard Glyn Williams. These four excellent climbs were destined to become classics which have delighted thousands of climbers over the years.

Richard Glyn Williams and E. Pentyr Williams were part of an increasingly active group of local climbers in North Wales that included Hal Jacob, Jake Cooke, P.L. Roberts and George Dwyer. They were all well known at the Idwal Hostel and to Colin, who was himself particularly admired by Dwyer as being a craftsman. Richard Glyn Williams, known affectionately as 'Taff', was later to marry the Idwal Hostel warden Connie Alexander.

In the Alps two very important ascents were made that year; in June Meier and Peters climbed the magnificent Croz Spur on the Grandes Jorasses, while in August, Allain and Leininger climbed the North Face of the Petit Dru.

7 Alpine Adventures and Guide-book Labours

In the autumn of 1935, the Mountaineering Journal included a further guide to Helsby written by Bob Frost and Frank Stangle, which contained 27 problems, variations and additions to Colin and 'AB's very thorough guide of 1930. Their comments of the time make interesting reading:

> It seems that the limit of human ingenuity at Helsby has now been attained, and it can almost safely be said that the crag is "worked out".

How many times have these sentiments appeared in a guide-book, only to be disproved within a few years. This was to be particularly true of Helsby over the next twenty-five years, as standards on the crag rapidly rose until in the late 1950s they were as high as any in Britain. Frost and Stangle's guide was again a thorough piece of work, and represented the fruit of continued exploration largely by Bob Frost and Colin himself, together with support from other regulars from the Wayfarers' Club. As his local crag, Colin must have known the place like the back of his hand by 1935-36 and Helsby certainly served him well in maintaining climbing fitness when away from the mountains. There exists a very good photograph of Colin taken at the time at Helsby, by Charles Douglas Milner. It shows Colin in a pensive mood looking out over the plain to the north while another climber starts up the wall to his left. Helsby has suffered a considerable decline in popularity since the mid-Sixties, as local climbers have been increasingly attracted to the rocks at Frodsham and Pex Hill: the situation has not been improved by the gradual invasion of green lichen onto much of the crag, thought to be caused by the presence of a fertiliser factory in the valley below.

After the publication of the 1935 guide, Colin continued to climb regularly at Helsby, most often in the company of Bob Frost. A most notable addition, thought to date from this period, is a bold line on the West Buttress now known as *Morgue Slab*. It is believed that the line was already well known to Helsby regulars and had been the subject of numerous top-roped ascents, but Colin is thought to have made the first lead of the route. It must have been an exciting ascent, for the climb still warrants a grade of E1 5b. The climb takes a delicate line to the left of *The Beatnik*. It takes the blank-looking slab directly, crossing the line of overhangs at mid-height at their weakest point, utilising what appears to be a drilled hole for a finger.

Writing in 'Mountain' more than thirty-five years later, sandstone maestro Martin Boysen recalled Helsby, and *Morgue Slab* in particular:–

> The crag has a forbidding character: it feels big, and the routes are steep and on smoke-blackened rock. A real bogey climb for me is *Morgue Slab* – a Kirkus route, and hard. At a height of 35 ft., whilst easing over a bulge, one finger stuffed into a tiny hole, my only foothold exploded into a puff of sand. For a moment, I maintained my position, contemplating a one finger mantelshelf. Then came the inevitable fall. By some instinct, I managed to perform this perfectly: turning round in full flight, I bounced off the lower slab with both feet and leapt for the steep bracken slopes, down which I rolled in a crazy bundle. I ended up wrapped round a birch tree, shaken but unhurt, glasses still on. Since then, I have only once plucked up enough courage to lead the route.

Like much of Helsby these days, the climb seems to get little traffic, and this situation is not helped by the particularly bad encroachment of green lichen on this part of the crag. Notwithstanding the place's current neglect, it is difficult to visit Helsby and not be touched by a sense of the pre-war period and the strange atmosphere of the place. The 1930s were perhaps the golden period on the crag, but some bold and hard climbs were later added in the 1950s by a talented group including Hugh Banner and Jim O'Neill. Helsby now seems to have largely fallen from grace, yet the place possesses some excellent climbing. Much of Colin's acknowledged excellence on rock was almost certainly due to the ready availability of Helsby's steep and fingery climbing, particularly in his early days as a climber. It is good to picture him there after work, climbing alone or with a few mates, deriving simple pleasure from the steep sandstone before enjoying a pint or two on the way home. Colin clearly had a great affection for the place, and that comes through clearly in the 1930 guide he wrote with 'AB'. He was also later to use photographs of the crag in "Let's Go Climbing!" Just as his name is forever linked with that of Clogwyn Du'r Arddu and Dinas Mot, so is it linked to the development of this unusual Cheshire outcrop.

To attempt to sum up Helsby, and its great significance in the 1930s, not only to Colin's climbing but to Welsh climbing as a whole, it seems appropriate to borrow another descriptive quote from 'Menlove'. Here Jim Perrin is describing an evening on the crag several years before Colin's ascent of *Morgue Slab*;–

> It is easy to imagine the twenty-year-old Menlove, on a summer evening in 1930, sitting below the rocks of Helsby, which glow warmly red in the light of a sun setting out over Liverpool Bay. He is watching the slight figure of Colin Kirkus composedly, perhaps slightly awkwardly on occasions, dealing with the problems

of, say, *Wood's Climb*. Kirkus is at the height of his powers, yet he stops at those difficult moves into the base of the groove – just as Menlove did a few minutes previously. He moves up, feels the holds, and moves down again. Just as Menlove did. And then he starts to climb, leaning his body out to the right, running his feet up, reaching up just a trifle hurriedly for those holds in the groove. "This is the man whose routes in Wales are beyond the capacity of ordinary mortals. Yet they are on rock, the same as this, and....did he really do those moves any better than I did?" muses the watcher, before he turns his gaze out west to where the hills of Snowdonia are a faint band of darkness on the farthest horizon.

Having been overlooked for the forthcoming Everest expedition, Colin turned his attention to two main climbing objectives for the following year. These were the completion of the Glyder Fach guide-book, and a proposed visit to the French Alps in the summer with Bob Frost. During the early part of 1936, Colin paid a number of visits to North Wales, and towards the end of March was accompanied on one such trip by Graham MacPhee and Earle Morgan. One intention was to get some fitness developed for a forthcoming Easter trip to the snows of Ben Nevis, but the weather took a turn for the worse and the three men splashed round a traverse of Lliwedd and Snowdon before returning to the valley. As was often the case in wet weather, MacPhee suffered badly with pain in his ankle.

Just over a week later on April 9th, Colin travelled up to Fort William with MacPhee for a Rucksack Club meet over the Easter weekend. Colin camped again at Lochan Meall an t-Suidhe in very cold conditions, with a great deal of snow on the mountain. Bob Frost was also camping nearby, with some of the Idwal group. Amongst those on the meet were Alfred Wood, Derrick Ritson and Dorothy Smith, and on the Sunday Colin joined these three for an attempt on Glover's Chimney at the Tower Gap (first climbed in winter a year earlier by MacPhee), anticipating some good sport with hard ice. It is not clear whether this weekend was Colin's first return to the cliffs of Ben Nevis since the accident of two years previously, but it is quite likely that this was the case. Unfortunately it was not to be an auspicious return, as the party met with an unfortunate accident on the approach to Garadh na Ciste, as Colin recorded in 'Let's Go Climbing.'

> We came to a great crevasse, where the snow had shrunk away from the cliff; it was nearly 100 feet deep and in the Alps would have been called a bergschrund.
> Then we had a 40-foot pitch of steep ice, which took some time. The snow-slope above was fairly steep and very hard; several blows of the axe were needed for each step. We were climbing on two separate ropes; Derrick and I were on the first, and Alfred and Dorothy were on the other. I was leading and cutting the steps; then we changed placed, and Derrick took over the lead.

North Face of Ben Nevis: the route up to Glover's Chimney follows the snow-slope in the right-hand half of the photograph   *Photo P. H. Hodgkiss*

We were ascending a kind of scoop. On the right were steep iced rocks; an overhanging line of dark crags rose above us on the left. Our snow-slope was about 30 feet wide.

Suddenly there was a great clattering, far above us. It grew louder, but sounded well away to the right. Then small stones began to whiz over the edge of the cliff on the left. This was just the beginning. Have you ever watched a cart-load of bricks being emptied? That is what is looked like. A great avalanche of stones crashed over the rocks, just above our heads. They came in an endless stream. They rumbled and sang past our ears, and split in fragments all round. It was terrifying to see them dropping thickly out of the sky. The slope above us became a heaving mass of grating rocks.

I think Alfred was the first to be hit. A large rock broke his arm, which he had put up to protect his head. He went down, but Dorothy held him. Then she too was hit and they were both swept down.

I tried desperately to reach the little crevasse on the left. There was shelter there, and I should be able to hold Derrick. I attempted to dig the pick of my axe into the hard snow; there was certainly no time for step-cutting. It was all in vain; I was swept down by the shooting stream of rocks.

I went head-first; it seems to be a habit of mine. I could see my camera going down in front. It was an easy winner; I never saw it again. Then I went over the 40-foot ice-wall and landed with a sickening jolt on the edge of the crevasse. Derrick must have arrived soon afterwards to complete the party. He went plonk into a hole, so that only his head and shoulders were visible. He looked rather funny. Alfred was a few feet down the slope, held by the rope. Dorothy was close to me.

The stones continued for another 500 feet. I cannot imagine why we didn't do likewise.

Alfred was the most cheerful of the party, although he had a broken arm and a gash that ran half-way up his face. He also had a bone broken on his ankle. He sat and smoked cigarette after cigarette. Derrick had concussion and looked grey and drawn. His hands were mangled. Dorothy had her face and one leg badly cut and various muscles strained. I had a shoulder torn so that one arm was useless. My ribs were damaged. I could not breathe sitting down and felt sick standing up. After a time the faintness disappeared and I felt quite comfortable.

We had all lost our axes, so we could not help ourselves at all. It was very chilly sitting there on the snow, waiting. At intervals we shouted for help.

Our shouts were heard by Hemming and McCallum of the Scottish Mountaineering Club, who climbed up to our rescue. We owe a lot to them; they were most skilful and efficient. They retrieved our axes; mine was broken in two.

The first thing was to get Derrick down. He was lowered on his back down the slope, his arms sticking out pathetically in front. I couldn't help being amused; he looked so ridiculous, although he was in a bad enough way, poor chap.

The procedure was for one or other of the rescue party to carve a great platform out of the snow every hundred feet. Then the whole party would be assembled there. I managed to descend on my own, cutting steps with my uninjured arm and the broken ice-axe.

The accident had happened at two o'clock. It was seven before we reached the hut, about 800 feet lower down. Without help we could never have managed it at all. It was really a miracle that none of us was killed, since we had fallen over 250 feet, apart from the bombardment we had suffered.

MacPhee had been busy himself that weekend having already done the Secondary Tower Ridge (1931 Route) and made the first ascent of the South Gully of Creag Coire na Ciste with G.C. Williams. On the Saturday he climbed *Long Climb*[1], finishing at 9 p.m. in a typical Nevis blizzard. On this particular Sunday MacPhee had not left the C.I.C. hut until 2 p.m., and with G.C. Williams and Colin Steven made an ascent of Gardyloo Gulley. MacPhee recorded that they reached the summit to be greeted by magnificent views, on a perfect spring evening. It was only on returning to the hut and finding Colin and his party there with Hemming and McCallum, that MacPhee learnt of the drama of that afternoon. It was quickly agreed that Wood was too badly hurt to be moved that night, and MacPhee and McCallum took care of him while Colin returned to his tent where he was looked after by Bob Frost:

1 In view of the conditions that can be inferred, MacPhee's ascent must have very nearly predated Marshall and Smith's first winter ascent by 25 years.

I had a poor night. I could not lie on my left side on account of my ribs, nor on my right because of my shoulder; so I had to try and sleep on my back. I gave up the attempt when it grew light, and read through the Ben Nevis guide from cover to cover.

Derrick Ritson and Dorothy Smith meanwhile were accompanied down to the hospital at Fort William by Hemming and Steven, who returned to the hut in the early hours of next morning. Later that day a pony was brought up to the hut to take Alfred Wood down to the Belford Hospital, on a particularly stormy afternoon. Having helped get Wood to the hospital, MacPhee returned to the hut that same night. Wood required several stitches in a face wound and suffered a badly fractured arm. Colin summed up the incident thus:

> This accident was pure bad luck. We could not possibly have foreseen it. It was freezing quite hard, so there was no reason for us to expect an avalanche. Whether the stones were loosened by the sun, or whether some one knocked them down, we were never able to discover.

The party were indeed fortunate that the Scottish Mountaineering Club men were on hand to help them down to the hut and then safely down to Fort William. The three casualties were detained in hospital for some time but, despite his battered condition, Colin was back at work in Liverpool on the Tuesday morning. Alfred Wood made a quick recovery, and was soon climbing again with Colin and MacPhee. Neither Colin nor his cousin Wilfrid Noyce enjoyed the best of fortune on the Ben, for in addition to Colin's two accidents there, Wilfrid suffered a broken leg on the mountain in 1939.

The Whitsun weekend saw MacPhee and Colin driving down to Wales together with Alfred Wood, now recovered from his injuries sustained on Ben Nevis. They stayed at Tal-y-braich, but the weekend did not begin well as MacPhee recorded of the Saturday:

> Pouring wet day, sat in the hut by the fire. It was very cold – we walked up to see Colin's brother but the tent was empty.

The following day dawned bright and clear, and Colin and MacPhee made for Idwal and the Bochlywd Buttress where they quickly climbed the Original Route (*Chimney Climb*) before walking over to the Glyder Fach Main Cliff. Here they appear to have had a busy afternoon, commencing with the very pleasant *Slab Route* (by the Spiral Variant) followed by what MacPhee described as 'two climbs to the right of Beta lower down.' The former of these was in fact a new route on the Alphabet Slab. It gave 160 feet of delicate, enjoyable climbing on small holds, and in line with existing route names Colin called it *Gamma*. It is likely that the other route they climbed that afternoon was *Delta*. *Gamma* is described in the current Ogwen guide-book as 'An absorbing climb of some delicacy on the clean smooth slab right of *Beta*'. It is the ideal way, and a total contrast in style, to reach Colin's classic routes *Lot's Groove* and *Lot's Wife*.

The following day (June 1st) was cold and showery, but the sun came through later and together with two Rucksack members, Duckworth and Gudgeon, Colin and MacPhee returned to Bochlwyd Buttress. Colin led the party up *Wall Climb*, Ted Hick's lovely little route of 1929, and despite a heavy shower they then continued up to Glyder Fach. Here Colin led them up *Hawk's Nest Buttress*, the Abraham brothers' classic dating from 1905, and MacPhee recorded that the remainder of the party found the route very hard. They finished the day off with the *Needle's Eye Climb*, Palmer's route of 1925, which was found to be strenuous in the conditions pertaining that day. In the Glyder Fach guide-book, which appeared a year later, Colin commented on this route amusingly:

> A thoroughly excellent course whereby a moderate party can sample many of the delights of the Hawk's Nest Buttress without its difficulties. In fact this route is often mistaken for the Hawk's Nest by jubilant cragsmen, who enlarge on the manner in which the old pioneers overrated standards of difficulty.

(A respectful nod to Ashley and George perhaps, the Abraham brothers' book 'British Mountain Climbs' having been Colin's inspiration as a schoolboy.) During the course of this weekend, MacPhee shot some film on his new cine camera, which later they all watched at MacPhee's home. Truly something of a rarity at that time.

In the middle of June MacPhee's wife and children were again on holiday at Borth y Gest, and while they were away MacPhee had Alfred Wood and Colin to stay for a while at his home in Liverpool..."the boys are very late going to bed, usually well after midnight." At the end of the week Wood returned to his home at Wilmslow, and the Friday evening saw MacPhee and Colin heading for North Wales where Colin was dropped off at Helyg. Amongst those there that weekend were Bob Frost, Robin Hodgkin and David Cox, and Colin and Frost managed a weekend of hard training as their departure to the Alps was now only a fortnight away. On Sunday evening MacPhee collected Colin and Frost and took them back to Liverpool. Alfred Wood and Colin moved in with MacPhee for a second week, when they appear to have had some fun, according to MacPhee:

> Took them to the Empire Variety Show, and ate strawberries afterwards until midnight.' and later in the week, 'Colin took us to the Stadium to see a boxing show. Two men were knocked out. I smoked a large cigar and felt ill.

Of historical interest, the following Wednesday (July 1st) saw a significant event enacted on the South Buttress of Tryfan. This event came about as a result of an exchange visit to Britain of seventeen members of the Deutscher und Oesterreichischer Alpen Verein, as described by Clark and Pyatt in 'Mountaineering in Britain.'[1]

> The Germans were at this time severely limited in their climbing by political and similar restrictions – they were, for instance, virtually forbidden to climb even in Austria by the currency restrictions which the Third Reich imposed – but their problem was overcome by an arrangement made between Dr. Walker Hartmann of the German Club and Mr J.E.B. Wright, the founder of the Lakeland Mountain Guides and in 1936 an employee of the Workers' Travel Association. The visitors, who included the cream of German rock-climbers, made light of most that could be shown them both in the Lake District and in Wales. Then they were taken to Tryfan. 'I had Belle Vue Bastion in mind', J.R. Jenkins wrote later, 'but on reaching the Heather Terrace I remembered an old project of mine to force a route up the wall bounded by the Gashed Crag climb and South Gully. There was a chance that no continuous climb would be found, but I egged on Teufel to try something. A rain-shower delayed operations, but he soon warmed up to it and worked out a route which far exceeded my expectations. It was a very fine lead under the conditions, and provided six excellent pitches, all of a consistently high standard. Two pitons were used.

John Jenkins was a member of the Rucksack Club and together with fellow member Priestly Phillips was responsible for directing the visiting climbers to suitable locations. Despite the obvious quality and difficulty of the new route, it was clearly felt by a number of Welsh regulars that the rock of Tryfan had been violated by the German's pitons, and feelings ran high in some quarters. Within a few weeks Menlove had safely led the route without the offending pitons, which had been duly removed by use of the Helyg poker. Thus was honour restored, the route being called *Munich Climb*.

It is quite likely that Colin would not have heard of Teufel's fine lead and the ensuing controversy until after his return from the Alps. Certainly it would have been interesting to hear his opinion of the incident. In many respects Colin was something of a conservative, but it is likely that he had already begun to realise the direction in which hard rock-climbing was heading and the need for a positive attitude towards the occasional piton (witness Linnell's peg placed on Scafell's Overhanging Wall, and the amusing invitation to would-be leaders to dispense with its use should they see fit!) Colin's developing thoughts on the matter later emerged in an article

1 'Mountaineering in Britain' Clark & Pyatt (Phoenix House – 1957)

Bob Frost on the Glacier d'Argentiere.   *Photo C. F. Kirkus (AC coll.)*

in the 1939 Warfarers' Club Journal[1] and formed a logical and sensible standpoint for the next generation of top climbers in acknowledging the changes emerging in the sport.

On the following Friday (July 3rd), Bob Frost and Colin set off for London, thence Dover, the ferry and the long train journey across France to the Chamonix valley. By all accounts it was a visit they had looked forward to with great anticipation; Frost had never previously visited the Alps (John Watson remembered Frost's delight at how far back one had to tip one's head in order to see the tops of the mountains) while Colin had not climbed in the Mont Blanc range before. At the time British climbers were far from numerous in the Alps, and those who did make the trip were usually University men with long holidays at their disposal. In general, British visitors gravitated towards the more traditional haunts of the Pennine Alps, and the overall level of attainment was rather modest. There were some notable exceptions, in particular the exploits of Graham Brown and Smythe on the Brenva Face of Mont Blanc, and MacPhee and Smythe's epic traverse of the Aiguille Blanche de Peuterey, but a high level of British competence in the Alps was not really the norm until the 1950s. Colin had almost certainly read about the wonders of the climbing above Chamonix and, armed with the French guide-book, they set about getting to know

1 'The Ethics of Ironmongery'

something of its mysteries. Colin covers this Alpine holiday in some detail in Chapters 12 and 13 of 'Let's Go Climbing!', and it would appear that he and Frost enjoyed a good fortnight despite a helping of the poor weather commonly found in the Western Alps.

Once established in the Chamonix valley, they commenced operations with a reasonably uneventful traverse of the Aiguille d'Argentière reaching the safety of the Argentière hut just as a dramatic storm broke. The following day they traversed the classic Forbes Arête on the Auguille de Chardonnet, experiencing some problems on the approach up the Char-donnet glacier. Some route-finding difficulties followed before they were able to savour the delights of the ridge itself, with its stupendous views towards the heart of the Mont Blanc range. They finally left the summit of the Chardonnet at 3 p.m. but in reality their adventure was only just beginning, as Colin recorded in 'Let's Go Climbing!':

> We were going down to north-west ridge, which was very much easier than our route up the mountain. There was just one difficult pitch before the col, which we had nearly reached when the storm broke upon us. A sudden gale had sprung up, it was snowing and hailing, and the lightning was flashing all around. The thunder was deafening; it ripped through the clouds and seemed as though it would burst our ear drums. It was a terrifying experience.

Gradually the threat from the lightning decreased but the high wind and heavy snowfall continued, and Frost and Colin were constantly aware of the threat from covered crevasses. It was still early in the season, a poor season at that, and conditions were most unpleasant. This, combined with the effects of the fierce storm, caused them to reach the Col Adams Reilly only by 7 p.m., with just two hours of daylight remaining. It was to be almost dark before they reached the glacier and by this time a further storm had set in.

> The danger was over, but we still had more trouble to come. There was another violent thunderstorm and a thick cloud descended on to the glacier. It was pitch dark and raining in torrents. We knew the hut was a few hundred feet up the slope on the left, but whether we had passed it or not we could not tell. We just stumbled on, in dazed exhaustion. We were quite resigned to spending the night out on the glacier. It would have been unpleasant, but not serious at this altitude. I had a torch, but I switched it on only now and again, to save the battery.
>
> We were wet to the skin, but so tired that we would have been glad to sleep anywhere. I shone the torch again – surely those were tracks in the snow!
>
> Fifteen minutes later we were in the hut. It was eleven o'clock; we had been out nineteen hours. We had half expected a search party, but the guardian was in bed. He didn't care.
>
> We spent most of the next day in bed.

Bob Frost on the Voie Normale of the Aig du Moine.   *Photo C. F. Kirkus (AC coll.)*

Altogether it had been something of an Alpine baptism of fire for Bob Frost, and the two men were glad of a few days' respite to recover. In fact the weather remained poor for the next ten days, and the only action they enjoyed was an ascent in unpleasant conditions of the Ordinary Route on the Auguille du Moine. Four days were spent at the Couvercle Hut, and by this time they were fast running out of holiday, with the return to England only a few days away. However, a walk up to Montenvers found them in rapidly improving weather, and they decided to attempt the South-West Face and Main Ridge of the Grands Charmoz. An early start enabled them to dispose of this classic AD route by 8 a.m., the beautiful weather serving as ample consolation for them not being able to climb the nearby Aiguille de Grèpon, which was heavily iced and out of condition.

> We stayed an hour on the top, eating and lazing. It was hot and sunny, and it was delightful just to lie on the rock and gaze at the scenery. The huge mass of Mont Blanc, towering high above everything else, looking dazzling against the deep blue sky. In front, the dark slender needle of the Grépon provided a striking contrast.

Despite an uneventful ascent, the day's excitement was far from over, as they decided to descend the North West ridge of the mountain direct to the Petits Charmoz, in the belief that this was a normal method of descent.[1] Colin and Frost left the summit at 9 a.m. and were soon confronted with technical and route-finding problems that almost attained epic proportions. Unaccustomed to the phenomenal exposure on this ridge and the complexity of route-finding involved, the two men were soon in trouble. Colin made no secret of their shortcomings in 'Lets Go Climbing', and it was with some relief that they retraced their steps, and regained the summit some five hours later, very tired and somewhat humbled by their experience. A rapid descent was made down the Charmoz-Grépon couloir, to the safety of the Nantillons Glacier.

> On the glacier a kindly French party gave us some tea they had made on a spirit stove. They laughed when I rushed forward so eagerly that I put my foot through a crevasse. It was delightful strolling down the lovely path. It was all so safe and friendly; we felt pleasantly tired and thoroughly happy and contented.

On arrival at Chamonix that evening they enjoyed the delights of a hot bath and a shave, before the long journey back to London, and thence Liverpool. Colin summed it up thus:

> It had been a most glorious holiday, in spite of the weather. People often find it hard to get on together through all the difficulties and discomforts of an Alpine holiday, but in Bob Frost I had found the perfect companion.

1 This route was not in fact done in ascent until 1950, by a party led by Pierre Allain. It is still regarded as long and quite difficult.

By the beginning of August Colin was back in action in North Wales, hard at work on the final push to complete the Glyder Fach guide-book. In fact the next few months were very busy ones in the Ogwen Valley, for not only was Colin exploring with Frost and MacPhee, but Menlove was working on the Tryfan guide-book together with Wilfrid Noyce, himself freshly back from a trip to the Pennine Alps. Amongst the new routes established by this strong team was *Scars Climb*, a bold route on Tryfan's Terrace Wall, which held a big reputation for many years.

Colin continued his work on the Glyder Fach area, with an investigation of the steep buttress situated under and right of Hawk's Nest Buttress, well below the Dolmen Buttress. Here, on August 11th, he and MacPhee found a splendid climb of Severe standard, some 200 feet in length, which they called *Little Buttress*. Colin described it as 'A fine steep climb, clean and strenuous and exposed. A route of character.' The climb is viewed by some Ogwen devotees as a little gem, rather like Colin's route of the previous year, *Marble Slab*. The dominant feature of the climb is a strenuous and energetic struggle with a steep crack which widens into a chimney higher up on splendid rock. Colin and MacPhee spent the remainder of the day on Glyder Fach main cliff before returning to Helyg.

Around this time Wilfrid Noyce and Menlove Edwards were camped high up in the heather of Cwm Tryfan, working on their own guide-book. In "Samson",[1] Noyce and Sutton describe an occasion when Colin visited the pair at their tent:

> One golden evening Noyce's cousin Colin Kirkus, who had just been up one of the buttresses and down another, joined them and sat smoking, in shorts, outside the tent. Menlove smoked too. "You're the only person I take a cigarette off, Colin". But the habit grew on him later. After Kirkus had left Edwards remarked that Colin had been 'very decent' to him at a time when others were stand-offish. They were an interesting contrast, Colin slim to the point of slightness, standing by a few principles in which he believed with all the strength of his modest, essentially straight-seeing character; Menlove rugged and burly, warm-hearted and lovable but also with the black well of loneliness inside him so that already the puckish laughter was growing less frequent.

Colin continued with his work on Glyder Fach, and visited the area four weekends in succession that September, establishing three further new routes. On September 6th he and P.M. Mahon ventured into the line of gulleys to the left of the *Direct Route*, to produce four pitches of damp

1 'Samson' G. Sutton/W. Noyce (published privately – 1960).

climbing. The early part of the climb is not particularly pleasant or distinguished, but it improves with height gained. A week later Colin returned with Bob Frost and George Dwyer to complete the route above a notable arch in the gully, the route's dominant feature. *Arch Gully*, as the route was named, was some 300 feet in length, and was graded Very Difficult. A route in the traditional mould, Colin had this to say of it:

> Dirty in parts but has a charm of its own. It gets mixed up with other climbs, fortuitously senior, but nevertheless follows as closely as possible the true line of the gully, which is conspicuous in its upper half, finishing to the right of the final pitch of the *Slab Climb.*

Today the route is graded Difficult, and can give excellent sport under winter conditions.

The following weekend saw another new route put up on Glyder Fach, when Colin visited the cliff with Bill and Robin Stallybrass. After graduating from Liverpool University, Bill Stallybrass had spent some time working abroad, and this was the first time he and Colin had climbed together for a number of years. Bill takes up the story:

> By the autumn of 1936, I was teaching at Hoylake and had a £60 Ford Car. Colin lived at Heswall and sometimes I used to take him down to Wales. Colin took myself and my brother up the first ascent of *Errant Route* while working on the Glyder Fach guide-book. The thing I remember was that at one point Colin went up a strip of very steep grass, brought me up and then went off in a totally different direction, hence the route name. I remember him way out somewhere, where I would take a big swing if I came off, and I had to descend some grass before I could go up to him. He called down: "The art of descending steep grass is to ascend at half the rate the grass is falling off!" (laughter) I was laughing so much, that I did it OK.

Errant Route climbs the area of cliff to the right of *Oblique Gully*, and gives a rather tortuous route of Severe standard, of which Colin wrote:

> An artificial climb which in its upper part labours, with many twists and turns, to preserve its individuality. Nevertheless it is excellent as regards its separate pitches and well worth doing by a party that has already gained some knowledge of the cliff.

In fact two of the climb's pitches, including a fine jamming crack, are highlighted in the current Ogwen guide-book. Bill Stallybrass recalled that he was back in Wales with Colin the following weekend, and commented on the diligence with which the guide-book work was undertaken:

> I did some routes with Colin measuring pitches for the guide-book. He was very, very thorough about this work. I think we did *Home Climb* and *Zig Zag* on the Gribin Facet.

Bill had this to say of Colin's climbing style:

> Colin didn't chat much as a climber but was very helpful when you were trying to do a move. He was a very neat climber – far more so than Menlove. It was a delight to watch him, his moves were thought out and fluid, he was a natural. He was about 5ft. 9 in. and no more than 10 stone in weight.

It is inevitable that comparisons were drawn between Colin and Menlove, on the basis that they, more than anyone else, defined the character of the sport in North Wales for virtually the entire 1930s. The contrasts between them were considerable and yet it is generally agreed that, although not particularly close and predominantly climbing with different groups, they remained friends for the duration of their association. As mentioned previously, Menlove maintained a very real admiration and affection for Colin, whilst Colin regarded him as the finest climber of the period. Both men hailed from Liverpool and both were born in June 1910, yet in rock-climbing terms they were not really contemporary. Colin's major exploits as a rock-climber from 1929 to 1932 pre-date the major achievements of Menlove, whose activities encompassed a much longer period. It is not the intention here to compare the two men at length, for this aspect has been adequately examined elsewhere (notably in 'Snowdon Biography'[1] and particularly in 'Menlove'), but 1936 is an interesting time to examine their respective positions in the climbing world.

At the age of twenty-six, Colin's great days as a climber were virtually behind him. To quote Alf Bridge, Colin was in the process of gradually 'climbing down' from his virtually undisputed position of pre-eminence of three years before. At that time the active life of a 'tiger' was usually regarded as only three or four years – before other factors came into play such as career considerations, marriage and family responsibilities. Colin was sufficiently conservative in character to be aware of these pressures, notwithstanding his great love of being in the mountains. Added to this was the effect of the aftermath of the Ben Nevis accident of 1934. Certainly the nature of Colin's activity throughout 1935 and 1936 does seem to confirm a more relaxed, broader approach to the mountains than was the case prior to 1934. Colin's importance in the history of the sport was established by the time he was twenty-two and, increasingly after 1934, he appeared happiest climbing at a more modest level, teaching novices to climb, and enjoying the mountains for themselves.

The position of Menlove in 1936 was very different, for he was at another

1 By G. W. Young, G. Sutton & W. Noyce: Dent 1957.

stage of his life and climbing career altogether. Then he was perhaps at the height of his physical powers, and was almost certainly the principal rock-climber in Wales, as shown by his audacious ascent of *Munich Climb*. Despite the acknowledged instability of much of Menlove's life, this does appear to have been a relatively happy and fulfilling period for him; involved as he was in professional work as a doctor, in extensive guide-book work in the mountains of North Wales and embarked on a relationship with Wilfrid Noyce that was to be a profound influence on much of the remainder of his life. Noyce's comment comparing Menlove and Colin is perhaps the most revealing snapshot of the two men at this time:

....like a turbulent current beside the clear pool of the other.

In early October Colin was again climbing with Graham MacPhee, and they attended the Fell and Rock Climbing Club dinner together. The next day they made for Gimmer Crag on a beautiful autumn day, and Colin effortlessly led MacPhee up *Gimmer Crack* and *'A' Route*. The following weekend (October 10th/11th) the pair drove down to Wales together. MacPhee recorded:

Colin came to dinner, and we then looked at photographs of the *Kaisergebirge*. Afterwards we drove to Helyg in the Riley. Made fast time after leaving Mold and the new automatic signals. Helyg has now been all electrified which makes things easier and cleaner.

The next morning saw them heading once again for the main cliff of Glyder Fach, where Colin led the first ascent of *Hawk Slab*, and what was thought to be the second ascent of Menlove's *Chasm Rib*. As the name implies, *Hawk Slab* is a short slab pitch just to the left of the clean steep edge of *Hawk's Nest Buttress* (climbed in 1940 by Nock and Harrison, to become the superb *Hawk's Nest Arête*). The slab gives a delicate little pitch, but Colin obviously did not think an awful lot of it:

90 feet. A rather pointless climb, delicate in places.

It is interesting to ponder whether Colin ever made a serious attempt on the Arête itself, for the challenge is obvious enough, and it gives a very fine 90-foot pitch.

Menlove's *Chasm Rib* had first been climbed in August 1931, when he was accompanied by his brother Hewlett, and Alan Sutcliffe-Kerr. Colin seemed to have enjoyed the climb, for he wrote in the guide-book:

115 feet. An exposed and delicate climb of fine quality on clean rock. Standard Severe.

Colin continued his work in earnest, and was back in Wales for the next two weekends. On October 18th he climbed two new routes with Bob Frost, *Main Gully Ridge* and *False Route. Main Gully Ridge* takes the crest above the *Alphabet Slab* on Glyder Fach Main Cliff. It is pleasant enough, but technically very easy. Colin obviously thought so...."Quite suitable for novices, since difficulties are avoided." *False Route* was found on the extensive, though broken, area of rock where the Gribin Ridge encloses Cwm Bochlwyd to the west. This east face of the Gribin had previously been climbed by a party including G. H. L. Mallory, R. L. G. Irving, D. Murray and H. E. G. Tyndale in January 1909, and it was in order to check this esoteric route that Colin and Frost went to this rather unlikely situation. *False Route* climbed the steeper rock to the right of the original climb and gave 160 feet of climbing, now graded Severe. Colin regarded it as "An interesting climb, though somewhat artificial, bristling with little overhangs, which provide good safe exercise."

The following weekend Colin returned with Alfred Wood, and completed the first ascent of the *Tower Rib,* on the eastern side of the Nameless Cwm, opposite the impressive cliffs of Clogwyn Du and above the Cneifion Arête. Colin dismissed it as a vague climb of no great interest, although its inclusion did serve to demonstrate once again his thorough approach to producing the guide-book. However, this constant checking of often indifferent routes and featureless areas of rock must have been gradually taking its toll. A few weeks later Colin wrote to Alf Bridge:

> I have nearly finished my Glyder Fach guide now. It has been a hard job. I have measured separately practically every one of the seventy odd climbs. Still it has been a labour of love.

In the introduction to the guide itself, Colin was even more frank:

> All kinds of things were climbed, some for their quality and others, mouldering slag-heaps, just to make the work complete. Enthusiasm gave place to weariness, then almost to despair. Like the Phoenix, from the ashes of endeavour, comes forth this guide.

The following weekend (7th/8th November) Graham MacPhee had a climbing friend from Glasgow, Arthur Murray, staying with him, and together with Colin they sped down to Helyg on the Saturday morning. In poor weather they walked over to the Idwal Slabs and did *Hope* and the *Original Route* on the Holly Tree Wall, '....in a deluge of rain and snow and sleet and a gale. We found ourselves perished with cold,' to quote MacPhee. They were certainly no fair-weather climbers and next day, in barely improved conditions, Colin had them out checking pitches on the Gribin Facet – speeding up *Slab Climb, Slab Recess, Gully and Slab* and *Zig Zag Climb.* Colin playfully claimed that the routes were suitable for the day as they were all sheltered ones. One has to admire their continued enthusiasm at this stage of the year.

Later that month Colin attended the Rucksack Club Dinner with MacPhee at Manchester, and on November 21st visited the MacPhee home in Liverpool. The occasion was the birthday of MacPhee's young daughter Hermione. Many years later in 1987, this lady remembered meeting Colin and recalled his kindness and interest in the children. Typically, Colin finished the year rather in the manner of returning to his roots – namely a solo ascent of a new climb high above Ogwen, that of the pleasant *Pinnacle Edge* in the Nameless Cwm, climbed on December 20th. This is almost certainly Colin's final new rock-route in the mountains of Snowdonia, the conclusion of nine years of exploration of very great significance in the history of climbing in the area. In some ways it is strangely appropriate to picture Colin at the close of that year, not on the windswept verticalities of Clogwyn Du'r Arddu or even the cliffs of Glyder Fach, but on this enjoyable minor route that hardly warrants a mention in the current Ogwen guide-book. Clad in old, ragged clothes and nailed boots, carrying a small rucksack and perhaps sporting a cigarette in a holder, Colin was probably in his element alone on these rocks high above the Ogwen valley. Just as he entered the sport as an eager schoolboy, so he was still able to find his own joy and self-expression in the mountains of North Wales.

Elsewhere in the climbing world, 1936 saw the British Everest expedition turned back by repeated heavy snowfall at the North Col, while in the Garhwal, Bill Tilman and Noel Odell made their magnificent ascent of Nanda Devi. In Britain the year saw the publication of Graham MacPhee's guide to Ben Nevis, A.T. Hargreave's guide to the Scafell Group, and a series of important first ascents on Tryfan by Wilfrid Noyce and Menlove Edwards.

During the mid-Thirties Colin had maintained his friendship with A. B. Hargreaves although the two men climbed together less and less. In 1931 'AB' had moved from Liverpool to Barrow-in-Furness and had by 1937 not only become heavily involved in the laundry business, but had begun to raise a family, both activities combining to seriously curtail his climbing activities. 'AB' recalled that Colin would sometimes come to stay with him and his family:

I remember that my wife was astonished at Colin's appetite for food! Although he

'AB'.   Photo Jack Longland

was not a big chap, he seemed to require an enormous amount of fuel! In 1937/38 I became even more pre-occupied with my Lakeland Laundries job, and on the back of that, I had several illnesses, including one period of nervous breakdown. Consequently through these years my contact with Colin gradually fell away. Indeed when it came to 1939 I almost had to give up climbing and was in a pretty low condition. War had begun, and I found it very difficult indeed just getting up and down the two easy terraces on Clogwyn Du'r Arddu. On that occasion Colin was very kind and understanding, helping me a lot, which of course was one of his characteristics.

That spring, the Glyder Fach guide-book at last appeared in print, the fruit of Colin's labours over the past two years. It was the first comprehensive guide to the area since Archer Thomson's 'Climbing in the Ogwen District' of 1910 (republished in 1921 with an appendix by H.E.L. Porter) and, typically, in his introduction Colin expressed thanks to those who had helped in its production:

> ....especially C.H. French for his magnificent and microscopically accurate drawings, and G. Graham MacPhee and R.C. Frost for noble work in all kinds of weather, measuring and shivering. And for his painstaking and sympathetic aid all gratitude is due to G.R. Speaker – counsellor as much as editor.

C.H.FRENCH

CLIMBS ON EAST BUTTRESS

		Standard
1	Square Chimney ..	S
2	Square Chimney But-tress	S
3	Oblique Buttress ..	S
4	Oblique Gully ..	VD
5	Errant Route ..	S
6	Arch Gully (Start)..	VD
7	Slab Route	VD
7A	Slab Route (Spiral Variant)	D
8	Arch Chimney ..	S
9	Direct Route ..	S
9A	Direct Route (Rec-tangular Excursion)	S
9B	Direct Route (Winter Finish)	S
9C	Direct Route (Final Flake)	VS
10	Lot's Wife (Approxi-mate Start) ..	VS
11	Lot's Groove (Ap-proximate Start) ..	VS
12	Chasm Route ..	VD
13	Chasm Rib	S
14	Chasm Chimney ..	D
15	Main Gully	E

ROUGH SCALE
250 feet

MAIN CLIFF OF GLYDER FACH

FEATURES

A–B Alphabet Slab
C   Capstan
L   Lunching Stone
SP   Shark Pinnacle
T–T The Terrace
W–X East Buttress
X–Y Central Mass
Y–Z Gable Buttress

MAIN CLIFF OF GLYDER FACH

CLIMBS ON CENTRAL MASS

		Standard
16	Main Gully Ridge ..	D
17	Alpha	S
18	Beta	D
19	Gamma	S
20	Delta..	VD
21	Arête of East Gully	D
22	East Gully	S

CLIMBS ON GABLE BUTTRESS

		Standard
23	Hawk Slab	VD
24	Hawk's Nest Buttress	S
25	Needle's Eye Climb	VD
26	Groove Route ..	D
27	Little Buttress ..	S
28	Dolmen Buttress (Route II) ..	D
29	Dolmen Buttress (Route I)	M
30	West Gully	E
31	West Buttress (Approximate Route)	M

C. H. French's drawings reproduced courtesy of the Climbers' Club.

The 1930s had proved to be an important period for guide-book production to various areas in the British mountains, and 1936 had seen the publication of three particularly significant ones; Graham MacPhee had completed the huge task of writing up the summer and winter routes on Ben Nevis, Menlove Edwards had written his classic work on Cwm Idwal, and A.T. Hargreaves' guide to the Scafell Group had also appeared. This latter work was the second of a new series of guides to the Lake District to be produced by the Fell and Rock Climbing Club (in parallel with the Climbers' Club's new series for North Wales) the first having been that to the Pillar Rock area by Harry Kelly, published in 1935.

To some extent it is difficult to compare the approaches adopted in these various guide-books, because of the very different areas involved and the characters of the respective authors. In particular, Graham MacPhee's Ben Nevis guide, containing both rock-climbs and snow and ice-climbs, was a monumental work, while Menlove Edwards in his brilliant guide to Cwm Idwal had adopted a singularly individual approach. This work of Menlove's is still greatly admired for bringing the area to life on the page, though it was an achievement that he was not quite able to equal in later work on Tryfan (1937) and Lliwedd (1939). His approach was to remain an inspiration to many guide-book writers right up to the present day. Here is Menlove introducing the delights of Clogwyn Y Geifr (Devil's Kitchen Cliffs):

> Holds are usually present in plenty, but almost all are the surface detail of weathering, and a good deep split is rare. Grass caps tenant most of the pocket holes, and the surface is usually smooth and slippery as well as moist. At the same time the main climbing thoroughfares are by now so excellently groomed as to be almost clean. Most climbs here get steadily safer and easier. Nails are usual, and otherwise stockings are better than rubbers on this damp cliff.

In sharp contrast to Menlove's approach was that adopted for the Fell and Rock Climbing Club series under the Editorship of Harry Kelly. Kelly's primary objective seemed to be a simplicity of style, resulting in a terseness perhaps more in common with some of the clinical guides of the Sixties (e.g. the 1963 guide to Clogwyn Du'r Arddu) than with the more flowery style of most pre-war guide-book work. One of the best summaries of the respective styles at this time came from H.E. Kretschmer in his chapter in 'The Mountains of Snowdonia'[1]:

> Colin Kirkus wrote the guide to Glyder Fach, and the contrast between this and the Edwards guide-books throws interesting light on the characters of their authors. In Kirkus's Glyder Fach guide, which is perhaps the best liked and most

1 'The Mountains of Snowdonia' by Herbert Carr and George Lister (Crosby Lockwood and Son Limited)

useful guide-book for the average climber, we have the same system which Kelly used in Lakeland guides, broadened and humanized perhaps, but essentially a type of description based on a system. This system was described by Edwards as the "tiny narrow spotlight moving in single line.....The rocks might be any rocks and the conformation of the cliff and climb might be any conformation, might be any climb in mid-air from which the spotlight sheds no rays aside......"Kelly's main objective in his Lakeland guide was to describe the climbs with the greatest possible clarity in the fewest possible words, assuming that the climber was not interested in literary style. He wanted a system which would be consistent, easy of reference and giving no scope to the fallible imagination of the compiler. He accepted the fact that such a system must be based on purely artificial conventions and left the particular qualities of a route and its wider perspective to discover themselves to parties as they climbed.

In Edwards' guide we have nothing of this system, the basic principle being summed up in a single sentence in the introduction to his Cwm Idwal – "It is hoped that the climber might get a good idea of things before seeing the cliff". This apparently simple and common sense intention in fact meant a sharp break with the system because it introduced into guide writing the fact of the guide writer himself.

Obviously, and to a large extent, the tone of Colin's guide-book is set by the nature and character of the area it covers – that of a traditional climbing ground. In fairness, the cliffs covered in the volume are not ones usually associated with the cutting edge of the sport even in the pre-war period, and with one or two notable exceptions (i.e. *Lot's Groove* and *Final Flake*), the climbs found here were not of the top order of difficulty. What was so important about this area, and what was affectionately recorded within the guide-book, was its role as a delightful climbing playground for the main body of climbers, rather than for the rubber-shod expert. In this way it clearly brings into focus Wales in the late Thirties in much the same way as Don Roscoe's 'Llanberis North' (1961) and Jimmy Marshal's masterful 'Ben Nevis' (1969) clearly define their respective periods and locations; the arrival of hard rock-climbing for everyone on the one hand, and Scotland's showpiece at the end of the traditional era before the ice-climbing revolution, on the other. In effect what Colin achieved with 'Glyder Fach' was to produce a delightful insight into Welsh climbing, celebrating a playful and mosty still innocent era, and the guide-book remains a good companion for a day on the rocks of the area.

Colin's humour and love of the area, which were to be displayed still further in 'Let's Go Climbing!', still shine from those pages of over fifty years ago. This is part of the introduction to the section covering the Facet of the Gribin:

The rock is excellent, clean and rough, and the climbing most unusual. The climber who wants to get the maximum amount of exercise into the shortest possible space of time should be well satisfied here. It must not be thought that technical difficulty and artistry of movement are lacking, however; some of the pitches are pretty problems, quite apart from the physical effort. But the keynote is exertion – safe usually, but exhausting. It will not be found, however, that excessive use has to be made of the arms; most of the muscles of the body are exercised fairly impartially.

Colin's feeling for the area is particularly well conveyed in this vivid description of the main cliff of Glyder Fach, the centre-piece of the guidebook:

Seen from the shores of Llyn Bochlwyd the cliff itself appears wholly insignificant; its 300 feet are completely dwarfed by the 1,400 feet of mountain-side of which it forms a part. Perhaps it is on this account that it has only just begun to enjoy the popularity it deserves. When the crag is actually reached, however, it is found to be of a quite unexpected magnificence, which absolutely belies the distant impression. One is struck by the clean vertical lines of the rock architecture. The first impression is of a noble line of pillars, sheer and lofty, square-cut and simple. In sunshine the rock is of an almost luminous silver, grey, bright and challenging. From the foot an immense impression of height is gained, a picture of fortress-like walls, receding in perspective – not austere, but sheer and lovely, rough-grained shining grey against the blue of the summer sky. Everything looks so attractive, so grand and warm, that the fingers feel an almost irresistible desire for the friendly touch of the rock.

Colin's balanced approach to the older climbs is displayed to good effect in his introduction to the great 1907 classic of Ward and Gibson, *Direct Route on Glyder Fach Main Cliff* – a route he must have known well from regular visits to the crag:

270 feet. Probably the best climb of its kind in Wales. It is a route of continuous interest on perfect rock, and seems much longer than is actually the case. It belongs to the old type of climbing, but has a satisfying degree of steepness; very quickly a sense of exposure is attained. If the Winter Finish be taken, only the Hand Traverse can be called Severe. The usual route by the Rectangular Excursion and the final crack is a splendid climb, honest and strenuous and thoroughly satisfying. The ascent of Gibson's Chimney is more spectacular and of much greater technical difficulty, whilst the Final Flake will probably satisfy the most advanced ambitions.

The description of Menlove's ferocious pitch the Final Flake, mentioned earlier, demonstrates Colin's responsible approach in dealing with the area's hard, and at that time dangerous, test-pieces. This is reflected also in the reasonable nature of the description of *Lot's Groove*, which still retained much of its aura some eight years after Colin's first ascent.

FINAL FLAKE
A layback of extreme severity, demanding both strength and skill in a high degree. For this reason a prior inspection on the rope is advisable before leading. The rock is perfect.....The main method of ascent is laybacking which becomes extremely exhausting towards the top, though a little relief can be obtained in places by wedging. The last few feet yield more easily with holds on the right.

LOT'S GROOVE
110 feet. A climb of great severity, including one of the most difficult pitches in Wales. A preliminary inspection on the rope is probably advisable. Skill and confidence are necessary and strong fingers are an asset. The groove is vertical and is both strenuous and delicate. Standard: Very Severe (exceptionally so). Rubbers.

In conclusion, perhaps the strongest quality of the guide-book is to consistently convey such a heady image of the delights of the place, as to make an invitation to climb impossible to ignore. This is demonstrated beautifully in the introduction to Sub Cneifion Rib:

The climb, besides being long, is entertaining and thoroughly attractive in character and finishes grandly with a clean and airy nose. The rock throughout is very sound and rough. This is an ideal climb for short sunny evenings.

Who, camped by Llyn Idwal or staying at the Hostel, could resist such an invitation to the delights of good rock in a wonderful setting! What a wealth of enjoyment the guide-book must have given, particularly in the early post-war years, when the numbers of people climbing in North Wales rapidly increased. Even now it is possible to spend a mid-week afternoon on Glyder Fach Main Cliff and have the crag to yourself, away from the crowds on Tryfan or at Idwal, and be unable to hear or see the traffic along the A5. Climbing there with a friend, I felt something of the atmosphere of the place and tried to imagine it fifty years ago. In truth the rock is luminous, silver-grey, bright and challenging, and irresistible to cragsmen of any period. Much of the Main Cliff seems quiet these days, although *Direct Route* and *Hawk's Nest Arête* remain popular. Grass even grows again in parts of *Lot's Groove*, yet the Gribin Facet and Bochlywd Buttress remain popular playgrounds, located in the hub of truly traditional Welsh climbing along with Tryfan's East Face and the delights of Idwal's slabs and walls. Long may it remain so, and long may climbers find that same delight – so evident in his classic guide-book – in the area that Colin and his companions clearly did.

Released from the demands of guide-book work, Colin resumed climbing for pleasure, most often in the company of Graham MacPhee or Bob Frost and members of the Idwal Group. After the usual springtime exertions at Helsby, Colin returned periodically to the mountains of Snowdonia. A typical visit took place in early June with Graham MacPhee, when the two friends travelled down one Saturday afternoon. The Sunday dawned reasonably bright, and they ventured out on to the Carneddau to the north of the Ogwen Valley, climbing *Western Gully* on the Black Ladders before traversing the tops in mist back to their base at Helyg. It is interesting to picture that particular area in the pre-war period. The Black Ladders (Ysgolion Duon) at the head of Cwm Llafar are quiet enough in summer nowadays, being predominantly a winter playground. It must have been a lovely deserted spot at that time, for there had been little development either on the Black Ladders themselves or on the nearby Llech Ddu, itself very much a 'modern' crag. *Western Gully*, now graded Severe, must have been quite a handful at that time. Regarded as one of the best gully routes in Wales, it rapidly becomes much harder and increasingly more serious in less than perfect conditions and must have made for an exciting first ascent in 1901! The whole of the Carneddau had a distinct air of seclusion and mystery in those days with only Craig yr Ysfa receiving much traffic and, certain recent abuses aside, these wonderful hills retain much of that atmosphere to this day. After a meal together, MacPhee returned to Liverpool, while Colin settled into Helyg for the next week. MacPhee returned for him the following Sunday, having spent the weekend with his family, again enjoying a summer holiday at Borth y Gest.

With little or no exploring for new routes by this stage of his life (summer 1937), Colin seemed content to enjoy climbing with various friends irrespective of the difficulty or status of the climbs done. Someone who remembers climbing with Colin around this time is Tony Giffard, then the Viscount Tiverton and a member of the Climbers' Club, now The Earl of Halsbury:

> Colin wasn't an intellectual like Menlove; just a very nice friend and companion, and a beautiful mover on rock. Climbs I did with him included the *Terrace Wall Variant* on Tryfan's North Buttress, *Alpha, Beta* and *Gamma* on Glyder Fach. the *Vertical Vice*, the *Holly Tree Wall* and the Devil's Kitchen. I remember an anxious moment (for me) at the slab by the Bollards on the *Terrace Wall Variant.* The slab is sloping upwards and downwards to the right and is approached from the left below. Your right foot has to be at a very awkward angle with a big drop below. "Move quickly and stand up immediately" instructed Colin. With my heart in my mouth I obeyed orders and all was well.

We had an awkward moment in the Devil's Kitchen. Colin was standing on one knob and I immediately below on another with my face level with Colin's heels. I was belayed to something level with Colin's head and his own belay was above mine on the same knob. The immediate manoeuvre was for Colin to remove his belay and move off to the right on to a shelf-traverse which ended the climb. My move was to get to the stance Colin had vacated, cast off my belay and follow him along the shelf.

In the preliminary run up to these manoeuvres Colin, most unusually for him, got our ropes into a tangle and I spent what seemed hours standing on that knob on one boot while he rearranged the ropes. I was beginning to get a bit wobbly by the time he was able to move off, but all was well in the end!

I wasn't of course anywhere near to being in Colin's class as a climber and it was characteristically kind of him to take me along with him "duo". I enjoyed climbing with him enormously.

Someone who had got to know Colin well at this time was his cousin Wilfrid Noyce who, writing in 1947, mentions Colin's gradual move away from hard climbing to a more general approach:

He became interested in what he was also supremely good at – the instruction of others. That helpful side of him, too, was more attractive than the restlessness which hustled him straight to Everest, the highest peak. If he had lived to approach the Himalaya again, the approach might have been by the greater enjoyment of the lower peaks. He had always found happiness in activity among the hills. He could now also enjoy being, without necessarily moving at top speed the whole time in their company.

Towards the end of the 1930s Colin visited Skye on at least one occasion and was clearly captivated by the 'Isle of Mists' judging by comments in 'Let's Go Climbing'. No doubt Colin's brother Guy had told him of the delights of the place after his own eventful visit to the island in the early Thirties, with a friend and an ancient motor-cycle – a journey of remote locations, unmade roads and beautiful scenery, among perhaps Britain's finest mountains. In his classic book 'The Cuillin of Sky'* Ben Humble recounts a visit by Colin:

Colin Kirkus, that supreme leader, whose feats in Snowdonia had astonished even the experts, was one of the campers of this period. As happened with many another "tiger", he was tamed by the magnificence of the Cuillin and the glory of the ridges. Alf Bridge, his companion, relates how they were so supremely happy that they did not even think of new routes, and quotes a remark of Colin's on the summit of Sgurr Alasdair:

"You know, Alf, going to the right place, at the right time, with the right people is all that really matters. What one does is purely incidental."

* 'The Cuillin of Skye' Ben Humble (Republished by The Ernest Press – 1986)

This particular quote by Colin, is also to be found on the title page of the 1982 Scottish Mountaineering Club guidebook to Rock and Ice climbs on Skye by J.R. Mackenzie – a rare and delightful honour for a mere Sassenach! As an aside, fellow members of the Wayfarers' Club, J.K. Cooke, F.B. Dutton-Walker and F. McGavin became the second party to complete the Greater Traverse of the Cuillin Ridge plus Blà Bheinn and Clach Glas (i.e. all the Skye Munros), in a single day in 1939. Their time of 23 hours was subsequently shortened when, in 1944, Menlove completed the same round in 12½ hours, returning to his starting point in twenty-four hours. This was regarded at the time as a quite remarkable performance. In these days of rapid, reliable transport and up-to-date guide-books, it is important to remember the esteem and air of mystery that Skye held amongst climbers of the 1930s, by virtue of its remoteness and the magnificence of its mountains. Colin's friend Bill Stallybrass summed it up perhaps best:

> In the period before widespread travel to the Alps, Skye was an absolute Mecca to our generation.

Late that summer there occurred a serious climbing accident on the East Buttress of Scafell, that had *connections* with Colin. On September 21st, Menlove Edwards and Colin's cousin Wilfrid Noyce, who were on holiday in the Lake District, took advantage of the first dry day for some time and walked up to Sty Head, *en-route* for Scafell and its impressive crags. Although the East Buttress was rather wet in places they elected to try *Mickledore Grooves*, Colin's classic route of 1930 which had paved the way for exploration on this most imposing area of rock. On the long (140-foot) slab pitch near the top, Noyce was leading in damp conditions, when a turf ledge on which he was standing, peeled off the rock. This caused the young leader to fall past Edwards, some 90 feet below, hitting several ledges before coming to rest just a few feet above the scree. There were no running belays to absorb any of the impact, Noyce had fallen 180 feet and two of the rope's three strands had snapped. That Menlove managed to arrest the fall at all was a near miracle, and it is a wonder that both men were not fatally injured. Menlove succeeded in getting the unconscious Noyce to the ground, and a rescue party rushed him to Whitehaven Hospital, where an emergency operation was carried out on his serious head injuries. After three days Noyce regained consciousness and gradually recovered, although this was to be the first of a number of climbing accidents he suffered, and ultimately he was to lose his life in the mountains.

Bill Stallybrass recalled a day climbing with Colin in early October, when they drove down from Liverpool to Helyg.

We had a marvellous day on Lliwedd, climbing *Mallory's Slab* and *Great Chimney*. We walked down to the Pen-y-Pass Hotel in lovely late afternoon sunshine. In those days there was no drinking alcohol on a Sunday, and the form was to arrive looking very thirsty because the lady there, Miss Williams, had a soft spot for climbers! She would look very shocked if you asked for a drink, and would say "Good heavens, it's Sunday!" After a while however, she would disappear and then come back and say "I think the policeman is down the road now, I'll get you both a pint!" This particular evening was so lovely that Colin suggested we round the day off with the *Nose Direct* on Dinas Mot, so we trotted off down the Pass and did the climb – a marvellous rounding off of the day. I had previously done the climb with Menlove, when he had had a little trouble with it. I can't remember any particular details of this ascent with Colin, just the sheer glory of enjoying it together on a perfect evening.

Sadly that autumn also brought great unhappiness for Colin, with the sudden death of his friend and fellow Wayfarer Bob Frost. There was little doubt that by 1937, Frost had matured into a considerable talent and at the age of twenty-five was approaching his mental and physical peak, with numerous mountaineering ambitions still to fulfil. Tragically it was not to be; on October 14th Frost set off with Geoffrey Furness on the latter's motor-cycle to visit the Blackpool Illuminations. Just outside Rufford they were involved in an accident, and both men were killed.

Bob Frost's death removed a great talent from the pre-war scene in Wales, and although not widely remembered today, he was much admired and liked by his contemporaries. One wonders what he and Colin might have achieved together over the next couple of years. Two obituaries of Bob Frost appeared in the Wayfarers' Club Journal, one written by Colin, the other by John Watson. Colin had this to say of his friend:

As a rock-climber he was in the first flight – far better than he himself realised. Imbued with a terrific underlying enthusiasm which showed but rarely on the surface, he had yet restrained himself to build up his skill slowly and methodically, never entering upon a new grade of difficulty until he had made himself master of its predecessor. The final product was a master craftsman in the art, qualified to compete in safety with any problem. Few climbers have combined brilliance with security in such a degree.

As a personality Bob Frost was less well known. Quiet and unassuming to the point of shyness, he had the rare attribute of silent companionship. The bonds of friendship that were felt had no need to be spoken. Perhaps his outstanding characteristic was that of dependability. He could always be relied upon in any emergency and remained unperturbed during periods of danger or long-sustained nervous tension.

One, at least, of Bob's ambitions was realised in a visit to Chamonix in 1936, when in a season of bad weather he showed an aptitude for Alpine climbing unusual in a first visit, besides being the ideal climbing companion.

Nobody had a hard word to say about Bob Frost – he had no enemies. This undoubted fact speaks more eloquently than any words.

In his comments about Frost, John Watson referred to his friend's renowned ability as a rock-climber:

One remembers overhearing the remark passed on by an onlooker, as he watched, that "he made it look so easy!" And truly, with his beautifully neat style and his perfect safety and composure on the most difficult problems, he did make it look easy, and therein stamped himself as a supreme artist.

The passing of Bob Frost was keenly felt by the regulars at the Idwal Hostel where he had been a key figure, and as John Watson recorded the original 'scene' there soon faded; the faces changed and the happy trips to the deserted beaches at Benllech Bay when not climbing, became less frequent.

In John's words:

Bob Frost was dead, and Colin did not seem to wish to undertake serious climbing with anyone else. I had married, and others had dispersed for various reasons. The hostel was still busy, and Connie was still in charge but somehow it was not the same place. Visits to Idwal became much less frequent for me between late 1937 and the outbreak of the war. The hostel continued to function until 1940, when it became used as a residence for child evacuees. By this time Connie had left, and married Richard Glyn (Taff) Williams, a climber from Bangor.

In late October Colin spent a weekend in the Robertson Lamb Hut in Langdale with Graham MacPhee, and Piero Ghiglione, an Italian mountaineer and friend of MacPhee. The Saturday was, to quote MacPhee, 'a pouring wet, horrid day', but nonetheless he and Colin walked up The Band and climbed *Bowfell Buttress* on a cold, wet and windy afternoon. Their Italian companion declined to climb in view of the weather! The next day the weather was better, and it turned into a lovely, sunny day. Together the three men enjoyed two routes on Oake Howe Needle, before returning to Liverpool.

As the year drew to a close Colin attended a couple of social events with MacPhee. On November 18th they attended the Rucksack Club Dinner at the Athenaeum, and MacPhee recorded:

I had a party of six; Richards, Noel Kirkman, Porter and Kirkus included. Pigott gave a lecture afterwards on rock-climbing which was good. Solly proposed a vote of thanks and Kirkus and I seconded it.

A month later MacPhee presided as Honorary President at a lecture given by Colin to the Liverpool University Mountaineering Club, on his Himalayan adventures of 1933.

Elsewhere 1937 was significant for the emergence on gritstone and on the rock of North Wales of a formidable new talent, in Arthur Birtwistle of the Manchester University Mountaineering Club. A series of exciting first ascents in the Peak District, notably in the Chew Valley area and on Laddow, culminated in the superb first ascent of the *Drainpipe Crack* on the East Buttress of Clogwyn Du'r Arddu. Birtwistle thought that the crack had already been climbed by Colin as a variation to *Curving Crack*, but of course this was not the case. As described earlier (see p.103) Colin had attempted to solo the crack in 1932, and had to be rescued by Alf Bridge. Birtwistle produced one of the most difficult and committing pitches in Wales at that time, and it remained unrepeated until Joe Brown's ascent in 1949 when attempting to climb what was later to become *Vember*. The year was also notable for another new route on the East Buttress, *Sunset Crack*, climbed in June by David Cox accompanied by Robin Hodgkin and the Mallory sisters, Clare and Beridge. A most significant event occurred in the Lake District that year with the opening of the first hut owned by the Fell & Rock Climbing Club, Brackenclose at Wasdale Head.

In the Alps that year two very significant climbs were made in the Bregaglia over the same period, 14th-16th July. While Cassin, Esposito, Ratti, Molteni and Valsecchi made their epic ascent of the North-East Face of the Piz Badile (the latter two men dying during the descent), across the Cengalo Glacier and almost within shouting range, Lehmann and Gaise climbed the superb North-West Buttress of the Piz Cengalo. A week later saw the first ascent of the North-East Spur of Les Droites at Chamonix by Authenac and Tournier. These three climbs were destined to become great post-war classics, much sought after by British Alpinists.

8 New Directions

New Year's Day in 1938 saw Colin in North Wales, enjoying cold winter conditions on the mountains of Snowdonia. It was here that an incident occurred which he later recorded in 'Let's Go Climbing!', in order to demonstrate the need for caution on snow and ice.

There was very little snow about; from below it had not looked as though we should need our axes. When we got above Glaslyn, however, we found the middle Trinity Gully quite well-filled with good hard snow, and had a pleasant bout of step-cutting.

We descended by the zigzags down to Glaslyn, an ordinary tourist route in summer. Now, it was impossible to descend without crossing a certain amount of hard snow. A little way down was a large and rather worried party, judging by all the shouting that was going on. They had come up equipped for a pleasant stroll and had got into trouble.

They had all descended separate tongues of frozen stones until they found themselves cut off by hard snow. So there they all were, each one marooned on his own little island of stones. They could move comfortably enough on the scree, but could not keep their footing on the hard snow.

One of them, bolder than the rest, made an effort to descend the snow. He succeeded. His feet shot from under him and he slid down with increasing velocity on his back. His feet caught on a rock and he was jerked upright and by a great effort managed to prevent himself from falling forward on to his face. He fell back again on another patch of snow and once more succeeded in regaining a standing position. There he was, running down the scree quite out of control, going faster and faster and having to take longer and longer strides to keep himself from pitching on to his face. Somehow he kept his balance and at last managed to stop.

Naturally the rest of the party did not feel very much encouraged by this performance. So we hurried to their aid and spent a hot half-hour cutting bucket-like steps for them. We were in no hurry and found the whole thing rather amusing. Now apart from the risk, you don't want to make a fool of yourself in this way. Therefore, when there is snow about, never venture on the mountains without an ice-axe.

Sound advice from Colin that holds good to this day, and yet, amazingly, often goes unheeded.

Bill Stallybrass recounted an amusing incident that occurred on the hill with Colin a few weeks later. Again they were in North Wales, with the mountains covered in a thick fall of snow. Bill takes up the story:

The Devil's Chimney.   *Photo C. F. Kirkus (AC coll.)*

Colin and I climbed *Parsley Fern Gully* in Cwm Glas in fine winter conditions, with a lot of snow about. We descended by way of the P-y-G track, and as we set off down, Colin recalled a previous visit when he had seen a party of very ill-equipped hikers fall one after another on the ice down the infamous zigzags. He thought that he had better go down and help them. He started to descend by glissading down, but was himself soon out of control and was tobogganing down on his stomach (laughter) only to finish up a few yards from the party he was supposed to be helping. He slowly picked himself up, dusted the snow off his clothes, and said to the hikers "you seem to have had a rather nasty fall!"

Bill recalled that Colin found this humbling experience a highly amusing example of how one should never take conditions for granted. Bill continued:

After Colin had told me this story, we started off down the same slope at the zigzags. I was soon off and out of control, and in trying to brake too soon had my ice-axe wrenched from my grasp. Fortunately a few yards lower the snow softened and I came to a halt. Colin was watching all this with great interest, and finally said:

"Ah, now I see it's safe to glissade!"

The following day we were climbing with a Doctor Russell, who I believe was killed on Ben Nevis in 1939. We did a gully to the right of the Crib Goch ridge, and then went over Crib Goch and glissaded down to the P-y-G track, and did the Left Hand Trinity Gully which Colin led us up, through a particularly good cornice. The following weekend we were in Wales again but the weather was so poor that we did nothing at all – almost unheard of with Colin!

Some weeks later, in late February, Colin and Bill were back in North Wales, staying at Helyg. The weather was once again dreadful, but they did manage an ascent of the *Ordinary Route* in the Devil's Kitchen before returning soaked to the hut. In early April they returned to Helyg, this time in the company of Graham MacPhee. The three friends tramped up to Craig yr Ysfa, where Colin led them up *Great Gully* in what might be termed 'traditional' conditions. Bill recalls:

Conditions were very wet and slimy, and there was an enormous party in front which kept knocking rocks down on to us. MacPhee was a good friend of Colin's, and a man with a marvellous sense of humour, capable of devastatingly dry comments! I liked him immensely, and my own contact with him was really through him being on the staff at Liverpool University as a lecturer, and having been the president of our rock-climbing club.

It is obvious from these fond recollections that Colin clearly still enjoyed climbing for pleasure, and that visits to North Wales in particular were still a regular feature of his life. His most regular partner, Graham MacPhee, was himself climbing less frequently due to increasing professional and family commitments (Graham was of course some twelve years older than Colin), and, following the tragic death of Bob Frost the previous autumn, Colin was climbing perhaps less frequently than at any time since he had left school in the summer of 1927. It was felt by some of Colin's friends, notably Alf Bridge, that he had in fact made a conscious decision to 'climb down' and restrict his activities to more modest objectives. Around this time Colin acquired an interest in Hafod Owen, an isolated cottage near Nantgwynant, south of Snowdon. In 'Menlove', Jim Perrin describes the cottage thus:

> Hafod Owen nestles into a thicket of rhododendron on top of the hillside above Llyn Dinas. The nearest road is half a mile away and the village of Beddgelert three miles distant. From the knoll above the house you look straight up the winding valley of Cwm y Llan to Snowdon, dome-like at its head. The cottage is whitewashed and small, out of sight from most angles until you are almost upon it. Its lop-sided arrangements of three windows at the front faces to the south-east. Huge boulders give foundations to the whitewashed walls; the roof slates are as irregular as if wind-rippled, and the tumbledown dry stone walling round about is mottled with pale green and grey lichens. There are few more lovely places in the whole of Wales.

Little remains known about Colin's motives for acquiring the cottage, other than his brother Guy's view that it was out of a desire for a little more privacy and seclusion when visiting Snowdonia. Access to the cottage cannot have been easy for Colin, as it was located some distance from the mainstream climbing areas around Ogwen and he did not own a motor car. Hafod Owen became better known after Colin rented it to Menlove Edwards during the early war years. The time Menlove spent at this beautiful but lonely place is well covered in Jim Perrin's biography.

In July Colin was staying at Helyg, when Graham MacPhee was visiting his family, again on holiday at Borth y Gest. On the Saturday MacPhee and Colin had walked up Snowdon together while the family travelled up on the train! The following day the weather was poor, and they all went to the beach, as MacPhee recorded:

> Colin was a great help playing with the children. We went to Black Rock Sands and Colin filled three bags with sand to take home for the girls' sandpit.

Although they were then not often climbing together, Colin continued to be a frequent visitor to the MacPhee home in Liverpool.

In early August, Colin set off from Liverpool for his annual holiday and this year he visited a new area – the granite sea-cliffs of Cornwall. He travelled down to the south-west with Bill and Peter Fallows, two climbers of average ability who were fellow members of the Wayfarers' Club. Bill

Fallows was also a friend of Bill Stallybrass, the two men having been contemporaries at Shrewsbury School. The journey down to Cornwall must have been a lengthy one, for in those days, long before the advent of today's motorway network, West Penwith was a remote place. This particular trip was almost certainly prompted by the recent leasing of the Count House at Bosigran to the Climbers' Club. Colin was one of the first club members to use this excellent new base on his only visit to the climbing grounds of Cornwall, but it seems to have been an enjoyable holiday and Cornish granite was to be mentioned kindly in 'Let's Go Climbing!'

Rock-climbing on the Cornish cliffs was already well-established by the late 1930s but in general the area had seen few climbers during the depression years. The opening of the Count House, leased to the Climbers' Club by the nephew of A. W. Andrews, was a considerable step in developing interest in the climbing offered by this delightful area. The first tentative exploration of the climbing potential on the granite coast came in the latter part of the nineteenth century, predominantly from A. W. Andrews, the father of British sea-cliff climbing, whose uncle owned Eagle's Nest, the prominent house above the village of Zennor. The 1890s saw visits by climbers such as Sir Bertrand Jerram, Donald G. Romanis and E. F. Bradby, but little is known of their exploits. It was Andrews who really got Cornish climbing established in the 1900s, and in 1912 the area was visited by Geoffrey Winthrop-Young and George Mallory, who climbed the ridge at Carn Lês Boel. Another notable explorer at that time was Professor J. Littlewood who added a number of routes at Chair Ladder. During the 1930s, A. W. Andrews wrote about the area in the Climbers' Club Journal and the article was accompanied by photographs showing the unique character of Cornish climbing. Interest was thus stimulated in acquiring the Count House for the use of the club. This building itself has an interesting history; reputedly haunted, it formed the inspiration for part of D. H. Lawrence's novel 'Kangaroo.' Lawrence and his German-born wife Frieda moved to Zennor in 1916, but aroused much local suspicion in those war years and were forced to leave Cornwall a year later.

In the course of his visit to the Count House, Colin produced five new climbs in a variety of locations. None of them was particularly difficult, but served to reflect the holiday atmosphere of the area. It must have been a delightful time to visit the Cornish cliffs, the locality being remote and totally unspoilt with hardly any other climbers to be seen. It is pleasant to imagine Colin and his companions lean and tanned, climbing in shorts on sun-baked granite; although no doubt the Atlantic threw wind and rain at them at some point in the holiday.

The first place they visited was the main cliff at Bosigran, itself not yet widely explored. *Bosigran Ridge* had been climbed in 1902, and *Alison Rib* and *Ledge Climb* were added in the 1920s, but there was little else. Together with Peter Fallows, Colin passed beneath the great walls that were to thrill later generations: they made their way to what is now called the Seaward Cliff. Here they discovered a superb 80-foot slab of rough rock set in an exciting situation above a convenient platform, with the sea pounding in beneath. The slab itself gave a delightful and quite straightforward pitch to good belays beneath the roofs above. An escape was made to the left up the easy finish to *Shallow Chimney*. *Black Slab*, as the climb became known, is now regarded as a miniature classic and a gem of a beginners' climb in a wild and impressive situation. The slab is covered in superb holds, giving a lovely set of moves up to perfect anchors at the top. No doubt Colin's eye was also drawn to the impressive sweep of slabs to the left, but those were not to be climbed for some eighteen years until the arrival of Pete Biven and Trevor Peck, who called the route *Ochre Slab*. No visit to Bosigran is complete without a wander up the Black Slab, for it is appropriate that Colin's legacy to this lovely place should be this superb little climb, available to virtually any climber and a classic of its grade.

Four days later, on August 7th, Colin added two more new routes; at Chair Ladder and Hella Point respectively. The morning was spent repeating some of the existing routes at Chair Ladder, before Colin led the Fallows brothers up a line on the South-east Buttress, immediately left of *Ash Can Gully*. The only previous route on this buttress was *Dexter Crack*, climbed the previous year by L.S. Powell. Colin's route started on the platform above sea-level on the west side of the gully, and climbed the exposed wall above on good holds. They called the climb *Original Route* and it is now graded Very Difficult. Later in the day, Peter Fallows accompanied Colin to Hella Point, some way east of Chair Ladder, where they took a look at Porthgwarra Buttress, the base of which was easily reached by means of a convenient gully. They climbed the face of the cliff to the left of the prominent arête that dominates the crag, and called it *Porthgwarra Face*. It gave a pleasant 100-foot route, now graded Very Difficult. They returned to the crag two days later and climbed the prominent crack to the right of the arête. This they called *Porthgwarra Crack*, a 115-foot Difficult. The buttress now has eight routes.

Amongst Colin's other activities on this holiday were a scramble over to Porthmoina Island, an ascent of *Bosigran Ridge* and repeats of most of the routes already established in the area. A number of Professor J. Littlewood's

routes that Colin repeated were thought initially to be first ascents, as the recording of climbs at the time was notoriously casual. Together with Peter Fallows, he also climbed one of the 40-foot chimneys at the Horse's Back at Zennor. However, perhaps Colin's best-remembered exploit in Cornwall was a solo exploration of the central part of the Main Cliff at Bosigran. Colin climbed up the rake that is now taken by the route *Nameless*, and reached a high point just below that route's final pitch. This was a notable effort, as *Nameless* was not to be climbed until 1953 (by Dennis Kemp and Nea Morin), but it was perhaps as well that Colin retreated. The top pitch of *Nameless* acquired something of a rogue reputation over the years, due to its tricky moves at the top of the Very Severe grade, on unpleasantly gritty rock. Colin's high spot, now the belay at the foot of this pitch, was to be the scene of a bad accident in 1972 when two Cambridge University climbers were killed on the route after a belay failure. Colin must have been impressed by what he saw of the central part of the cliff, and it is perhaps surprising that he did not return after this most enterprising solo excursion, showing once again his eye for a good line up impressively steep rock. For one brief afternoon it was almost a return to his halcyon days of the early Thirties. The completion of the climb would have resulted in the most significant route in Cornwall until well after the war.

1938 proved to be a most notable year in the evolution of the sport, giving in hindsight clear indications of future achievements on a wave of activity delayed for only a few years by a World War. During the summer best remembered for the increasingly grave political situation in Europe and the infamous meeting of Chamberlain and Hitler at Munich, mountaineering history was being made.

In Britain some very significant new routes pointed the way to a new, harder era. In North Wales, Menlove Edwards pioneered a number of new routes on Lliwedd as part of his ever-diligent guide-book work. However, the most important addition that year came from Arthur Birtwistle, with his ascent of the superb *Diagonal Route* on the Nose of Dinas Mot, in August. Birtwistle, fresh from some exciting new routes on gritstone, notably at Laddow and in the Chew Valley, produced this magnificent slab climb which was to remain unrepeated for ten years. It formed a delightful companion route to Colin's seven year-old *West Rib*, both routes giving the ultimate in delicate climbing for the time. Birtwistle's route finished up the final part of *West Rib*, the true finish being added in 1946 by Peter Harding and Tony Moulham. About this time Birtwistle also made a very enterprising attempt to climb what became known as the *White Slab*, on Clogwyn Du'r Arddu. In the Lake District two important new climbs were established on the cliffs of

Colin leading on the first ascent of Black Slab (Bosigran) Cornwall.   *Photo Fallows Brothers, AC coll.*

Scafell by a climber destined to be of great significance in Cumbrian climbing for the next decade and more, Jim Birkett. May saw the first ascent of his *May Day Climb*, followed in August by the exciting girdle of the East Buttress. These two climbs were impressive products of the period, and in the view of some commentators the balance of British climbing began to swing once more towards the Lake District, not to be redressed until the emergence of Joe Brown in Snowdonia a decade later.

In the Himalaya, another British expedition attempted to climb Everest from the Tibetan side, led by Bill Tilman and Frank Smythe. This was intended to be a more modest enterprise than the 1936 affair, and the team members included Eric Shipton, Charles Warren and Noel Odell. Operating in particularly cold conditions the expedition eventually performed with some distinction. The North Col was attained by a new route up its western flank, and from here the conventional route was followed to Camp 6 at 27,300 feet. Two summit attempts followed (Shipton and Smythe, followed by Tilman and Lloyd) but the unstable snow conditions and an early monsoon drove the climbers back. This was the last serious expedition to Everest until the 1951 Reconnaissance led by Eric Shipton.

Meanwhile, in the Western Alps, three particularly famous first ascents were made in 1938 that were to show the way forward in modern alpinism and paradoxically served to demonstrate how far behind their leading European counterparts British climbers were. At Chamonix the North Face of Les Courtes in the Argentière basin was climbed by Cornaz and Mathey at the end of July, while a week later Cassin, Esposito and Tizzoni climbed the magnificent Walker Spur on the Grandes Jorasses, regarded for many years as the finest and most sought-after route in the Alps. In the Oberland, the North Face of the Eiger was finally climbed by Heckmair and his team over five days in July. It is sobering to recall that neither of these latter routes received a British ascent for more than twenty years.

Sadly the view had developed amongst British climbers that such climbing was the work of 'North Wall fanatics' climbing to further the glory of the Fatherland, and this sadly insular standpoint was not fully eroded until British climbers began to find their feet in the Alps from 1954 onwards. It then became fully realised just what brilliant mountaineers people such as Cassin and Heckmair were. One parallel in Britain with this move forward was the gradually increasing use of pitons and, by the late Thirties, karabiners (or snap-links). The use of such items on British crags was still treated with great suspicion, although some historical precedents had been established (i.e. Linnell's piton for aid on Scafell's Overhanging Wall). In the latter part of 1938, Colin was approached by the Editor of the Wayfarers'

Club Journal, to produce a paper examining the issues involved.

Colin's article (which appeared in the Wayfarers' Journal of 1939) was entitled 'The Ethics of Ironmongery', and is reproduced here in its entirety:

The piton has long been prevalent in Central Europe and now it is winging its way to this country like the germ of a deadly disease or the beginning of a glorious climbing renaissance ... who shall say which? The question at issue therefore, is whether pitons are to be encouraged on our homeland crags.

To begin with, some clear definition is necessary of the functions of a piton. A piton is an implement usually of metal and commonly but not necessarily, having a ring at the blunt end. It is used either solely as a belay or else also for the purpose of providing handhold and foothold. A very clear distinction must be made between these two uses, for they present cases which are entirely different from an ethical point of view.

As to history, the Piton Route on the Holly Tree Wall provides an early example. This venerable relic had too many historical associations to be regarded with any great distaste by even the most rabid purist; but alas! when getting frail and weak with advancing years, it was uprooted by some ruthless vandal having no respect for the antiques of a bygone age. Whereupon a dauntless enthusiast decided that another piton must be inserted in the Piton Route. Nor was this done by stealth at night. Far from it, for a photographer was brought up specially to immortalise the ceremony, and the whole procedure was carried out with almost medieval pomp and splendour. Unfortunately the new piton was put some four feet above the site of the old one and about two feet below a large belay, so that its purpose was purely sentimental unless one admits the horrible possibility that it was intended to be used as a hold.

The new arrival did not long survive. A note in a certain log-book records of its passing that it "came out quite easily". One cannot regret its decease since at the best it was merely pseudo-antique, like a Tudor garage. Still it served to justify the name of the climb, as an inn-sign may do for a pub.

Then there is the famous broomstick piton of Pigott and Morley Wood on the East Buttress of Clogwyn Du'r Arddu, which surely could not have lent more than moral support. And on the Chimney Climb on the same cliff a piton of sorts was used as a handhold for the first ascent. This was unnecessary on a subsequent ascent when the grass overhang had disappeared, and was removed. In any case this was an action of no more than semi-immorality, since the piton was so inadequate as to bend double in use.

On Craig yr Ysfa too, a piton was used, or misused, on an attempted first ascent. The implement on this occasion was a thin piece of steel, originally intended as a marble-chisel. This chisel was inserted into a thin crack and a rope loop some four feet in diameter placed round it. The leader then hauled horizontally on the end of this loop in order to overcome a very considerable overhang. The natural result followed. There was a loud metallic ringing sound as the piton took leave of its uncongenial situation and the climber landed on his stomach on a grass ledge thirty feet below and spent the next five minutes with groaning intake of the air which had been so suddenly and forcibly expelled. There is a moral to this story, but whether it is that pitons should not be used at all or else that only properly constructed ones are permissible is left as a debatable point.

And now we come to the matter which has really started the controversy – the Munich Climb. The first ascent of this route on the South Buttress of Tryfan, was made in the summer of 1936 by a party of German climbers, who used three or more pitons on holds, one of which they left behind. The whole climb was later led "clean" by J. M. Edwards, that indefatigable extractor of pitons, who removed the remaining offender. No one questions the rock climbing ability of the German leader – his brilliant direct lead of the Flake Crack on Scafell puts this beyond all doubt – but the whole question is raised as to whether a new era of exploration should be initiated by the use of the piton.

It is probably better to take the narrower and simpler issue first – the use of the piton solely as a belay. This will not, of course, revolutionise climbing or make possible a lot of new routes. It will act purely as a safeguard.

It is hard to see how the use of a piton on an old climb can be excused. Any climb belongs in part to its pioneers; it should be climbed as they climbed it. "Gardening" of course is inevitable and not undesirable, since it makes a climb pleasanter and safer, without removing any sense of isolation. It may be argued that similarly a piton makes a climb safer by splitting a long pitch. But here the personal equation comes in. If an ascent has already been made it is safe to assume that there are some leaders who can repeat it in perfect safety, whatever the runout. And the climber who cannot manage the long lead in safety has no right to spoil it for those who can by sticking in his offensive ironmongery. He should instead choose a climb which is within his capacity. It may seem a selfish view, on the face of it, that a good climb should be reserved solely for experts, but any climber, whatever his standard, will find a plentiful supply of good climbs which he can do in safety and without extraneous aids. For the sheer joy of the isolation of a long run out – a joy which only the most bigoted armchair expert will deny – is rudely shattered by the sight of a piton which it may seem foolhardy to neglect, even though no need of a belay would otherwise have been felt. And in any case the illusion of aloofness from a mechanical world is completely destroyed.

On a new climb, however, the situation is rather different. The pioneer party has a certain right to choose its tactics and if it seems probable that the full length of the rope will be used without any belay being reached, then a piton may be justifiable. Also, if a very desperate move has to be made, it may be very desirable to have the second man close at hand in case the leader meets an unforeseen obstacle higher up and is forced to return. This argument applies of course only to routes of great difficulty, as any new climbs on our overworked crags are likely to be. In a virgin land it would be a crime to neglect the natural belays in favour of the artificial.

All this leads up to the major question – the use of pitons as holds for hand and foot. So far such use has been negligible but now that the big crags are becoming worked out one can foresee a time when the problem will assume serious dimensions.

In a few years, perhaps, the crags will be completely exhausted unless there is a very considerable increase in the maximum standard of performance. Each generation has claimed that the limit of human skill has been reached and each succeeding generation has disproved the claim of its predecessors. And nobody has the right to climb with pitons a route which is conceivably possible without. If he does he will be depriving a more worthy contender of the honour of the first ascent, leaving for him only the rather bitter pleasure of proving that the climb can be done unaided.

But some day the human limit must be reached. Are the men of that generation, then, to be deprived of all the thrills of pioneer exploration? Obviously this cannot be so; they will take the law into their own hands. There seems to be little doubt that some day, be it a matter of years, or of decades, piton-climbing will come to be a recognised practice in this country. It is better to realise this rather than fight blindly against the inevitable and divide the British climbing community into two hostile camps. If piton-climbing is not officially recognised it cannot be controlled; and if it is not controlled its partisans will be free to spread their ware indiscriminately over all the rocks and all climbs, old and new.

Firstly it is essential that pitons should be used only on faces that are impossible without. When all the precipices are truly exhausted this problem will solve itself. Until that time let their use be confined to rocks that are obviously otherwise unclimbable. One can think of cliffs that do conform to this limitation; border line cases that might conceivably be climbed should be left unsullied. In time it may become a point of honour to observe this rule.

But the most important rule of all should be that no one must insert a piton in any climb that has previously been ascended without artificial aids.

The disadvantages of piton-climbing are many. Firstly, there is the physical danger, which is almost certainly greater than in ordinary climbing. But this is not an ethical question and can be dealt with only when the tragic need arises. The spirit of adventure cannot be stifled and perhaps the responsibility for the accidents that are likely to occur must rest with over-elaborated guide books which leave for the future generations no mysteries to be rediscovered.

Another danger is that ordinary rock-climbing may tend to die out; that every slight difficulty may be overcome with pitons; that natural belays may be disregarded. This can be avoided only by preserving inviolate the old climbs.

The natural conclusion, then, seems to be that one day piton-climbing will take root (literally and figuratively) in Britain. Therefore it is best to prepare for its advent, not wage a hopeless war against it. The old climbs must be preserved and it must be made a point of honour to respect them. Let the climber who uses a piton unnecessarily be ridiculed as though he had used a rope on Crib Goch or Striding Edge.

And when the Piton Age has come – Goodbye to the old peaceful age of natural exploring! Hail to the new era of clanging metal and eager restless youth that would risk death rather than fail! But may it not be in our time.

A. B. Hargreaves remembered that Colin's article was very widely read at
the time, and was regarded as highly authoratative:

> It was a highly intelligent commentary on how artificial climbing was developing,
> and for the time it was a wise look into the future. Colin was in his prime then, and
> he knew what he was talking about.

With the obvious benefit of hindsight, Colin's paper makes most
interesting reading, particularly in the light of his own climbing experiences,
and position at that time in the climbing world. What seems to be particularly
heartening is the reasonable and forward-looking viewpoint that he adopted,
together with his generous comments regarding Teufel's climbing on Scafell
and Tryfan. Colin made the clear distinction between the use of pitons for
security in the form of reliable belays, and that for direct aid in assisting
upward progress or for resting. By 1938 Colin would have certainly enjoyed
a measure of well-earned respect from within the climbing world as a
consequence of his endeavours in the early 1930s. Although no longer in the
forefront of the sport, particularly in the light of recent achievements by
climbers such as Birtwistle and Birkett, Colin adopted a generous and
positive attitude regarding the future of rock-climbing. To a person of
Colin's intelligence, it would have become clear that the limit of
performance, with the occasional technical grade of 5b, had probably been
reached in relation to the footwear and means of protection then available.
Indeed Colin, among others, had attempted to improve the performance of
his 'rubbers' by wrapping a number of elastic bands around the toes (the first
sticky boot!?) The improvement in performance gradually came after the
war, commencing with Chris Preston's brilliant lead of *Suicide Wall*. Much
of this improvement was due to the availability of better equipment (e.g.
rubber-soled boots, nylon ropes and increasingly reliable pitons and
karabiners) and, consequently, to the more positive mental approach that
leading climbers were able to adopt. Part of this process was a generally
sensible approach to the use of the odd piton, usually for protection, built
firmly on the traditions of climbers such as Jack Longland, Colin, Menlove
Edwards, Ted Hicks and Maurice Linnell. It should not be forgotten,
however, that these men displayed great courage in putting up bold new
climbs, with indifferent equipment at their disposal.

In the early autumn of that year, Colin was approached by the BBC to take
part in a series of radio broadcasts regarding different aspects and areas of
the British mountains. He was invited to talk about Snowdon, while other
speakers included Jack Longland who described the Pillar area, and A. B.
Hargreaves who spoke about the Scafell group. One intention of these

broadcasts was to draw wider public attention to the rapidly increasing interest in the outdoor movement, and to rally support for the forthcoming Access to Mountains Bill. This enlightened piece of legislation found its way on to the statute book in the following year, having seen a chequered history for many years. It was finally passed by both Houses of Parliament after having been introduced as a private member's bill by A. Creech-Jones. The object of the bill was to give the public the right of access to many areas of upland and mountain country from which they had been excluded by land-owning and sporting interests. The outbreak of the war in the same year had the effect of preventing the passing of many Access Orders, but the Act was seen as a triumph by the many outdoor groups that had fought for its passing, and it paved the way for the National Parks and Access to Countryside Act ten years later. It seems thoroughly in character that Colin was involved in such work, along with Jack Longland and A. B. Hargreaves. These were crucial pieces of legislation that all walkers and climbers would do well to remember, particularly in light of the current threats to established access posed by the proposals to privatise the water industry.

The talk Colin gave on the radio was a delightful little piece, that demonstrated his humour and modest nature while still projecting his deep affection for the Welsh Mountains. The broadcast, made at the BBC studios in Manchester, was entitled 'The Spirit of Snowdon,' and was reproduced in an article in The Listener that September. The text, included here in its entirety, shows the emergence of the style of writing that was to make 'Let's Go Climbing!' so endearing in revealing that to Colin climbing mountains was basically about fun, companionship and joy coupled with a spiritual feeling for the hills and their many different moods.

It is fitting to have the bread and butter (or should I say dry bread?) before the cake, so I will begin with the Snowdon Railway. It is a very safe railway, I am afraid, and I have even given up hoping that it will one day be blown over the cliff at Clogwyn Station. And that is all I have to say about the Snowdon Railway. On the summit of Snowdon is a hotel which swallows all that the railway disgorges. Perhaps I should have begun with that.

Many people think it to be a great improvement on the old wooden huts and remark kindly that it would not look out of place on Blackpool Promenade. But I must confess to having been seen inside.

This disposes of Snowdon the holiday show-place. And now for Snowdon the mountain! Of all mountains I have known, both home and abroad, it is the one which combines best, to my mind, both grandeur and friendliness. The ordinary pedestrian will enjoy the walk from Pen-y-Pass on the Capel Curig side, up by the dark hollow of Glaslyn. But any person used to mountains will choose to scramble over the four peaks round the Horseshoe of Snowdon, beginning with the narrow ridge of Crib Goch, which still gives me a thrill every time I cross it. But those who do not wish to be disillusioned I should advise to miss out the crowded actual summit.

But it is only in winter time that you get the real spirit of the mountain, when there is a blizzard raging and everything is sheeted in snow and ice. Some years ago three of us went up one March night to test some new sleeping bags. We had some step-cutting above Glaslyn – an ordinary pedestrian route in summer – and arrived on the ridge about 11 p.m. There were 18 degrees of frost and it was blowing a gale which whipped the snow stingingly into our faces. We made an effort to build a wall of snow, but it was not a great success; it blew down almost as fast as we built it up. We then crawled into our sleeping bags and closed them right up, since we had no tent to protect us. These bags were made of eiderdown with a waterproof cover, and at first you felt as though you were in a coffin and expected to suffocate. Then we had supper, each of us in our own separate bag. The food was frozen so solid that I could not distinguish between fruit cake and corned beef. We had a warm and comfortable night and next morning made our sleepy way over Crib Goch and down to a well-earned breakfast at Pen-y-Pass.

Few people realise what a difference snow may make even to our own British hills. For ordinary tourists' routes it may be necessary to have full Alpine equipment – warm clothing, ropes and ice-axes. An incident that occurred a few years ago illustrates this. Two of us were coming down the zigzags to Glaslyn when we saw three people some 500 feet below us, apparently in trouble. Near to them we could see a great patch of red in the snow. This did not alarm us unduly, for a little blood goes a long way in snow; a cut finger may easily have the appearance of a major tragedy. We began to make our way down towards them, and I rather carelessly was not digging in my heels deeply enough. That was in my young and foolish days. Suddenly I came on some hard snow, and the next instant was sliding with rapidly increasing speed on my back. I made frantic efforts to dig in my axe, but it was torn from my grasp, though the sling prevented it from being lost. Then I got going head-first and had to wait until I was right way up again before I could make another attempt to stop myself. Each time I got the axe in I would fly past it to the full length of the partly broken sling and then the axe would be jerked out over my head. Then once more I was descending head-first at 30 or 40 miles an hour. I saw the top of an ice-cliff ahead of me – smooth green bulges like bottle glass. It was about 20 feet high, and I went over head-first with a pleasing switch-back sensation and hit the steep snow-slope below without a trace of a jar. A little farther on I was able to pull up on some frozen grass just short of some rather unfriendly-looking rocks. I had had a slide of four or five hundred feet, and the only damage was one torn glove. With great presence of mind I picked myself up as though I had meant to come down that way, and moved as casually as possible towards the party in distress. They had been attempting the ascent in ordinary shoes and had got quite close to the ridge before they had all slipped. They were not very seriously hurt and we managed to help them down without a great deal of trouble. Two of them are now quite keen climbers.

CFK contemplating ice-axe braking!   *Photo C.F. Kirkus (AC coll.)*

Last December two of us were descending the same place when my companion decided to try a glissade – that is, a controlled, standing slide, with his ice axe held behind as a brake. I thought it quite a good way of finding out, at no risk to myself, the condition of the snow. As soon as he started moving, however, he lost control, began sliding on his back and parted company with his ice-axe. I immediately plunged down after him, risking my life to save him. At least that is what I would have done had I been a film hero. As it was I just stood there and wondered with a detached and rather callous interest, how far he would go. He stopped quite soon in some soft snow. I believe in keeping cool in an emergency – providing it is someone else's emergency – so I asked him quite calmly what impulse prompted him to throw away his axe. His reply is best left to the imagination. A little lower down we had to come to the aid of several tourists. A stream had frozen over the path and covered it with a thick layer of ice for about 20 feet, so that any people without axes had to take to the frozen snow and stones below. When we reached them they were all helplessly marooned on separate islands of rock and we spent an energetic half-hour cutting steps for them across the hard snow. These little incidents illustrate the need for experience, care and proper equipment on the homeland hills in winter time.

The gullies under the actual summit of Snowdown provide excellent sport in winter. You usually get 500 feet of snow at 40 or 50 degrees, steepening up to vertical at the top and often ending in a cornice; that is, an overhang of snow or ice. It is an interesting problem to overcome a cornice. The snow is often nearly as hard as ice and you continue cutting ordinary steps as high as possible. When it becomes very steep it is necessary to cut grooves for the legs, so as to avoid being thrown out of balance.

By this time one will be quite close to the cornice, which may overhang for five feet or more. Then the cornice has to be cut away – very gingerly, so that it will not all fall at once and take the party with it. It is very tiring work, cutting above the head with one hand. The leader gets boiling hot, whilst the second man stands shivering below, half-buried in chunks of snow and ice. Then a large niche is cut, the ice-axe plunged in and the body dragged laboriously up. When the cornice is very large it is sometimes necessary to dig a tunnel, an operation which may take several hours. When the summit is reached it is found to be covered with piled-up snow, and every rock is festooned with feathers of ice-needles sometimes several feet in length. The contrast with popular summer conditions is ludicrous.

Sometimes in March you get good hard snow in the gullies and then come out into the sunshine and find it is hot enough to sunbathe. And sometimes in the middle of our English summer you may get it hailing and miserably cold. In summer the rock-climbing on Snowdon is very good, for it possesses perhaps the finest cliff in Britain – Clogwyn Du'r Arddu – known affectionately among climbers as 'Cloggy'. Practically all the climbs here are extremely difficult, and on one of them in particular, known as the West Buttress, there have been several hectic adventures. This climb starts with a narrow slab, overhung above and below and inclined at about 70 degrees. When this slab narrows to nothingness it is necessary to make a very difficult step to the right and then cross a short but very tricky section, known as the "Faith and Friction Slab", above an overhang of 200 feet.

On the ascent in question the leader and the second man had got over the difficulty and the latter was ensconced just above the overhang. As the third man was crossing the "Faith and Friction Slab", he slipped and the second was not able to hold him until he had gone over the edge and was dangling in mid-air. It was impossible to pull him up and the only thing to do was to lower him down to the full length of the 120 foot rope. This was done and he was still dangling in mid-air, some distance from terra firma. Anyone who has been in such a situation will know that it is not a comfortable sensation to be suspended by the waist on a thin climbing rope. Luckily there was a young and expert climber watching below and he was able with great difficulty to climb up on the left, lasso the suspended man and draw him in to comparative safety.

One of the favourite climbing grounds on the Snowdown massif is Lliwedd. This cliff rises at an average angle of over 60 degrees for 850 feet. We started up the Slanting Gully one March day at about 12 noon. All went well for some time and then, after cutting steps in snow and ice at about 70 degrees, we were stopped by vertical ice-covered rocks and took to the buttress on the right. Much of this was vertical and I had some hectic moments digging my ice-axe into frozen turf and pulling myself bodily up on it. At about 6 o'clock, when it was fairly dark, we were above the most difficult part and some 400 feet up the face. Just as we were resigning ourselves to a very cold night on the mountain – a rather dangerous expedient in such conditions – we found a fairly reasonable gully leading down on the far side of the buttress and reached the bottom of the cliff at 8 p.m. – defeated, but with the satisfied feeling of having put up a good fight. As it was, one of the party got two fingers slightly frostbitten. And I still remember vividly the sparks that flew off our boots as we ran and stumbled down the snow-covered scree at the bottom.

My aim in giving these personal reminiscences has been to convey something of the spirit of Snowdon. It has always had a special appeal for me and I still regard my first proud ascent at the age of nine as one of the most thrilling days of my life, only equalled by the occasion, two years later, when I crossed Crib Goch, with a walking stick in one hand and a tea basket in the other. In those days I thought that anyone who appeared on a mountain without a walking stick was entirely ignorant of mountain-craft.

Since then I have known the grandeur of the Alps and the breath-taking magnificence of the Himalaya; but Snowdon seems to give me something that is entirely its own. To those with eyes to see, every mountain has its own distinct personality. There is a story of a well-known Alpine guide who was taken up Crib Goch on a winter's day and was asked how long he thought it would take to reach the summit of Snowdon. "We cannot possibly do it today" was his reply; "it will take at least six hours". Yet one hour later he stood on the top of Y Wyddfa, the highest peak of Snowdon. That is the beauty of it; it all looks so grand and impressive and yet one is able to enjoy it to the full, with a mind untroubled by the worry about the descent, which is always present in Alpine climbing.

To look across Glasyn and see the rocks rising darkly into the mist, then to look up and up and to see, incredibly high and remote, a gleaming snowy point sticking up above the clouds, dazzling against the deep blue sky – that is an unforgettable sight, ethereal and lovely, almost an another world. And for a space everyday life is banished and forgotten. It is an escape from reality. But for such an escape one must be in harmony with one's surroundings – and I can find that harmony on Snowdon.

Colin's recollections here refer to adventures already described with, amongst others, Marco Pallis and Bill Stallybrass. The exciting incident described on Clogwyn Du'r Arddu concerns an attempt to repeat Longland's West Buttress route in March 1934. The party involved consisted of Jack Longland himself, his brother-in-law Paul Sinker, and a Professor Turnbull. It was Turnbull who had the misfortune to fall beneath the overhang on the climb, almost pulling off the remainder of the party in the process. The young climber who came to his rescue was John Hoyland of Oxford University M.C. who was on Pigott's East Buttress route when the incident occurred.

Towards the end of the year, Colin continued to socialise and occasionally climb with Graham MacPhee. They attended a couple of club dinners together; in December the Rucksack Club dinner, at which Colin was the

Tryfan from Tal-y-braich.   *Photo C. F. Kirkus (AC coll.)*

Climbers' Club representative, and in January that of the Liverpool
University Mountaineering Club (no longer simply a rock-climbing Club), at
which Colin gave a speech, together with Messrs. Solly and Greenwood.
After the dinner several of the party, including Colin and MacPhee, drove
from Liverpool to the Rucksack Club Hut (Tal-y-braich) in the Ogwen
Valley. The next day (January 21st) Colin and MacPhee climbed together on
the East Face of Tryfan.

Colin returned to Wales with MacPhee on March 10th, when they drove
down from Liverpool together, being delayed rather by a breakdown to
MacPhee's car *en route* to Helyg. The next day, March 11th, they climbed
the *Pinnacle Rib* on Tryfan in freezing cold conditions. The following day
dawned bright and sunny, though still very cold. Colin and MacPhee
enjoyed a good day on the rocks of Glyder Fach, doing *Beta* and *Chasm
Route*, before walking over to Idwal to romp up *Charity* and *Holly Tree Wall*.
MacPhee recorded that these climbs were enlivened by a liberal helping of
ice on many of the holds. This was probably the last time these two friends
climbed together, and it is poignant to picture them walking back to the hut
late in the afternoon at the end of a good day's sport.

Later that month Bill Stallybrass drove Colin down to Helyg from
Liverpool, and they spent a day together on the rocks of Lliwedd. Bill
recalled:

We climbed *Mallory's Slab* and *Great Chimney* closely followed by John Jenkins and Gilbert Peaker. That was the last time I climbed with Colin.

During the late 1930s, the publishing company Thomas Nelson and Sons was in the process of compiling a series of hardback handbooks for young people, known collectively as the Nelsonian Library. These books covered a wide range of hobbies and activities and included such titles as 'The Young Steamship Officer', 'Adventurous Women' and 'A Book of Escapes and Hurried Journeys'. Other books were entitled 'Let's Go ......' followed by an activity such as Riding, Fishing, or Camping. Following discussions with Nelson and Sons, Colin agreed to produce a book for this series, to be entitled 'Let's Go Climbing!' and a contract was signed in July 1939 requiring the book to be completed by the end of October. Due to delays caused by the outbreak of the war, the book was not published until February 1941 but it then sold very well, and was reprinted in 1946. Such was the classic nature of Colin's book, that it was reproduced in paperback form as late as 1959 and only fell out of print in January 1964.

By the summer of 1939 both Colin's brothers had left home and had married. Guy was living in Accrington, working in the textile industry, while Nigel was continuing his service in the RAF, having joined in 1929 and qualifying as a pilot for 101 Squadron in 1936. Guy Kirkus recalled that Nigel quickly became deeply involved in the wonders of aviation once he was employed in the RAF, and conveyed his huge enthusiasm for it to his brothers in turn. Meanwhile, as the international situation worsened through that July and August, Colin, now twenty-nine, continued working at the Royal Insurance offices in Liverpool and living with his parents at Acre Lane in Heswall. He had also become engaged to Eileen Foster, also from Heswall, and the couple were to marry the following year.

In Europe the inevitable finally occurred and, following Hitler's invasion of Poland on September 1st, war was declared on Germany on September 3rd. Britain then embarked on a strange period known as the 'phoney war', before the real onslaughts began a year later. The evacuation of children, food rationing, the blackout, gas-masks and air-raid drills became part of everyday life in and around Liverpool, as they were throughout the country.

As the war opened, the British Government adopted a cautious approach to the use of its (albeit limited) air power. Indeed, to a suggestion that the RAF might bomb the Ruhr, the then Air Minister, Sir Kingsley Wood, made the time-honoured remark that factories were private property! It was due to this attitude to Germany that in the opening weeks of the war the RAF limited its bombing operations to attacks on the German Navy. This was clearly perceived as a military target, but an early raid on September 4th on the naval base at Wilhelmshaven, by RAF bombers of 2 and 3 Group, showed clearly the dangers posed by Germany's modern fighter aircraft, when of the 29 bombers dispatched 7 failed to return. By the last few days of September, Bomber Command had introduced the concept of reconnaiss-ance in force, in which nine or more aircraft swept the Heligoland Bight with orders to attack any warships or U boats they might find there. On September 29th, eleven Hampden bombers from Nos. 61 and 144 Squadrons were attacked by German fighters based at the North Frisian island of Wangerooge, as they prepared to attack two German destroyers. Five of the Hampdens, all from 144 Squadron, were shot down into the sea and with awful suddenness the RAF was to comprehend the utter stupidity of sending vulnerable bomber aircraft to fly unescorted on daylight missions. For the Kirkus family, and for Nigel's young wife Mary, there was to be no 'phoney war', only heartbreak and grief; one of the pilots lost that day was Nigel Miller Kirkus, with the war barely three weeks old. It was almost certainly this family tragedy that subsequently prompted Colin to volunteer for the RAF, despite being nearly thirty years old and with defective eyesight, resulting from the 1934 accident on Ben Nevis. For the time being he continued to work in the Insurance Office but it was only to be a matter of time before Colin joined the forces, as the situation in Britain and Europe worsened in 1940.

Obviously, 1939 was dominated by the lead up to and the outbreak of the war, and for most people thoughts of climbing and mountains were overtaken by far more serious matters. Nonetheless one or two notable events occurred that year, notably Jim Birkett's discovery of the splendid *Overhanging Bastion* on Castle Rock of Triermain and the publication of Menlove Edwards' and Wilf Noyce's guide-book to Lliwedd. Birkett's climb was very modern in concept and looked firmly to the future, while the Lliwedd guide-book was the standard work on the crag for many years, and was a unique piece of work in its own way. Strangely, Lliwedd was never a favourite haunt of Colin's although he repeated most of the main courses on the cliff. That year also finally saw the publication of Marco Pallis's book 'Peaks and Lamas' by Cassell, which of course included a full account of the 1933 Gangotri Expedition. In the Western Alps, Ratti and Vitali climbed their magnificent route on the West Face of the Aiguille Noire de Peuterey, a fortnight before the outbreak of the war. Sadly however, mountaineering and its attendant pleasures now had to take a back seat in most people's minds, and be at most a source of happy and inspiring memories, as the world became engulfed in a terrible war that was to last for six years.

9　RAF Pathfinder

The winter of 1939-40 was a fairly bleak and miserable time for many people in Britain as rationing and limitations on travel began to impinge on day-to-day life, increasingly dominated by the war with Germany. In addition, that winter was particularly harsh, with bitterly cold weather and heavy snowfall over much of the country. After the outbreak of the war, and the death of his brother Nigel in September, Colin effectively ceased regular climbing. Understandably, he now spent most of his leisure time with his fiancée Eileen Foster. His occasional visits to North Wales or the Lake District were now light-hearted affairs, teaching Eileen to climb and trying to enjoy life to the full in the knowledge that he would soon himself be joining the war effort. Colin continued to make every effort to join the RAF, and was somewhat concerned when initially certain aspects of insurance work were classified as reserve occupation, and he feared that he might not be called up.

At Easter, the Climbers' Club organised a meet at Helyg which served to gather together many of the most active climbers of the past decade, including Colin, Jack Longland, A. B. Hargreaves, Bill Stallybrass, Stuart Chantrell, David Cox, Nully Kretschmer and Menlove Edwards. The weather that weekend was not good, as the severe winter lingered on into spring, and there was some heavy rain. However some climbing was done by the company, and it was on this meet that Colin climbed for the last time with Menlove Edwards. In 'Menlove', Jim Perrin describes this event with admirable feeling:

> On the final day, the Easter Monday, fittingly Menlove and Colin Kirkus climbed together for the last time. There is something immensely poignant about these two men, the great rock-climbers of their time, being ushered into each other's company on a fine spring morning, setting out for Cwm Idwal, making their way up *Hope* on the Slabs, then the *Holly Tree Wall* and afterwards traversing across to scramble up the *Cneifion Arête* and walk across the summits of the Glyders – the two men who had set the tone and the standards for an era coming together for a last day of simple pleasure at its very close.

Poignant indeed, when one reflects on the contrasting fates of these two men who had established such a magnificent collection of memorable climbs over the previous decade.

The following weekend, Colin and Eileen were married at Heswall Parish Church, with the reception being held at the Hotel Victoria. Bill Stallybrass

did the honours as Colin's best man, having taken him out in Liverpool the previous night to enjoy a Gilbert and Sullivan concert, 'The Yeoman of the Guard'. Colin and Eileen set up home in a house in Mere Lane, Heswall, which they named 'Mickledore' after the col between Scafell and Scafell Pike. The house retains the name to this day.

Colin and Eileen were married shortly before the Dunkirk evacuations, and their short period of domestic married life sadly coincided with an increasingly serious situation in Europe. In June, France accepted the terms of an armistice offered by the German High Command and capitulated. Britain and the Commmonwealth countries stood alone, the remainder of Europe having fallen to the forces of the Reich. It was against this sombre background that Colin attended his medical examination for entry to the RAF that summer. As a legacy of the 1934 accident on Ben Nevis, Colin's eyesight was permanently out of alignment, which in itself would have prevented him from being selected for air-crew duties. The queue for the eyesight test was a long one; it gave Colin the opportunity to memorise the order of letters on the board and when his turn came he was able to recite them correctly, and conceal from the RAF doctors the limitations of his vision. As a result, he was passed as physically A1, and entered the service on August 1st 1940 at No. 3 Recruits Centre at RAF Padgate (near Warrington) as No. 1109511 Aircraftsman 2nd Class/Aircraftshand/ Observer in the RAF Volunteer Reserve, and was put on reserve for basic training. Colin's entry into the RAF came just two days after the first German bombs fell on Liverpool and the Wirral, and it was also at this time that the Battle of Britain was raging over South-East England, as 'the few' sought to control the skies against the German attackers. Shortly after enlisting, Colin met his old friend Graham MacPhee in an Air-Raid Shelter in central Liverpool on September 9th. On that particular day, there were four air-raid warnings in the City – an already common occurrence.

Menlove Edwards had earlier that year registered as a conscientious objector and was continuing his psychiatric work in Liverpool. That August, Menlove produced two highly significant climbs on the steep and complex central buttress on Clogwyn y Grochan on the north side of the Llanberis Pass. The first, climbed on August 5th with John Barford, was called *The Brant*. Three days later a second route was climbed with Gilbert Peaker and R. G. Donaldson, and this was called *The Slape*. Both climbs were destined to become classics after the War, with famous pitches that would tease and frighten many would-be leaders, notably the fierce wall pitch of *Slape* and the steep initial traverse and V-Chimney on *Brant*. These climbs are now

Eileen Foster on Troutdale Pinnacle, Borrowdale. *Photo C. F. Kirkus (AC coll.)*

recognised as the start of a new era in Welsh climbing, the first really hard routes on the north side of 'The Pass'.

As the summer of 1940 merged into autumn, it is likely that Colin found his initial weeks in the RAF to be a considerable contrast from the regular routine in the Insurance Office and from travelling into Liverpool daily from Heswall. This was of course an experience now being shared by many, as thousands of ordinary men and women entered the services in the defence of the way of life they had left behind. What is clear with hindsight is that Colin joined the RAF at a particularly grim stage of the war. Despite the triumph of Fighter Command in the Battle of Britain it must have seemed almost inevitable that a German victory would follow as a relentless stranglehold surrounded the British Isles. In the Atlantic, marauding packs of German U-boats were attacking the convoys daily, killing many seamen and causing thousands of tons of essential supplies to be lost, while in Europe the overall situation was grave. In the latter part of 1940 and into 1941, Bomber Command was the only force available to the Allies that was capable of taking the war to the enemy. However, the cost in aircrew lives at this stage of the war was truly terrible and between July and October 1940 Bomber Command lost 220 aircraft. And yet, despite the gravity of the situation, Berlin was successfully bombed in late August when 81 aircraft were dispatched there. In general, however, Colin would not have found morale to be high in the service at this stage of the war. Military service was clearly going to be hard work.

The winter of 1940/41 was a bitterly cold one and not the least of Colin's worries would have been the increasing severity of the bombing of Liverpool, and the obvious concern for his loved ones. The whole series of Luftwaffe raids on the great city and its surrounding area was part of a long drawn-out engagement by the Germans in the context of the Battle of the Atlantic. It was an attempt to put out of action one of the main ports for which the convoys were making – one of the keys to western approaches. There were sixty-eight major night raids on the Liverpool area in this period, the first bombs fell on the Wirral on July 29th 1940, the last on January 10th, 1942. On eight successive nights (May 1st - 8th 1941) the raids culminated in what became known as the May blitz after which they became fewer and milder. In this overall period of some eighteen months the Liverpool area suffered considerably, with almost 4,000 people killed, 3,800 seriously injured and more than 200,000 forced to leave their homes. More than half the City's housing stock was damaged, and in excess of 10,000 houses totally destroyed. In the midst of this period, Colin was placed in No. 1 Reserve Wing in 54 Group on January 11th 1941, and a month later he was sent to No. 3 Initial Training Wing at Torquay. After a few weeks there on April 18th he was reclassified as a Leading Aircraftsman and remustered under training as an Air Observer. The following month, on May 17th, he was sent north to No. 8 Bombing and Gunnery School at RAF Evanton in Ross-shire.

The training of RAF bomber crews was an arduous and often dangerous process, with constant pressure on personnel as new crews were often needed before they were ready to become operational. In early 1941 it was laid down by the Air Ministry that an operational tour should be 200 hours, followed by six months rest normally spent instructing at an Operational Training Unit. After this, a second 200-hour tour would be undertaken – this length of tour equating to 30-35 operational sorties. After an initial three-day air-crew selection board, at which those who passed were categorised into pilot/navigator/bomb-aimer and wireless operator/flight engineer/gunner, some ten days were spent kitting out at the Air-Crew Reception Centre at Regents Park in London. Twelve weeks would then be spent on ground training at an Initial Training Wing (Colin's period at Torquay) before time at flying school. This particular period for pilots and some navigators often took place in the U.S.A., Canada or in South Africa. Once trained, airmen were sent to an Operational Training Unit to be formed into crews. Here they would carry out specific training on the type of aircraft they would fly in an Operational Squadron, in Colin's case the Vickers Wellington.

Naturally enough some men fell by the wayside during this training period through unsuitability, injury or death. Indeed more than 5300 crew were killed and 3100 were injured during training in Bomber Command during the war, so one could conclude that it was a hazardous business even prior to confronting the enemy.

After the period at the Initial Training Wing and at RAF Evanton, Colin was stationed in August 1941 at No. 3 Air Observer Navigation School at RAF Bobbington (near Wolverhampton) and here his particular talents at this type of work began to emerge, for by November he had been promoted to Temporary Sergeant, and remustered as an Air Observer.

While Colin was embarking on the serious business of RAF training and of acquiring the skills that were to result in him becoming a top-class aviation navigator, Thomas Nelson finally published 'Let's Go Climbing!' in February 1941. The book, the bulk of which was written in the latter part of 1939, was intended for what were then known as 'young people', in the period before the term 'teenager' came into regular use. The first edition in hardback, with its distinctive artwork, sold quickly and a second edition soon followed. The book is now rightfully regarded as a little classic of British mountain writing, and functions well on three counts; as a basic and very friendly instruction book, as a 'period piece' successfully depicting a specific time in the sport's evolution and, perhaps most significantly, as an evocation of the spirit of the sport and the gifts it has on offer to those willing to venture forth and learn the basic techniques described in the text. In my view this latter factor is the key to the book's quality and the affection in which it is still held by generations of climbers. When researching Colin's life I contacted all the senior (pre-war) members of the Climbers' Club. Many of them referred to 'Let's Go Climbing!' and it was obvious that it had been widely read and well received. Perhaps the most interesting comment came from Elliott Viney who remembered:

> Colin's book was an inspiration and a source of joy to several of us in a German prisoner-of-war camp during the war.

When I told Colin's brother Guy of this reply from Elliott, he smiled broadly and told me that Colin would have been delighted to have known that.

Throughout the book, Colin displayed the gift of writing in a simple manner designed to appeal to a readership in the 12-20 age group. He achieved this objective quite brilliantly and although parts of the book are now dated (equipment, aspects of technique and so on), the spirit of the book remains undiminished and its essence is quite timeless. There is something to bring a smile and a happy hill memory to almost anyone who cares to read this little volume, be they elderly hill-walkers or some young lycra-clad thruster out on the crag. Everyone will recognise something of themselves, particularly in Colin's ability to tell a story about his own occasional misfortunes, which he did in order to bring out a point and stress the need for vigilance and safety when out on the hill or crag. Although 'Let's Go Climbing!' went out of print in January 1964, it is still available through second-hand dealers. Thomas Nelson probably never realised that they had such a classic on their hands: it was conceived as one of a series of children's instruction books covering a wide range of subjects. It is unlikely that any of the others in the series are remembered all these years later, but mention of 'Let's Go Climbing!' amongst older climbers in particular is still greeted with a smile and an acknowledgement of the book's obvious qualities. I make no apologies for using quotes from Colin's book throughout this account of his life, for I feel that he left much of himself in those 200 pages, written as Europe descended into war. In 'Menlove', Jim Perrin acknowledges a debt to 'Let's Go Climbing!' and touches on the nature of Colin himself:

> Kirkus's character comes over supremely well in his instructional book for boys, 'Let's Go Climbing!'. (It was a copy of this book in the library of my school in Manchester which first enthused me about the sport.) Its lyrical freshness, the generous enthusiasms of its author and the sharp, deft, uncluttered pictures he evokes, make this book, for all its great simplicity, one of the very best about the climbing experience. The man who wrote it cannot have been other than an utterly likeable, honest and brotherly soul, and one whose friendship and company Menlove must have held very dear.)

'Let's Go Climbing!' opens with an account of a night ascent of, and the sunrise over a snow-covered Snowdon. The chapter is entitled 'Why do we Climb?' and the passage referred to does indeed explain much of what draws people to the hills. It effortlessly displays a sensitivity and love of the mountains, that is still reflected in the enduring affection for Colin within British climbing. To demonstrate the attraction of the sport Colin doesn't describe a thrilling rock ascent, or a steep ice pitch in bright sunshine, but instead the simple pleasure of a night walk alone, from Helyg to the summit of Snowdon on an Easter weekend.

> It was wonderful to be walking across the crackly frozen bog, all alone in the night. I experienced a satisfying sense of freedom and all sleepiness was driven away by the keen air; I felt I could keep going for ever.

The walk takes him past Llyn Cwm-y-Ffynnon and down past the Pen-y-Pass hotel, where he is anxious not to disturb anyone. The image then forms of this solitary spirit happily making his way in darkness up to the summit of Crib-Goch and along the pinnacle ridge, to Crib y Ddysgl and the summit of Snowdon as, all around, Wales sleeps:

> It was 5.30 now and beginning to get light. The moon seemed to have lost its brilliance and the snow was a dead unearthly white, cold and spectral. A chilly wind had sprung up and I shivered as I forced my way into the old wooden hut on the summit. The door was jammed with frozen snow and it was a tight squeeze to get in.
>
> There was no furniture inside nor glass in the windows, and the floor was covered with a thick sheet of ice. I ate a little food, but my fingers got frozen as soon as I took off my gloves, so I just stamped my feet and shivered and waited for the sunrise.
>
> The east window was almost covered by a framework of feathery icicles, and I kept watch through a ragged hole that was left in the middle. All the valleys were filled with mist, with the peaks standing up clear above, like islands. It got slowly lighter, but no warmer. Then presently a scarlet glow appeared above a level

purple bank of cloud lying on the horizon, and soon the red sun, looking queerly oval, came into view. As soon as it rose above the cloud it changed to gold and made the icicles in the window gleam like diamonds. I could feel its warmth immediately and grew cheerful and comfortable again in an instant.

Throughout its length, 'Let's Go Climbing!' is wholly encouraging and friendly in tone, without a hint of being condescending or patronising to the novice to whom it is aimed. Colin adheres to a simple ideal that climbing is all about fun, and is a source of shared or of solitary delight, often in wonderful surroundings:

> To be poised on a steep smooth face, concentrating with every nerve, and then to stretch cautiously up and to come unexpectedly on a large handhold which solves the problem – that seems to be the most thrillingly satisfying moment of your life each time it happens.
>
> As an exercise climbing is unrivalled, since every muscle in the body is used. It teaches judgement and courage and coolness in an emergency, and makes you forget completely all the worries of everyday life. It is a wonderful chance for adventure in pure air and magnificent surroundings. Few who start climbing ever give it up. Once a climber, always a climber.

After the introductory chapters describing some of his own adventures, and a few hair-raising exploits as well, Colin commences the instructional element with the basics of simple hill-walking, on a journey along part of the Berwyns ridge – a place he would have known well from his childhood. He describes a walk from the valley of the Dee, up on to Cader Fronwen and then along the ridge to Moel Sych, before encouraging the newcomer to investigate the North Ridge of Tryfan, and other delights in Snowdonia. Advice is given on what to wear, what to take with you, and a request is made (even fifty years ago) not to leave litter.

> But if you set out to know the mountains you will learn to love them, and it will be quite a different tale. You will be happy just to be amongst them, whether you are tackling a hard or an easy climb, or merely wandering freely over the tops.

From simple hill-walking, the book moves on to the mysteries of rock-climbing. Colin escorts the reader up a make-believe climb, and so the character of the book is established. He acts as a kindly instructor who stands at your side, as the various mysteries and delights unfold for the reader. Clear, though now dated, guidance is given regarding footwear, equipment and belaying techniques. The various techniques of rock-climbing are clearly explained, along with amusing suggestions for practising at home, and Colin also touches on the 'delights' of first ascents:

You have to clear grass out of the holds and throw down loose rocks and insecure ledges, until you have made the place safe for yourself and future climbers. There are few more cheering sights than seeing your second half-buried under a large and slimy sod.

No doubt this struck a chord at the time with characters such as Grahan MacPhee, 'AB', and Alf Bridge! This section of the book also contains Colin's famous (and gripping) account of the first ascent of *Great Slab* on Clogwyn Du'r Arddu – a classic piece of rock-climbing writing that has not diminished in impact, despite the changes on the crag itself. Later, the reader is introduced to and climbs alongside Graham MacPhee, 'AB', Alf Bridge and Maurice Linnell as *Central Buttress* and *Curving Crack* are described to illustrate certain points, and particular aspects of techniques. In closing the chapter, Colin acknowledges the good times he and his mates had on such climbs:

> I don't suggest that you should start off with climbs such as these. By the time you are fit for them you won't need a book to tell you what to do. But it is a pleasure to me to live these adventures over again, and I hope I have succeeded in passing on to you some idea of the excitement and enjoyment they have given me.

Colin's standpoint of climbing as innocent adventure and fun continues with a chapter about the delights of bivouacs, and some recollections of notable nights out, ranging from the rubbish dump next to Helyg, to high camping in the Gangotri Himalaya, and the pleasures and the discomforts involved. He then discusses the issue of accidents in the mountains, dealing with it in a mature and reasonable fashion not designed to put the reader off, but guiding one simply and trying to show the kind of places where danger might be found. On describing his own accident on *Great Central Route* on Dow Crag, Colin warns the reader in a simple, modest manner of one particular danger in the sport:

> This fall was, of course, due entirely to gross carelessness on my part. I had suddenly found myself able to do the hardest climbs and had grown over-confident. I had had a number of falls without serious injury and had begun to be less frightened of accidents. That is to say, I was willing to take risks; I thought boldness a better policy than discretion. That is a most dangerous state of mind, and one that is very common among young climbers between the ages of nineteen and twenty-one; that is why such a lot of accidents occur amongst university students.

Colin skilfully uses accounts of accidents and mishaps involving both himself and his friends to guide the newcomer carefully, and at the same time is able to find amusement in his own predicament or misfortune and not take the whole matter too seriously. However, he does end the chapter on a grave note, and touches on the matter of a fatal accident. Whilst not dwelling on the issue, Colin reminds the reader that such things can happen in the mountains. No doubt his own mind went back to that fateful day on Ben Nevis, and to the death of Maurice Linnell, as he wrote those words and recalled a personal tragedy of his own.

From climbing in Britain, the book then moves on to the exciting world of Alpine climbing, and the considerable differences the novice will experience from climbing at home. Colin uses a delightful account of a make-believe climb, set in the Zermatt Valley, to demonstrate the various stages of an Alpine ascent, and what to expect. The account of the rigours of an Alpine start ring as true today as before the war:

> "It's a lovely morning; get up you lazy brute." You almost wish it was raining; you feel sure you've only been in bed ten minutes. "Come on; it's one o'clock." Off come the blankets, and you are hauled onto the floor. Beastly hearty blighter!
>
> You sleepily pull on your boots with cold fingers. The candles make weird flickering shadows of the rucksacks on the table. You eat a silent, gloomy breakfast of boiled eggs and tea and hunks of bread. The two lanterns are lit and you set off at two o'clock. There is not a cloud in the sky and millions of stars are gleaming coldly down.
>
> You get on to the moraine, a ridge of stones of all sizes, from great boulders to dust, that have been carried down by the glacier. They slip and slide under your feet, and you bang your shins. The lantern is always shining in the wrong place. How you long for your warm bed! Surely nothing can make this nightmare worth while!

Of course it can! – Colin continues the account of a typical Alpine climb, and describes the delights of the hard-won rewards:

> A little more easy scrambling, and you are on your first Alpine summit – too proud and happy for words. It is only nine o'clock, yet it seems ages since you left the hut. You just sit and drink in the view. You have lived for this moment.
>
> All the well-known Alpine giants, about which you have read so longingly, are grouped around. The sun is very hot, and you spend the happiest hour of your life basking on the burning rocks .... By two o'clock in the afternoon you are down in the valley once more. You feel you have earned the delicious French pastries you get at tea-time. You have your tea at a table set among the trees, listening to the band and feeling thoroughly contented and pleased with life.

Colin continues with practical demonstrations, and accounts of Alpine adventures in the Chamonix area, notably from his 1936 trip with Bob Frost. Once again the stories, both here and in the later chapters on the Himalaya, are low-key, modest affairs designed to demonstrate a particular point of safety or technique, but are throughly self-effacing and serve as an ideal introduction. In particular, the Himalayan section is notable for Colin's stress on the humdrum hard work involved in expedition climbing, and on his sense of wonder at being amongst really large mountains. His own triumph on Bhagirathi III with Charles Warren is dismissed in about four lines! I particularly like his description of Shivling from the Gangotri base camp:

> It was a fearsome yellow tooth of a mountain, rising to 22,000 feet. Smooth rocks rose giddily up; it was a strain to look so high. The peak narrowed almost to a point. Perched on top of this was an ice-cap – fully 500 feet of vertical ice. It was a breaktaking sight, the savage glaring yellow rock, rising to this delicate and remote summit of ice. We could hardly believe our eyes when we first saw it. I cannot imagine anything more unclimbable. My idea of a mountaineering nightmare is to find myself stuck in those smooth merciless yellow slabs, with avalanches of ice showering down on me – as they probably would.
>
> So there we were, surrounded by unclimbed mountains. At last my dreams were coming true. What adventures lay ahead of us!

The book concludes with a chapter entitled 'Goodbye and Good Luck,' as Colin moves from the reader's side, and indicates the way ahead for the novice climber. He once again spells out his deep love of the sport:

> You would expect that when I returned from the Himalaya I would find the Welsh hills very uninteresting. Not a bit of it. It was like meeting old friends after a long absence. I had a lot of lectures to give, and a lot of articles to write, so that I was pretty busy for a time. But I seized every possible opportunity of getting down to my beloved Wales.

Colin encourages the novice to read 'Mountain Craft' by Geoffrey Winthrop Young, while girls are pointed in the direction of the delightful 'Climbing Days' by Dorothy Pilley. Advice is then given about joining a club to get further guidance, and mention is made of club huts and the facilities they provide, including this classic (and innocently chauvinistic) description of a typical club hut such as Helyg:

> When you first come in you will think what an extraordinary crowd the others look. Some have just arrived and are in city clothes. Others are in ragged climbing clothes, their big boots in every one's way. But nobody minds; you just do as you like here. A steaming curtain of wet clothes hangs in front of the fire. The owners are lolling about in pyjamas or old football jerseys and shapeless flannel trousers.
>
> The plain wooden table is strewn with all kinds of weird dishes. This is a grand place to experiment in cooking. I once ran out of dripping, and made some excellent fried bread in vaseline.
>
> The whole place looks in a terrible state of confusion and untidiness. Then comes the grand wash-up, and order is once more restored. Everything is spick and span – except the climbers themselves. You get things done properly when you haven't got any women messing about.

No doubt the ladies of the Pinnacle Club, or some of Colin's female friends at Idwal would have had something to say about that! Colin concludes the book with a firm promise for the novice:

> Whether you turn out to be a daring expert on the British crags or the great ice-faces of the Alps and Himalaya, or whether you are content to potter about on the easy climbs, I wish you the very best of luck. I hope I shall meet some of you on the hills.
>
> If mountaineering gives you have as much pleasure as it has given me, you will never regret having taken it up.

I feel sure that, had he lived, Colin would have been amazed by the rapid surge in standards both on rock and ice in Britain, and of British climbers in the Alps over the following two decades. Many of the young people in the vanguard of this post-war movement were no doubt inspired by the gentle and encouraging tone of Colin's book, which became almost a bible for the next generation of British climbers. It is no accident that the book is mentioned in the autobiographies of both Joe Brown and Don Whillans, characters at the very forefront of the great revival of British mountaineering in the 1950s and 60s.

While Colin's life was now increasingly dominated by the demands of his RAF training and the logistics of travelling back and forth to Liverpool to see his family during his short periods of leave, Menlove Edwards had continued his psychiatric work in Liverpool. He had been officially recognised as a conscientious objector in July 1941 and, following a reduction in his work-load at the Child Guidance Clinic where he was employed, he resolved to pursue his research work to the full. Menlove came to an agreement with Colin to rent Hafod Owen for five shillings a week, and set about moving into the beautifully located, albeit isolated cottage some three miles from Beddgelert. Menlove departed from Liverpool (after the city had ex-perienced the worst of its attentions from the bombers of the Luftwaffe) and moved into Hafod Owen on 2nd August – the same day that Colin was posted to No. 3 Air Observer Navigation School, at RAF Bobbington near Wolverhampton.

Menlove was to live alone at Hafod Owen for the next fourteen months. It is not known whether Colin ever visited him there, but it seems unlikely as Colin's visits to the mountains were now rare or virtually non-existent apart from occasional contact with Alf Bridge, who was working in Snowdonia training commandos in mountaincraft. The idea of Colin and Menlove chatting together one afternoon at this beautiful place, and exchanging experiences over a cup of tea, is an intriguing one, but it seems most unlikely that they met or corresponded during the period. It is likely that Menlove's period of solitude at Hafod Owen was far from idyllic despite the beauty of the place and its outlook. As someone who had turned his back on the war, Menlove chose to live an ascetic life style: he eschewed all luxuries and had few visitors.

One positive consequence of Menlove's period at Hafod Owen was the addition of a major new route on Clogwyn Du'r Arddu, climbed some six weeks after his move down to Wales. After detailed exploration the weekend before, Menlove climbed *Bow-Shaped Slab* on September 19th/20th with Jack Cooper of the Manchester University Climbing Club. In 'The Black Cliff', a particularly poignant passage served to describe Cloggy and its surrounding during the early part of the war:

> Quiet descended on the British Hills. The Snowdon Railway ceased to operate: gone were the summer tourists who had thronged the summit. Activity of a type did continue — khaki-clad figures with weapons and packs toiled through the rain, and no doubt hated the mountains and everything connected with them. For a few years the Black Cwm of Arddu became again the exclusive haunt of the raven, unless visited by some climber on his precious leave from the services or by those few who for some reason were still able to climb.

The new climb Menlove added to the West Buttress was his last climbing of any consequence for a year. His route, typically undergraded at the time, turned out to be a classic teaser with a considerable reputation for difficulty without good protection, in a most exposed position. *Bow-Shaped Slab* was not repeated until the late 1940s and by that time climbing standards in Wales were rapidly on the increase. The crucial pitch involving the traverse across the Bow is now most commonly linked with the initial pitches of Colin's *Great Slab* route of 1930. This gives what is possibly the best Very Severe route in Wales and one of the finest in Britain, and it is a fitting memorial to these two contrasting characters. At that time Menlove also produced with John Barford what became the 1942 guide to Clogwyn Du'r Arddu. Colin's great routes of the early Thirties were now written up in detail for public consumption together with the subsequent important additions to the crag (i.e. *Narrow Slab*, *Sunset Crack*, *Drainpipe Crack* and the *Bow*). This guide also contained the following overview of the place, the memories of which might have sustained Colin in his separation from his beloved mountains:

> When one is not immediately climbing, there is the magnificent beauty of these crags and the Llyn, unvarying, never the same, at all times, and in any weather.

While most of Colin's energies throughout 1941 were spent preparing to go to war, it was a particularly difficult and disappointing time for Bomber

Command prior to the very real breakthrough that was to be achieved in 1942-43.

This was still, of course, the very early days of the larger four-engined bomber aircraft, with both the Short Stirling and The Handley Page Halifax making their operational debuts early that year. The bombing of German cities was, however, still a fairly primitive business and so, in particular was air navigation at night. By the summer of 1941, it was becoming clear that the accuracy of bombing on targets was depressingly poor due to the sheer difficulty of achieving accurate navigation. A report to the War Cabinet indicated that moonlight was still essential for securing an acceptable percentage of crews bombing on target, but then of course the danger from the enemy's night fighters was substantially greater. During the summer of 1941, Bomber Command's losses began to increase rapidly, with over 350 aircraft being lost between the beginning of August and the end of October. On one night that November, following a raid on a north German city, no less than 37 aircraft failed to return.

In 'The Bombers'[1] Robin Cross describes this part of the war particularly well, and gives an insight into the situation in which Colin was about to find himself once his training was completed:

> On November 12th Churchill concluded that it was pointless to attempt to defeat both the Germans and the winter weather. Bomber Command was instructed to scale down its operations in preparation for a new offensive in the spring. The tonnage of bombs dropped fell from the August level of 4,242 to 1,001 in February. By the winter of 1941 Bomber Command had passed through two crises. The first had revealed the inadequacy of unescorted daylight bomber formations when pitted against cannon-armed German fighters. The second had demonstrated that the command remained too primitive an instrument to mount a decisive campaign by night. Bomber Command had reached a low point in its fortunes, but new aircraft and navigational aids were waiting in the wings.

This, therefore, was the context of Colin's service life in the autumn of 1941. Following his promotion to Temporary Sergeant on November 8th, he enjoyed one of his infrequent periods of leave at home in Heswall. In his diary (his last entry referring to Colin) Graham MacPhee recalled that weekend thus:

> November 13th: Colin Kirkus called and I took him to lunch at the University Club. Colin has just been made a sergeant observer in the RAF and is home on leave.

Following this period of leave, Colin was reposted to No. 12 Operational

1 Bantham Press 1987.

Training Unit at RAF Benson in Oxfordshire on November 18th. Here his training was completed by three months' concentrated work on Wellingtons prior to being posted as operational on 28th February 1942.

His entry into operational service came at a major turning point in the night bombing campaign against the Reich. Just a week previously, Air Marshal Sir Arthur Harris had taken over as Commander-in-Chief of Bomber Command Headquarters at High Wycombe. One of the outstanding operational commanders of the war, 'Bomber' Harris swiftly imposed his formidable personality and unshakeable belief in strategic bombing, and set about restoring the sagging morale in Bomber Command. At the time he had at his disposal only 518 crews and barely 400 aircraft but, encouraged by the development of the crucial navigational aid GEE, and the gradual emergence of the superb Avro Lancaster Bomber, Harris quickly established a highly sophisticated programme of area bombing that was soon to rain awful devastation at night upon many of Germany's towns and cities. In retrospect, this major development, together with the arrival in Britain in August that year of the United States Eighth Air Force to complement the efforts of the RAF, was perhaps the beginning of the end for Hitler's Germany.

Colin was to spend his operational service with No. 156 Squadron of 3 Group, and was initially stationed at RAF Alconbury in Huntingdonshire. This particular squadron had been used for day bombing in World War 1, and had then been disbanded. It was newly formed in early February 1942, and flew its first operations only a couple of weeks prior to Colin's arrival. No. 156 Squadron was destined to become one of the elite bombing squadrons in the RAF and was to achieve a considerable award list including 22 D.S.O.'s over the next 3½ years. It was also to lose 162 aircraft on operations. In its early days No. 156 was a Wellington Squadron (gradually switching to the four-engined Lancasters over the next year) and all Colin's operational duties were carried out in these robust and highly reliable Vickers aircraft. The Vickers Wellington was a twin-engined medium-weight bomber, and had been one of the mainstays of Bomber Command prior to the arrival of the four-engined heavy bombers in 1942-43. Known affectionately as the 'Wimpey' the aircraft had considerable virtues, in particular a tough geodetic structure and a robust vice-free character that enabled it to sustain colossal amounts of damage and still return to base. The 'Cloth bomber' as it was also known, was well-loved in the RAF and Colin would have done much of his training in one; no doubt astonished at how small the aircraft was. Fresh from his intensive training at Benson, Colin would have been accustomed to working inside such machines: the difference now was that it was for real, with a skilful and resourceful enemy to confront in the darkness high above northern Europe. Those of us who fly commercially today can really have no notion of what it must have been like for Colin and his fellow crew members to go to war in such a machine. Despite the superb quality of the Hercules engines, the noise and teeth-rattling vibration within the Wellington was phenomenal. Air turbulence would sometimes cause the whole airframe to flex and creak, and there would be a numbing cold with icy draughts seeking out chinks in the crew's clothing. The situation was not helped by having to wear an oxygen mask which made every breath reek of wet rubber, or by the common occurrence of cramp which the flight harness made it impossible to relieve. Coupled with this physical discomfort were the ever-present companions of bomber crews, uncertainty and fear. This latter emotion was best confronted by the need to keep busy and alert at all time while in the air. As a navigator (one of a crew of six in a Wellington) Colin would have had to concentrate hard, despite the physical discomfort, in order to provide the pilot with a constantly updated set of positions and course corrections. At this stage of the war, air navigation at night was still a rather primitive business, calling for mental confidence and a great nimbleness of mind on the part of the navigator. By early 1942 the only real aid to course accuracy available was GEE, which utilised radio beams. Colin would almost certainly have been accustomed to working with GEE, which, although it had limitations farther away from England, was a great help in guiding crews back home as the strength of the signal increased, and was therefore highly regarded by crews as a considerable safety aid. It was Colin's proud claim that as a navigator he never failed to guide his pilot to the target. 'AB' volunteered the opinion that:

> As a navigator, Colin would have been thoroughly professional and ruthless in carrying out his duties.

As a navigator in a Wellington bomber, Colin would sit in the nose of the aircraft once over the enemy coast, and would also sometimes act as bomb-aimer when over the target. On at least one occasion, Colin was called upon to take over the controls of the aircraft when the pilot had been injured, and he was to experience a crash-landing, a ditch in the sea, and a 'baling-out' during his operation flights. The Wellington could soak up huge amounts of damage, and sometimes, after a raid, they would resemble a flying birdcage with the cloth shot or burnt away to reveal the complex framework beneath.

Colin's operational flights at night over Germany commenced in early March and he was to fly 26 operations. At this stage of the war, provision was made to provide operational air-crew with six days' leave every 6-7 weeks, depending upon circumstances. This would enable Colin to make the long cross-country journey by slow train through Nottingham and Derby, back to Liverpool to his wife and family in Heswall. At other times he was sometimes able to visit his sister-in-law, Mary, who was working in a hospital in the Cambridge area. Of course the emotional strain of long periods separated from one's loved ones was commonplace at this time, but it must have been an austere and often comfortless period to live through, worrying about the safety of those left at home whilst engaging in what was already clearly known to be a highly dangerous and unpleasant form of warfare. It says a great deal for Colin's character and his personal courage that he took on such a role voluntarily, in the clear knowledge that he could have avoided it because of his impaired vision.

Colin quickly gained operational experience and was soon regarded as one of the finest navigators in the squadron – navigating on occasions for the squadron-leader. However, he was soon to discover that bombing German cities from 20,000 feet at night was a brutal business and it served to brutalise many of those involved, such were the stresses, both physical and mental. After the war, much of Bomber Command's efforts were played down – some would say devalued – to pacify public opinion, but the truth was that early in the war it was the only effective way to take the fight to the enemy. The night fliers, both allied and German, were brave men often barely out of school, working at the edge of the then available technology. The odds were heavily stacked against the bombers due to increased sophistication in the defence of German cities, the speed and manoeuvrability of enemy fighters, and the often dreadful weather and industrial haze over the Ruhr cities. There was nothing very glamorous or romantic about this type of warfare: it was grim, hard work with fear and danger constantly in attendance. In the course of the war, Bomber Command was to lose some 22,500 air-crew, and the statistics of survival did not bear close scrutiny, particularly early on in the hostilities. Certainly, Colin appeared to have few illusions and confided in his brother Guy that he did not expect to survive the war. For Colin, who at thirty-one would have been considerably older than most of his fellow air-crew members, all this must have seemed light years away from the happy carefree days at Helyg or Idwal of 10 or 12 years before, or from the beauty and uplifting inspiration of the Western Alps or the Himalaya. One can but hope that happy memories of his family and of

SGT. WRIGHTSON SGT. MYALL.
WILMSHIRST SGT. KIRKUS.
SGT. WILSON SGT. ALEXANDER
THATCH F/SGT BLACK SGT. DUKE.

RDS P/O DANDO P/O RICHARDSON
F/LT. WOLFE P/O REENBERG P/O. SMITH.
TS & OBSERVERS.

friends in the mountains would have comforted him during his initial flights, for the early part of an operational tour was known to be particularly dangerous and the most likely period for a crew to come to grief. When 'AB' was asked about this particular time in Colin's life, he was clearly of the opinion that Colin would have coped well:

> Despite Colin's relative lack of success in the world of insurance, he *found* himself as a man in the service of his country in wartime. I am sure he would have applied himself rigorously in that direction, spurred on by the tragic loss of his brother Nigel, and a very real belief in what we were fighting for at that time.

An interesting insight into Colin's attitude towards the war is provided in a comment he made in a letter to Alf Bridge, written only a few days before he was reported missing.

> ... I wish I could go back to the hills again, but I shan't really enjoy them until after the war, when all this business is behind me instead of just ahead.

One highly significant event in which Colin took part was the much-vaunted 'Thousand Bomber' raid on the city of Cologne on the night of May 30th/31st. It was Colin's eleventh or twelfth operation. The raid itself had been the subject of considerable planning by Bomber Command's top brass, who were particularly eager to demonstrate their capability to administer a massive blow on a major German city. What was proposed was that Bomber Command would throw the whole of its front-line strength and reserves in to a huge raid on a single strategic target. It was obviously a tremendous gamble, but it was felt by Bomber Command's leaders that the whole future of the strategic air offensive was at stake, and that the war could not be won without it. A huge and successful gesture was urgently called for with the largest number of aircraft previously dispatched to a single target having been only the 272 which flew to Hamburg on the night of April 8th/9th 1942. In order to mount 'Operation Millennium' as it became known, Bomber Command drew heavily on the Operational Training and Conversion units, courting considerable risk for the future if large numbers of instructors and advanced pupils were to be lost. In the event, 1047 aircraft were finally dispatched to Cologne that night, of which some 370 were from training units. 599 of the aircraft sent that night were Wellingtons.

In his excellent book 'The Bombers' Robin Cross described the Cologne raid:

> The first aircraft of the leading wave, GEE-equipped Wellingtons of 3 Group, arrived over the target at 0047 hrs. At 0225 hrs the last aircraft flew away from a blazing city on which approximately 870 bombers had dropped 1445 tons of

Colin in an RAF Bomber Command Group, Spring 1942.   *Photo courtesy Guy Kirkus*

Muriel Kirkus with Guy (left) and Nigel in 1930.   *Photo courtesy Guy Kirkus*

bombs. Air-crews flying at 17,000 ft could see the framework of white-hot building joists glowing below them in the immense fire raging in central Cologne. The aircraft flying beneath them were silhouetted against the flames. Some of the tail gunners reported seeing the glow of the burning city at distances of up to 150 miles. Forty-one aircraft failed to return. .... When the smoke cleared over Cologne, the recently introduced photo-reconnaissance Mosquitos of 2 Group returned with confirmation of the raids success: 3300 houses had been destroyed, more than 2000 badly damaged and a further 7000 partially damaged. Thirty-six factories had been destroyed and 70 had suffered severe damage. The docks and railway system had been severely hit and the City's trams put out of action for a week. In the midst of shattered water and gas mains, severed power cables and a wrecked telephone system, 12,000 fires burned on for several days. About 475 people had been killed, 384 of them civilians, and 50,000 of the towns inhabitants had to be "rehoused".

What he saw and experienced that particular night made a considerable impact on Colin and shortly afterwards he wrote to his brother, Guy, referring to the incident at some length. In his letter Colin asked after Guy's own efforts to join the RAF, but at the same time urged him for the sake of their family to try and avoid serving in Bomber Command. Colin went on to describe the awful and awesome sight from the skies over Cologne that night, with the great city seemingly ablaze from end to end and rent by explosions. Colin's wish that his younger brother serve elsewhere in the RAF came to pass however, and on entry into the service later that year Guy went on to serve in Coastal Command. He was to spend most of his operational time based in Gibraltar, doing convoy and reconnaissance work, mine-laying and air-sea rescue duties. Despite a number of exciting incidents and his own share of drama, Guy survived the war and left the RAF in 1946 to become a school teacher.

In a letter written to Graham MacPhee some six weeks later, Colin again referred to the Cologne raid. In the intervening period there had been two further 1000 bomber raids, although neither was as successful as that of May 30th/31st. By this time, however, further adventures had befallen Colin and his crew as the letter reveals:

> Sgt. C. F. Kirkus
> Sergeant's Mess
> RAF Alconbury
> Hunts.

Friday 17th July 1942
Dear Graham,

How are things going with you? It is ages since I have seen or heard from you. The trouble is that when I am on leave (only 6 days) I don't usually go to Liverpool at all, especially lately when Eileen has been lucky enough to get off at the same time (she is teaching at Heswall Children's Hospital).

I have now done 15 ops, so I am quite a veteran. It is interesting work, scares me still sometimes over the target (just like climbing) but isn't bad on the whole.

Coming back from Osnabruck on June 19th I got a few splinters from an explosive bullet in my face. There was a lot of bleeding but no damage and they soon got the bits out (except one, that they left in for luck) in hospital, where they left me a week. There are practically no marks and my personal beauty is unimpaired!

The same stream of bullets (from a fighter) put out the lights in my cabin, and put the oxygen, flaps and undercarriage out of action, so that we had to make a crash landing at about 100 mph. However, the pilot brought us in beautifully without a bump and we ploughed through the grass for about 300 yards, with a lovely smell of earth and vegetables.

I really think we are hitting the Huns now. Cologne was a colossal night – one mass of flames. I think the old town is pretty well worked out. The trouble is that there are so rarely absolutely clear nights around the Ruhr, there is always either cloud or industrial haze. For a "1000 raid" to be an absolute success it must all be concentrated on one town, so that the fire-fighters haven't a chance. A thousand-bomb load scattered all over the Ruhr will do immense damage but not nearly as much as when they are all dropped on one town, as at Cologne.

I am fully operational again now, and I was on the Duisburg trip the other night.

I hope you have good news of the children from America. Please remember me to Mrs MacPhee.

Yours Colin.

It is most likely that this is the last communication between the two friends, Colin deeply involved in RAF operations, while Graham MacPhee continued to work long hours doing dental work in war-torn Liverpool. It is interesting to contrast this letter of Colin's with that he wrote to Graham MacPhee in the summer of 1930, just before they made the first ascent of *Great Slab* on Cloggy. Gone is the jaunty 'Dear MacPhee' and the carefree tone of Colin's earlier letter. This is now a far more serious and preoccupied man writing, although Colin's delightful self-deprecatory humour is still in evidence. The letter is honest and self-revealing, yet betrays no hint of regret or unhappiness on his part, simply a professional willingness to continue his dangerous work. It is not without significance that this letter remained in Graham MacPhee's possession until the end of his life, and I was particularly grateful to his family for the opportunity to see it.

As Colin's letter indicated, he resumed his operation work in mid-July. On June 15th, shortly before being injured on the Osnabruck raid, he had been granted an Emergency Commission as a Pilot Officer (on probation) in the General Duties Branch of the Royal Air Volunteer Reserve, in recognition of the quality of his work. However, Colin's resumption of duties following his injury came at a time of considerable change for his squadron. It had become increasingly apparent to the Bomber Command Head-quarters that the accuracy of night bombing on targets was very variable and was particularly influenced by the prevailing weather conditions. In particular, the common factor in the successes of the bombing offensive thus far was that they occurred when the target could be visually identified, as opposed to bombing on an estimated position in poor visibility. There now developed a growing conviction that only an elite target-finding force could solve this problem, and so emerged the concept within Bomber Command of what become known as the Pathfinder Force.

Long deliberations had taken place over the previous twelve months as to how such a unit might be put together, and the Pathfinder Force was finally set up in mid-July 1942 under the inspired leadership of W/Cdr Donald Bennett. Initially fears were expressed – justified as it turned out – that there would be resentment from operation Squadrons asked to release their best crews or individual personnel for such a purpose. Certainly, the idea of forming an elite of this type was not initially well received among Bomber Command air-crews as a whole. It was proposed that the Pathfinder Force be administered from the bases at Wyton and Oakington, and each of these was to have a satellite, Graveley and Warboys respectively. It was made clear from the outset that the highest standards were expected within the Force, and that all air-crew were to be volunteers. This latter factor remained the practice even after the Pathfinder Force became a group and crews could be posted in directly. Established bomber-crew members, such as Colin, would have been in little doubt as to the dangers and difficulties of the work involved in this new set-up: namely the need for very high quality navigation and the hazards attached to not only being first over the target but often remaining there for some time, until satisfied that the target indicators had been correctly placed to guide the main stream of bombers over the next couple of hours.

The founder members of the Pathfinder Force consisted of five squadrons, one of which was the bulk of Colin's 156 Squadron, the majority of whose crews had been given the opportunity to volunteer for this new and exacting role. For various administrative reasons the Pathfinder crews did not fully assemble until August 17th, but prior to this, on 5th August, Colin's Squadron's previous base at Alconbury was swiftly taken over by the arrival of the first wave of bombers from the United States Air Force. Four days after their arrival at their new base at Warboys, 156 Squadron took part in a night raid on Osnabruck: this was their last operation prior to the commencement of Pathfinder duties. Around this time Colin would have enjoyed his last spell of leave, prior to the Pathfinder operations getting under way. During this brief period away from uniform Colin visited Great Hucklow Gliding School in Derbyshire. Here he was photographed – probably the last ever taken of him – with his close friend Alf Bridge.

As a navigator Colin held a key role within a Pathfinder crew, and it must be stressed that it was no mean achievement to fill such a position. The self sufficiency and coolness, developed over many years in the mountains, now served to help Colin in a totally different context. In his fine book 'Pathfinder Force'[1] Gordon Musgrove describes particularly well the role of the navigator and the qualities the job would have demanded of Colin:

> At first, because they knew the odds, only experienced crews had any chance of being accepted. PFF had to open the attacks and this meant it had to brave the flak before the Main force swamped the defences. Crews had to be 'press-on' types but they had to be more; they had to keep calm and assured because a TI (Target Indicator) in the wrong place was worse than no TI at all. Reliability was another essential characteristic as not only the Main Force but others in PFF depended on each aircraft being at a certain place at a definite time. Timing was the navigator's responsibility but even the best navigator depended on the pilot maintaining a good course at a steady air-speed. Navigation was a skilled trade carried out under trying conditions: plotting on a chart; measuring angles and

1 *MacDonald and Janes – 1976*

distances precisely, although cramped for space and with poor lighting; working to a regular time-schedule taking fixes, then calculating new course and ETA's were a full-time occupation. Maintaining a good air plot and keeping an accurate log were essential to good navigation, but the best navigators had that something extra – confidence in themselves. To use a wind which was entirely different from the forecast wind needed moral courage. If you were wrong and the night fighters didn't have you for breakfast then you were meat and gravy for the Squadron Navigation Officer. On the other hand, if you used the Met wind you knew you would not be alone.

All Pathfinder Force air-crew were volunteers and were expected initially to complete 50 operations instead of the usual 30 without a break. In effect, men such as Colin were being asked to face a 1 in 20 risk of failing to return fifty times. Whilst the risk of being killed was substantially less than that of ending up as a prisoner of war, those were clearly daunting odds. As a reflection of this extended length of tour and the acknowledged risk of Pathfinder work, crews were given one step in rank regardless of establishment, once they were considered proficient. This tiny increase in pay hardly compensated for the nature of the job, but was considered appropriate at the time.

The Pathfinder Force commenced operations on the night of August 18th/19th when 31 crews set out to mark Flensburg. Weather conditions were very poor, and it was not an auspicious start for the new force. Frankfurt was the next target on August 24th/25th, but cloud was again very low and the attack was a failure, resulting in the loss of five PFF aircraft. The Operations Book of No. 156 Squadron indicates that Colin carried out his first Pathfinder operation on the night of August 27th/28th when Kassel was the target. Flying in Wellington No. BJ789, Colin's crew was:

Squadron-Leader R. T. Collier, Pilot Officer C. F. Kirkus, Pilot Officer J. Barritt, Sergeant A. F. Mortimer, and Flight-Sergeants Comery and Greenwood. The raid as a whole was a partial success despite poor visibility, and much of the city was left in flames. Colin's crew was unable to positively identify the target due to cloud and therefore dropped no flares, but bombed from 11,000 feet on to large fires.

Colin's crew was again in action on the following night (August 28th/29th) when Nuremburg was attacked on a clear night, giving the Pathfinders their first real success. Colin's crew was one of several that dropped flares right on the target, and the marking was of great value to the attacking force. Colin's aircraft also bombed from 12,000 feet, and experienced severe flak over Bad Kreuznach. Whilst in that locality, the aircraft was also attacked by a German Fighter (an ME 109) but was able to get away with little damage done. Another 3 Pathfinder aircraft were lost that night, and during that August, from 175 sorties flown by PFF, 16 aircraft had failed to return – a depressing statistic.

Colin's crew missed the next two raids (on Saarbrucken and Karslruhe) possibly due to repairs being required to their aircraft after the brush with the fighter. On September 2nd, following his initial forays into Pathfinder work, Colin wrote to Alf Bridge who was still working at the Commando Mountain Warfare group in North Wales:

> ......I have now done 22 "ops". Since getting shot up in the face (a week in hospital and 10 days' sick-leave) I have had another shaky do. Coming back from Hamburg we were caught near .... and engaged in flak and searchlights for over 30 minutes. We got shot up and three of the crew wounded. We finally baled out over the Old Country, the only part of it I really liked.

On the night of September 4th/5th Colin's crew took part in the first of two highly successful attacks on the north German port of Bremen, noted for being a particularly well-defended target. On that particular night the Pathfinder Force put down Primary Visual Markers to clearly illuminate the industrial and dockland areas of the city, and by the early hours of the morning the main force had left vast areas of Bremen in flames. Several factories were totally destroyed, together with extensive areas of warehouses and railway buildings. Colin's crew flew that night without Flight-Sergeant Greenwood, and reported successfully dropping flares on the target, much of which was soon on fire. Flak was reported as being particularly heavy that night.

Two nights later, with Greenwood back in his gun turret, the crew was sent as part of a raid on Duisberg (September 6th/7th). Colin's crew reported bombing at 16,000 feet through heavy cloud, dropping a 4000 lb bomb into the target area despite once again suffering heavy flak. There was now little respite, and on the following night the crew was part of an attack on Frankfurt (September 8th/9th) when they successfully bombed bridges from 16,000 feet. The crew also had the misfortune to report 'Squadron-Leader Avesnes aircraft seen in flames, crashed and exploded.' The pressure continued and two nights later (September 10th/11th) Colin's crew was again in action, bombing Duisberg from 15,000 feet. The crew was unable to note the bombing results, but reported seeing two aircraft shot down by flak.

It was three days before suitable weather returned to allow the Pathfinder Force to resume its work. On the night of September 13th, with a reasonable weather forecast, 446 aircraft were dispatched back to Bremen. 156

Squadron was heavily involved in the target-marking that night, and late in the evening several of their Wellingtons roared away from the rural seclusion of the RAF Warboys *en route* for northern Germany. The bravery of the Wellington crews in particular was becoming increasingly apparent, for it was already clear that this aircraft, despite its ability to soak up punishment from flak, was really unsuitable for the demands of Pathfinder Work. The Wellington's lack of defence (only four 303 machine guns) and its relative lack of speed had begun to make it easy prey for German night-fighters, unless escape could be made by skilful evasive action and, by early 1943, 156 Squadron had switched to the faster and safer Lancaster bomber. It is not known what befell Colin's aircraft that night, other than that it failed to return and that there were no survivors. The RAF has no record of any known graves for the crew members and it seems most likely that the aircraft came down in the North Sea. This particular raid on Bremen was a heavy and spectacular one, with extensive damage being done to much of the city's industrial area, including the Lloyd dynamo works and the Focke-wulf aircraft factory. Two square miles of the port area was left as one huge fire, with heavy loss of life and damage to public buildings and services. Of the 446 aircraft dispatched that night of 13th September, 21 failed to return, 15 of which were Wellingtons. One of these was BJ 789, containing Pilot Officer Kirkus and the remainder of his crew; Squadron-Leader Collier, Pilot Officer Barritt, Sergeant Mortimer and Flight-Sergeant Comery.

For the family and friends of a missing crew, there would be an agonising period of waiting to find out if any of their loved ones had been reported as having become prisoners of war. On September 25th, Alf Bridge wrote poignantly to Graham MacPhee:

> Many thanks for your letter. I have now to go to Northern Ireland on business and am flying from Speke. On my return (approx 5-6 days) I will write to you. I would like to see you again and would like to cram in a Lakes show before winter sets in. Have been in North Wales working, and climbing with Wilfrid Noyce who has now gone abroad. Colin "missing" from raid on Bremen, night of September 13/14. We must hope on.

No word of Colin or his fellow crew members ever came from occupied Europe, and for their families and friends came the awful realisation that they had indeed been lost in action. Amongst Colin's possessions left in his locker at RAF Warboys was a sealed letter to Alf Bridge, written in the event of him failing to return from an operation. The base chaplain, the Reverend J. W. Buller, subsequently forwarded the letter to Alf, who later wrote movingly to Graham MacPhee:

And now that Colin has gone on to The Last Great Adventure, I am glad of the privilege that was mine, in being so close in friendship to a man whose qualities of courage, kindness and loyalty were of a noble standard. How should I write of Colin? As a climber with whom I shared many fine experiences on the mountains and crags, or, as the friend who always stood by me with loyalty and who always was ready with sympathy and help in troubled times? As a climber his influence on British climbing will be realised more and more as the years roll by. Colin and I climbed often together with Maurice Linnell, Alan Hargreaves, and Teddy Hicks, and many times with Jack Longland, Ivan Waller and Menlove Edwards. But it was Alan Hargreaves who coached Colin in the early days and whose sound judgement in climbing resulted in the development of Colin's natural gift for mountaineering.

And it was with Colin that I seemed to be most happy on the crags. We seemed so perfectly in tune with each other's thoughts. No matter if the situation was grim, for we were together on the rope. No matter how great the difficulty for I was following a man who played to the rules of the game and whose judgement was well-balanced. To be his 'second' on a crag like Clogwyn Du'r Arddu, and to see him forging a route on an almost vertical face, and at the end of a long run-out, was indeed a wonderful experience. Perfect balance, smooth movement and safe manipulation of the rope, sound leadership and a perfect eye for a route, made him the greatest climber of his generation, and possibly of all time.

The mountains were a very important part of Colin's life. A love inherited from his parents. May we be worthy of him and all those who laid down their lives that we might live. Staunch, true and gallant "CFK". Let our earnest desire be to try and emulate his appreciation of simple things – his willingness to do all he could for others – and, above all, his belief in human nature. Our hearts go out to his wife, his parents and all those near and dear to him, for we share their sorrow and pride.

Often will my thoughts travel to the mountains, crags and valleys where I spent so many glorious days and nights with my friend; for they will always be to me a shrine to his manly endeavour and of true comradeship for all who follow on.

To G.G.M. who was always a true friend of my best chum CFK.

AWB.

Colin and his fellow crew members were part of a total of 3,730 Pathfinder Force personnel lost in action between 1942-1945. This total formed about one sixth of Bomber Command's total air-crew losses during the war of some 22,500. The sheer danger of this type of work, in particular for those of the Pathfinders who out of necessity arrived over the target first and were often there for some time, is reflected in these cold statistics. All bomber crews, from the very best to the mediocre, were really at the mercy of fate, and for Colin and his crew luck simply ran out on that September night over Bremen. For Colin's family it was an awful blow, coming only three years after the death of his brother Nigel in almost identical

Alf Bridge and Colin in 1942.   *Photo courtesy Guy Kirkus*

circumstances. Eileen Kirkus was tragically widowed after barely two years of marriage, precious little of which she had been able to spend with her husband. Such were the dreadful demands imposed on the lives of so many ordinary people in those troubled times.

Colin's parents, Cecil and Muriel Kirkus, both survived the war, as did Colin's brother Guy, who returned from RAF service in Gibraltar. Guy and his wife Vera re-settled in Heswall, where he became a school-teacher and only retired as recently as 1984. Nigel's widow, Mary, continued her nursing career, and went to work for several years in the United States. The war over, Colin's widow, Eileen, remarried and later raised a family. For the Kirkus family, it had indeed been a terrible war, with the tragic loss of two talented young men in the prime of life. In the context of British mountaineering, Colin's death drew a sad parallel with that of Siegfried Herford in the trenches of the First World War. Perhaps the greatest rock-climbers of their respective generations, both were taken by the cruel demands of warfare and the service of their country.

10 'The Last Great Adventure.' Alf Bridge

The war years of 1939-45 extracted a sad toll both from the membership of the Climbers' Club and the Wayfarers' Club. Colin was one of twenty-seven Climbers' Club members who died in that period, and was included in the Roll of Honour printed in the CC Journal for 1945-46. Colin was also one of eleven Wayfarers lost during the war, and a memorial to these men is to be found in the Robertson Lamb Hut at Langdale. An oak settle was installed by the fireplace of the hut, with an appropriate ceremony in 1949, and is inscribed thus:

> It is impossible to write adequate words in honour of them. Let it suffice to say we are content to know their names are always before us when we visit the hut.
>
> | | | |
> |---|---|---|
> | G. J. Baker | F. M. Beck | A. G. Spencer |
> | C. F. Kirkus | J. L. Hicks | |
> | V. J. Derrick | J. W. Cooke | |
> | N. Buchanan | W. G. Moffat | |
> | G. R. B. Simmons | F. B. Dutton Walker | |

Colin was the subject of two lengthy obituaries in the Climbers' Club Journal for 1943, written by A. B. Hargreaves and by Jack Longland. That written by 'AB' also appeared in the Journal of the Wayfarers' Club. Obituaries of Colin were also published in the Alpine Journal and the Himalayan Journal.

In his affectionate recollections of Colin's life, 'AB' wrote of his friend with great tenderness and respect, and summed him up thus:

> It remains to attempt an assessment and appreciation of his climbing. He was practically always first class as a leader, being confident, solid and safe whatever the conditions. He was not merely a "gymnast" although, as his record shows, he was a brilliant technician. There was nothing showy about his climbing, in fact he liked to take things slowly, and was occasionally awkward and ungainly in his movements. He was not temperamental and never got rattled under even the most difficult circumstances. His principle physical characteristic was his extraordinary endurance and insensibility when having to sustain himself on small awkwardly shaped holds for a long time and for a long distance. One never saw him flapping about, kicking with his feet, or hauling himself up by main force. Everything seemed to go according to plan, up or down. He was always very careful and ingenious in the handling of the rope and the arrangement of belays, but so far as I know he never descended to the use of pitons except by way of a joke. It did not

Getting the car as far as possible! (En route to Cloggy)   *Photo C. F. Kirkus (AC coll.)*

seem to matter to him what he had on his feet or whether he had anything on them at all. Cold and wet did not seem to affect him as much as other people. He was a wonderful route finder on rocks and some of his climbs bear the hallmark of genius in that respect, notably Mickledore Grooves, Dinas Mot Direct, Lot's Wife and the Great Slab Route. Unlike many expert leaders he was also a very good second; that is he was content to follow someone less good without showing impatience or tactlessly making little of pitches which his leader had found difficult. He always tried hard to make things easy for his followers according to their ability and many and ingenious were his methods of getting weak climbers up difficult places.

His confidence in himself was such that except on the hardest climbs it did not seem to matter much to him whom he had got following; anybody would do to hold the rope if they would follow his instructions; he even put up with grumbling and defeatism.

As a man he was a delightful companion on the hills, full of fun and interest in the things about him. He was kindliness itself and also most unassuming about his climbing, yet never carrying his modesty so far as to appear to be fishing for adulation. To those who did not know him well he may have appeared dull, but this was not so ..... he was a simple soul, not much interested in the complicated ways of modern life, finding his escape and true expression in his mountaineering. In a better ordered world he would have been able to become an explorer or something of that sort, where his rare talents could have been used to the full, but in fact he was a clerk in the office of an Insurance Company, where, though he

worked hard and with some success, he was rather out of his element. In the
R.A.F. he seemed to have found himself properly and if he had survived I think he
would have become a man famous in other ways.

He died doing his duty for his country and he leaves a great name in the fine
sport of mountaineering, with very many friends to mourn his passing.

The other obituary in the Climbers' Club Journal was a very lengthy one
written by Jack Longland. Although Jack professed not to know Colin very
well, and only climbed with him on a few occasions, this is a very well written
appreciation of Colin not only as a climber, but as a man. Colin's
contribution to the climbing world and his context within it is examined, but
the most interesting and revealing parts of Jack's thoughtful obituary cover
the latter years of Colin's life:

> People who had put Colin down as a quiet and perhaps not very interesting
> person, or as only interesting because of what he did, were always getting shocks.
> For instance, after they had got him neatly docketed as a man who found his only
> escape from an unexciting job in the mountains, they discovered that he was really
> doing very well in his job after all. Or if they thought that he could not easily
> express what he felt about hills and climbing, they suddenly came up against his
> logical and clearly descriptive writing in the Glyder Fach Guide, or heard him
> give an admirable lecture to a mountaineering club. But the best proof of him
> being a fine person, and not just a fine performer, is seen in the years following his
> bad accident on Ben Nevis in 1934. We have grown used to shrugging our
> shoulders over brilliant rock-climbing leaders who do a wonderful season or two
> and then lose heart or interest, after which the pull of the mountains as mountains
> is not enough to hold them, once the competitive spur of doing new climbs is
> gone. And this happens very often to the leaders who have had a smash or a near
> escape. With Colin, there was never any doubt that his genuine devotion to
> mountains would survive the bitter memories and the physical handicaps resulting
> from that accident. In this he gave a valuable lesson to many of us, that being
> among the hills is in the long run more important than continuing to lead new
> climbs, although it is perfectly clear that, in order to give full expression to his
> feeling for the hills, Colin had had to make himself first into a great rock-climber.
> To the end of his life, he never wavered in his simple delight in mountains, and he
> showed this not only by continuing to visit them in all weathers, but by his quick
> and unaffected interest in the doings of other climbers, in the details of a new
> route, or in hearing or reading of explorations in ranges beyond this country. As
> Alan Hargreaves notes, he was always modest about his own doings, without that
> habit of deliberately underrating them that some climbers adopt so as to extract
> the greater applause – and this modesty was quite genuine, because in his own
> eyes the hills, and being among hills were more important things than the
> climber's own performances.

One particularly gratifying aspect of Jack's appreciation of Colin, was the

Colin relaxing in the hills.   *Photo Eileen Foster (AC coll.)*

attention he chose to draw to Colin's gradual move towards the teaching of climbing to others. In my view, Jack covers this aspect particularly well:

> From inclination, as well as perhaps partly from circumstance, Colin turned more and more in the last few years of his life to the task of introducing other people to the pleasures which he had found in mountain climbing. Weekend after weekend he was to be found patiently and carefully coaching novices up Welsh climbs, and thereby adding immeasurably to the happiness of those who had found their way to the threshold of adventure, which but for him they would never have tasted. And here again, without need for moralising, he had something of a lesson for the rest of us. Perhaps the biggest problem facing climbers today is to find means, without giving ourselves airs, of sharing what we have ourselves been taught of good and safe mountain-craft, among the thousands who are coming into the hills and who want to make themselves into climbers. Neither individually, nor in the somewhat self-satisfied communities which are our climbing clubs, have we done much to tackle this big new demand. Colin Kirkus, simple and quietly as was his habit, set about the practical job of communicating his love of the mountains and something of his own superb mountain method to people who, without his help, would never have learnt at all, or who would have learnt wrong things in the wrong way. It is not only a fine thing in itself, but also another of Colin's contributions to the future that so great a climber should have wished to spend so many of his hard-earned mountain hours in this way. And it was typical of Colin that he was prepared to act on the belief that the future of the craft was more important than his own great reputation as craftsman.

Writing in the Alpine Journal in 1946, in a piece entitled 'In Memory of Colin Kirkus', Charles Warren recalled numerous adventures Colin had, and made the following observations:

Colin Kirkus was a rock climber whose name will always be associated with one of these waves of development, particularly when Welsh climbing history is under consideration. Although he was never a member of the Alpine Club, he was a rock climber of such outstanding merit that some record of his achievement is called for in the pages of our Journal. There was something thoroughly genuine about Kirkus, whether one considers him in the light of his explorations, his writing or his toughness. His explorations in their own sphere have never been surpassed; and these he accomplished without taking unjustifiable risks or courting notoriety. He was successful because of a real enthusiasm for his favourite sport of rock-climbing which he combined with extreme perfection of technique in this particular branch of mountaineering.

A further obituary of Colin appeared in the 1946 edition of The Himalayan Journal, based on a memorial written by Alf Bridge. Although not a member of the Himalayan Club, the inclusion of Colin's obituary in that particular journal is significant, and a recognition of the particularly fine performance he put up when visiting the Gangotri in 1933. Writing of Colin in a Himalayan context, Alf had this to say:

He was not selected for the 1933 expedition, to his great disappointment. But he did in that year visit Gangotri on Marco Pallis's expedition, and with Dr. Charles Warren climbed the Central Satopanth peak (22,060 feet). On this climb he was able to demonstrate that difficult rock-work is possible above 21,000 feet; and had he had the good fortune of further experience on smaller expeditions he would have fitted himself supremely for the assault on the Second Step. The late General C. G. Bruce used to assert strongly that he was exactly the man for the job.

This reference to General Bruce is an interesting one, and recalls the strong support the General lent to Colin's inclusion for both the 1933 and 1936 Everest expeditions. An obituary of the venerable General was also included in that same expedition of the Himalayan Journal, and it does seem that he perceived in Colin similar qualities to those admired by Tom Longstaff, in the context of climbing at altitude. What is of significance in all the obituaries of Colin, are the references to his many qualities as a man, and not merely as a skilled climber of rock and ice. In particular, Colin's qualities of humanity and of humility have persevered down the years, and strongly shaped how he is remembered.

As discussed earlier, with reference to 'Let's Go Climbing!', Colin's influence was strongly felt by the immediate post-war generation of climbers in North Wales. His book was widely read at the time and Alf Bridge was particularly active in encouraging and helping the next generation of hard young climbers. Alf was acquainted with most of its leading figures, such as Chris Preston, John Lawton, Tony Moulam and John Disley, and became a particularly close friend and mentor to Peter Harding. The Derby-based Harding, together with Arthur Dolphin in the Lake District, were perhaps the key figures of the mid-late 1940's and formed a most important link between the form of rock climbing done in the 1930's, and the very real changes that came in the early 1950's with the emergence of Joe Brown, Don Whillans and Ron Moseley. Peter Harding recalled that Alf was a raconteur of note with a wealth of varied and hilarious stories. He was particularly fond of recalling the doings of Colin, Maurice and 'AB', and the great adventures they had shared in the 1930's. Peter felt that Alf, in his own way, kept Colin's memory alive by often talking of him, and making young climbers aware of the great deeds that had been done in the previous decade. In due course, Colin's great climbs became much sought-after, as the general standard of climbing rapidly increased, assisted by the emergence of improved footwear and clothing, nylon ropes, and the gradual reduction in rationing – most particularly that of petrol. I suspect that there was much in this period that Colin would have admired, for his generous spirit would have been quick to acknowledge the rapid rise in standards taking place and he would have been impressed by the talent, fitness and courage of people like Peter Harding, Arthur Dolphin, Jim Birkett, and most particularly Joe Brown and Don Whillans.

Peter Harding was particularly forthcoming regarding the influence Colin had on him and his contemporaries, through contact with Alf Bridge and Graham MacPhee.

> My generation were the caretakers really, carrying on with keeping the hills alive until the war and its aftermath were over. We were much affected by the influence of Colin by the linking contact of men such as Alf Bridge, A. B. Hargreaves and Graham MacPhee, all of whom had been close friends of his. Perhaps Colin's greatest contribution to climbing, was the notion of the long run-out on very exposed and difficult rock, particularly virgin rock. His routes clearly demonstrate this and I think this aspect is particularly important. Before Colin came on the scene, the hard parts of VS routes tended to be bounded closely by good belays and stances. Anything having a crucial move more than 30 feet above a good stance and belay was regarded as being extremely serious, which of course it was if one happened to fall off! Colin was able to develop the concentration and strength of mind to cope with the demands of really long run-outs at the top level of the day. This was a really important psychological breakthrough that led the way to the development of rock-climbing after the war. In Colin's day, plenty of leaders

had the strength and ability to deal with short difficult sections close to the safety of a stance and belay, but he succeeded in taking matters considerably further. I believe that Colin's early solo scrambles up dodgy places gave the hint that he was someone who would ultimately press on coolly and unworried by exposure even on stuff that was at the limit of its time.

Following on from Peter Harding, rock-climbing in Wales was dominated for a long time by the brilliance of Joe Brown. Like Peter, Joe was also a friend of Alf Bridge, and his comments regarding Colin and Alf are of considerable interest:

> In my opinion Colin's contribution to rock-climbing in Britain is second to none. One only has to glance through the guide-books of his period to see this. I think that had he not been killed during the war, he would almost certainly have been in the forefront of developments when I started climbing in 1947. He certainly was an influence on me, as the first climbing book I ever read was 'Let's Go Climbing!' I don't know if Colin's enthusiasm comes across to modern youngsters, but it certainly did to me and my friends. Regarding Alf Bridge, I don't think that he ever really got over the death of Colin, and he always talked to us about him and the adventures they shared. On many occasions, Alf would produce from his inside pocket the last letter he received from Colin, and I think that he always carried it with him.

It became very clear, in researching for this book, that Colin's memory had been cherished by many people this past fifty years, for he touched many lives with his humility, kindness and example in the hills. As is the case in particular with Arthur Dolphin, who died young in the Alps in 1953, Colin's friends have jealously guarded his memory and he is still widely recalled with honour, respect and, most of all, warmth and affection. As well as acting as a most important influence on the following generations of young climbers, he left an important legacy in his writing within the pages of 'Let's Go Climbing!'. By the time he wrote his book it seems that Colin had reached a stage in his life where he clearly understood that the mountains' most valuable gift was the ongoing joy and wonder they can provide throughout one's life. It is an acknowledgement of the spiritual dimension that complements and underpins the obvious physical pleasures that mountain-eering, and particularly rock-climbing, can provide. It comes as no surprise that 'Let's Go Climbing!' opens with a graphic description of a walk over the hills from Helyg to the summit of Snowdon, for an important grasp of the beauty and eternal mystery of mountains is evident in Colin's words here. In his obituary of Colin, Jack Longland was quick to grasp this particular aspect of Colin's writing, and of his overall attitude to the hills:

> It is one thing to have a deep and simple affection for the hills, but quite another thing to have the power of expression and conviction that will transmit such an

affection to ordinary readers. That was the great merit of the book. It made the specialised attraction of mountains seem real and important and of general application, and so the book will take its place with that very small collection of volumes which have actually turned non-climbers into climbers, and brought walkers in the flat lands and even those who before had not walked at all into a world of new experience .... It is safe to prophesy that it will bring many new recruits to climbing, and that, ... it will go a long way to ensure that they come with a sound grounding in attitude and technique.

I think that Colin was trying to convey in simple terms, how one's humanity can be enhanced by contact with the mountains, and how one's humility develops with the experiences gained. The hills are seen as the means of providing uplifting experiences that can enrich one's existence, and help sustain one's spirit though the more difficult and darker sides of life (usually not readily appreciated in one's youth). This theme of the ability of the hills to sustain us is central to an understanding of the message of Colin's book, and of his basic character. Recently the same idea was touched on particularly well by Dave Brown and Ian Mitchell, in 'A View from the Ridge'[1] who updated something of what 'Let's Go Climbing!' is trying to convey:

> We came to climbing in our youth, not to understand it in relation to the meaning of life, but to seek and to find the romance of adventure. And it was not just the rock: it was the hills, the pubs, the weekends, the travel, and perhaps most of all, the people. Adventure, of course, is a relative concept. Something which can be adjusted to one's abilities and inclinations in any period of one's life. It has been the constant rediscovering of this which has kept me going into middle age, overcoming periods of inertia and disillusionment. Given my timidity and physical limitations, I was never going to get near the standards of the friends of our youth. Yet I have travelled on many a mountain track, and along the way there have been a few minor triumphs.

This quote conveys a deep love for climbing and the mountains as a whole, expressed over a quite long period of time. It is that same notion of love for the outdoors that Colin expressed so skilfully more than fifty years ago.

Colin's own human qualities of kindness, patience and modesty are, I hope, already well documented in the pages of this book – along with the details of the physical qualities that enabled him to become such an outstanding mountaineer. Almost without exception, everyone who was contacted in the preparation of this work described him in the highest possible terms as a man, and not simply as a climber of rock, ice and snow.

1 'A View from the Ridge' (Ernest Press – 1991).

He was very warmly recalled by the senior members of both the Climbers' Club and the Wayfarers' Club, and one of the best responses was quite simple:

Colin? Oh he was a gem of a bloke!

That is no mean way to be remembered after fifty years, and a good indication of the way he touched many lives. An hour spent in the delightfully friendly and humorous company of Colin's brother Guy, gives a fairly clear indication of the kind of man he was and would have become later in life. There are a number of images of Colin that have passed down the years and which have helped make him one of the great legends of British climbing:

The young boy learning how to use a rope on a haystack with his brothers in tow; the youngster striding across the Welsh hills alone and then toiling back to the farm on his heavy bicycle; the assured first flush of youthful confidence burning off the Cambridge 'A' Team on *Lot's Groove*; the brilliant four years of first ascents that followed throughout the crags of Snowdonia. In parallel with these are recollections of the boldness of Colin's lead on Bhagirathi III and the real beginnings of Alpine-style climbing in the Himalaya; the solitary figure exploring above the Ogwen valley; the shy bridegroom in the shadow of the news of the Dunkirk evacuations; and the keen-eyed officer, senses all tensed, peering out into the night sky over Germany.

To my mind, perhaps the sharpest image is the recollection of 'AB', describing the day he spent with Colin on Clogwyn Du'r Arddu in the summer of 1939. The two men had been close friends for more than ten years and the first five of those had been spent climbing at the highest standards of the day. Now, years later 'AB's usual fiery and direct approach is severely reduced by the combined effects of stress, overwork and illness, and all he feels able to cope with is to scramble up the Eastern Terrace for an easy day. 'AB' remembered Colin's kindness and patience as they made their way slowly to the top of the crag, and his pleasure in simply being out on the hills with an old friend, talking over past times, as they strolled up to the summit of Snowdon. It is not difficult to picture the two of them there alone, gazing out towards Ireland and the setting sun, with the outbreak of the war that would claim Colin's life, only weeks away. There is a sense of both humanity and humility in this story of 'AB's that is as vivid and important as any of Colin's great achievements on the crags.

Two particularly astute quotes regarding Colin were written in the Fifties by Geoff Sutton and by Wilfrid Noyce respectively. They capture something of Colin's essence very well, and something of the qualities for which he is remembered:

> His climbs are characteristically clean, sound, exposed, in fine position ..... They have architecture: they were this quiet man's means of expression.'
>
> His (Colin's) style was likened to that of Herford, substituting a slow adhesive trimness for power in balance. The movement agreed well with his neat figure, close wavy crop, and large tranquil eyes. On any new attempt he moved gradually, steady in his readjustments, and reassuringly.

Colin's influence on Welsh climbing is still to be sensed to this day, most particularly in the Ogwen valley and on Clogwyn Du'r Arddu. Regarding both Colin and Menlove Edwards, Jim Perrin* has reflected that such is the power of their influence that, in a strange sense, they still inhabit the atmosphere in parts of Snowdonia – what they did and who they were still resonates strongly around the place. I have to agree with this view, for although most of us are subject to some nostalgic views of the past, the loving and intimate association with the hills that Colin passed on to others still shines through strongly to this day, both from his writing and from people's recollections of him. Perhaps this is the core of the reason why he is still recalled with such affection many years after his life was cut short.

Towards the end of this work on Colin's life, I was in North Wales looking over Colin's old haunts, and recalling the many anecdotes that had come to light regarding his life. One evening I went alone up to Cloggy, walking across from Halfway House to where I could sit above the still waters of the Llyn and gaze across at the details of this magnificent crag. One or two teams were still at work on their routes; their voices echoed about the place as a late train chuffed down the mountain railway towards Llanberis. It was a still summer's evening, with parts of both the East and West Buttresses picked out clearly in the low slanting sunshine. Like most climbers, I have my own very happy memories of the place, and there is little doubt of the esteem in which it is held in the development of British rock-climbing. Gradually, the sun went lower in the sky and some cloud developed, giving the place a more sombre feel, accentuated by the calls of some ravens flying high above the Llyn. I recalled the words of Jack Longland in his fine obituary of Colin:

> Clogwyn Du'r Arddu is a big enough memorial for any man, and without any sort of doubt or threat of rival claims Du'r Arddu is Colin's cliff.

* In 'Talking about Colin Kirkus' from *Yes, to Dance: Essays from Outside the Stockade*. (Oxford Illus. Press, 1990)

To be remembered with great honour in the history of such a place as this is no small thing to have achieved. To be recalled with such regard and genuine affection as well is the mark of a considerable spirit, and of a man well out of the ordinary. As I walked back towards the railway line I glanced back occasionally at the cliff, now almost in darkness: perhaps there are ghosts up there, and perhaps that same spirit touches all those who come to climb there.

Index